Teaching
The Way
of Jesus

Other Recent Abingdon Books by Jack L. Seymour

Mapping Christian Education: Approaches to Congregational Learning

A Deacon's Heart: The New United Methodist Diaconate,
with Margaret Ann Crain

Teaching
The Way
of Jesus

Educating Christians for Faithful Living

Jack L. Seymour

Abingdon Press™

Nashville

TEACHING THE WAY OF JESUS:
EDUCATING CHRISTIANS FOR FAITHFUL LIVING

Copyright © 2014 by Abingdon Press

Library of Congress Cataloging-in-Publication Data

Seymour, Jack L. (Jack Lee), 1948–
  Teaching the way of Jesus : educating Christians for faithful living / Jack L. Seymour.
    pages cm
  Includes index.
  ISBN 978-1-4267-6505-6 (binding: soft back, adhesive perfect binding : alk. paper) 1. Christian education—Philosophy. 2. Jesus Christ—Person and offices. I. Title.
  BV1464.S483 2014
  268.01—dc23

                                                                  2013036463

14 15 16 17 18 19 20 21 22 23—10 9 8 7 6 5 4 3 2 1

MANUFACTURED IN THE UNITED STATES OF AMERICA

Contents

Contents

Acknowledgments

I thank the administration and my colleagues at Garrett-Evangelical Theological Seminary for two sabbaticals over which this project was conceived and executed. Garrett-Evangelical is an outstanding place to teach and engage in teaching and research. Faculty support and community are greatly appreciated. Passionate and bold students who commit their lives to study and service call those of us who teach to make a difference and to be faithful to following the way of Jesus in the church and world. I appreciate the integrity, enthusiasm, and creativity that they show each day.

I also thank the administration and faculty of Hood Theological Seminary, particularly Dr. Mary Love, who invited me to deliver the Ruben L. Speaks Memorial Lecture series in 2010. These lectures, focusing on "teaching the way of Jesus" became a frame for three chapters in this book.

I thank the Christian education colleagues with whom I have served on faculty and/or have co-taught. These colleagues have enhanced my teaching and research: Charles Foster, Robert O'Gorman, Linda Vogel, Reginald Blount, Margaret Ann Crain, Virginia Lee, and Elizabeth Caldwell. Several of these friends and colleagues have read sections of this manuscript. I particularly thank Lib Caldwell, Chuck Foster, Diane Olson, and Linda and Dwight Vogel, whose careful reading of the manuscript has enhanced its comprehensiveness and clarity.

I also thank colleagues in the editorial board and executive committee of the Religious Education Association: An Association of Professors, Practitioners, and Researchers in Religious Education, for the ways they embody deeply their faith commitments and, at the same time, partner with people of other faith traditions in impacting public life. I am honored with the trust they have shown me as I have edited their journal, *Religious Education*.

Most of all I thank my colleague and life partner Margaret Ann Crain. We have engaged in research together, have written together, have built a home together, and have celebrated the lives of our respective daughters and our eleven shared grandchildren. It is a wonderful journey with deep commitments to faith and public life. In the lives of our children and grandchildren, we see the struggles to fulfill vocations and to serve others in a world that distracts, replacing service with status and community with division. May God guide them.

May this volume help in some small way as we each seek faithfully to live our vocations for a living, hope-giving and community-building God.

Introduction
Christian Education for the Realm of God

Teaching fills the pages of the New Testament. Jesus is identified as a master teacher, combining concern for the lives of people with prophetic witness. He drew on the sacred works of the Law and the Prophets to guide people in God's ways of living. Many he met referred to him as master and teacher.[1] Jesus taught people how to live in an oppressive and conflict-filled time. People who followed his way of abundant living were transformed. He pointed to the realm of God that was breaking into everyday living, calling people to abundant living.[2]

The disciples taught because they wanted the world to know about *Jesus and his way*.[3] Their encounter with him had transformed their lives. They saw the lives of others profoundly changed. He was a powerful healer and prophet. They wanted all they met to know how this Risen One called them into faithfulness and new life—to live the promises of the realm of God.

Teaching was a primary reason the gospel writers put into writing their faith perspectives and stories of Jesus—so others could learn. They wanted the way of the realm of God that had claimed them to be proclaimed. The writer of Luke made it explicit: "I want you to have confidence in the soundness of the instruction you have received" (Luke 1:4). In addition, the writer of the Gospel of John explicitly calls Jesus a rabbi to indicate his status: "Rabbi, we know that you are a teacher who has come from God" (John 3:2).[4]

While Paul's letters focus on issues in the midst of particular communities, Paul also is always teaching, seeking to help people be faithful. In his first letter to the Corinthians, he highlights the work of those who teach Jesus' way as a central task of Christian living (1 Cor. 12:28). Teachers of the faith offer people hope-filled ways of living. Teachers connect Jesus' ways with new people.

Teaching was the vocation for many early church leaders. They wanted to understand the way of Jesus in depth. They studied what others had written about this Jesus and his transforming ways. Moreover, they mined their own experiences and the wisdom of their cultures to connect the way of Jesus to new times and new communities.

At the same time, we need to admit that many of the conflicts in the early church resulted from teachers who taught conflicting messages about Jesus and his way. Paul highlights the emergence of different groups in his letters to the Corinthians (1 Cor. 1:11-13). In fact, the author of the letter from James almost discourages those who teach when he writes: "My brothers and sisters, not many of you should become teachers, because we know that we teachers will be judged more strictly" (Jas. 3:1). Teachers shaped the ways believers interpreted the signs of the times, understood the way of Jesus, and lived faithfully day by day.

The same is true today. If we claim to be Christian, we are called to teach the way of Jesus. Clergy and laity teach to help others follow Jesus' way of the realm of God. We seek to be faithful to a message, a vision, and a way of life that we know profoundly transforms lives and communities. The field of Christian religious education is explicitly responsible for understanding how that faith is taught. Since the time of the followers of Jesus, Christian educators have sought to understand how the redemptive and renewing experiences that came from Jesus into our history could be taught, learned, and lived. Teachers have explored how the meanings, values, and visions are passed on to the next generations, how the wisdom of the tradition could be connected to new times and in new contexts, and how the power of the way of Jesus could renew the world.

Our task as leaders of the church and as faithful people is to teach today the way of Jesus so that lives and communities are transformed by its abundant living. For the 150th anniversary of the congregation I attend, First United Methodist in Evanston, Illinois, hymn writer Brian Wren wrote "Carry the Flame." Its first verse poetically communicates the depth of this commitment to teaching the way of Jesus:

Since Jesus, who was mocked and killed
by Roman might, is raised, alive, above all power and thought,
we'll tell the story, sing the song,
and live the promise, true and strong, of all he did and taught.*

The task is to "tell the story . . . and live the promise." Living the promise and telling the story are precisely what Christian educators do on a regular basis.

The good news is that Jesus pointed to what God was doing in the world—the good news of the "kingdom of God," transforming humanity and community. Jesus' ministry of healing, feeding, and freeing sought to embody what God desired. The good news, the gospel, he proclaimed is that we do not owe our allegiance to the powers and principalities of the world that tell us who is of value and who is not. Instead, our allegiance is owed to the Creator of the world, who calls us children and heirs, and is seeking continuingly to create life and value in individuals and the world—a redeeming God.

nor do we get to decide

Christians proclaim that Jesus is God's creative and redeeming Word in the world—God's anointed one. For us to experience new life and to work to build new ways of relationship and community, we need to know and understand his ways. Therefore, through biblical, historical, theological, and educational scholarship, this book seeks to understand the ways of Jesus.

We also need to know how to teach those ways. This book then probes deeply the scholarship about teaching and learning, the practices of Christian religious education. How does one learn the texts of the faith, how does one learn the history of interpretation, how does one know what was affirmed in the past, how does one address conflicting interpretations, and how does one learn to follow? Jesus' way is the mission of Christian education.

The extraordinary importance of teaching and the responsibilities of our churches are highlighted in a passage in The United Methodist Church's *Book of Discipline*:

---

* Taken from "Carry the Flame" by Brian Wren ©2001 Hope Publishing Co., Carol Stream, IL 60188. All rights reserved. Used by permission.

The people of God, who are the church made visible in the world, must convince the world of the reality of the gospel or leave it unconvinced. There can be no evasion or delegation of this responsibility; the church is either faithful as a witnessing and serving community, or it loses its vitality and its impact on an unbelieving world.[5]

There can be no "evasion" of this task. Teaching invites people to claim an identity—a family name—and a vocation—a way of living. The people of God must be taught the meanings of the faith and learn to interpret them for everyday life. We all know how the church has, at times, failed to be the yeast of God's creative and redeeming word in the world.[6] If we fail to teach and live the way of Jesus, others will not see the fruits offered for transformed and redeemed living—providing hope, wholeness, and thriving in the midst of the world. Our educational task is very important! It cannot be evaded!

Therefore this book is a dynamic exploration of both what we know and have learned about Christian education and what we know and have learned about the way of Jesus. With humility and prayer, we seek to be teachers of that *way of Jesus*.

The Context for Teaching the Way of Jesus

Just as Jesus' early followers, as Paul, as the early church, and as the church throughout history, we seek to teach and live the way of Jesus in the midst of our everyday world. We live in an amazing time of almost instant global communication. We live in a time of extraordinary diversity where peoples across the world know about each other and the ways of each other. We live in a time when health care can extend lives and when technologies increase food production and provide shelter. Yet, we also live in a time where communication is broken and groups of people refuse to speak to each other. Diversity can also breed conflict as values contrast with each other. Technology creates weapons of mass destruction, and its by-products damage the earth. What does it mean to live the way of Jesus in this time?

That is a question posed to Christian education. Our responsibility is to seek to understand the way of Jesus today, to teach it, and to live it. As we engage in this task of teaching, we all must admit that too often religions have contributed to the lack of communication, fueled the divisions, and encouraged violent conflicts. This is in stark contrast to the message of the way of Jesus—pointing to God's grace, to redemptive living, and to healing and abundant living.

In fact, the historian Martin Marty has demonstrated that "in all religions" elements of extremism are growing that distract us from opportunities for redemption. These elements are not reflective of the grand ideas guiding these faiths; rather, the extremism is rooted in "fear, reaction, and aggression." Paraphrasing the journalist Harold Isaacs, Marty wrote: "Around the world there is a massive convulsive ingathering of peoples into their separatenesses and over-againstnesses to protect their pride and power and place from the real or presumed threat of others who are doing the same."[7] A fear of losing status, of having power positions challenged, or of questioning long-held convictions, fuels division.

Concomitant with these reactionary forms of religion is a nonbelieving consumerism that captures and motivates much of the developed world. This consumerism also creates hierarchy and division. Turning everything into individualism, consumption, or getting ahead, consumerism is willing to walk over others to hold on to privilege, control, and benefits. Wealth grows with little sense of responsibility to others and to the common good. Again, fear, reaction, and aggression are the response as the privileged seek to hold on to privileges.

An alternative pattern of religious faith is needed that offers hope and new life at the same time it honors historic and time-held traditions about how humans are responsible for each other and for the world in which we live. That is precisely what is offered by the great religious traditions, and I believe is central to Christianity. These profound religious traditions have given birth to people of goodwill who seek to build community and to develop patterns of care and justice so that "the-least-of-these" may be sheltered. As Susan Brookes Thistlethwaite, theologian and former president of Chicago Theological Seminary, recently wrote in a *Washington Post* blog:

> In the Bible, hope comes from the capacity we actually do have to "love one another." Compassion is the well from which we actually can draw hope for the future. Biblical truth teaches us that selfishness is profoundly destructive. . . . Freedom isn't selfishness. My freedom

ultimately depends on my capacity to feel compassion for you, and the freedom we achieve together in mutual responsibility.[8]

Compassion, mutual responsibility, and building community are at the heart of major faith traditions. They clearly fuel Christian commitments to hope, justice, love, and redemption. Also, the freedom of which the gospel speaks is a freedom from separation and selfishness. Freedom is a gift of living for God and for others.

Educator and theologian Letty Russell connects these commitments to the way of Jesus: "The church that does not see a direct Biblical mandate to serve in the ministry and life-style of Jesus Christ has lost the heart of the story of God's service." All that a church does should be "in the service of God's actions toward New Creation."[9]

Affirmations

This book hopes to be that kind of Christian religious education seeking "to serve in the ministry and life-style of Jesus Christ . . . in the service of God's actions toward New Creation." Christian education helps us understand how to teach and live the ways of Jesus. It celebrates the role Christian faith can play in redeeming individuals and the world.[10] Let me begin with the three affirmations that ground this study:

1. I believe in the transformative power of "following Jesus." Following Jesus does make a difference in lives and communities. People are changed and communities are renewed.

2. I believe that our understanding of what "following Jesus" means is enhanced with historical study and theological reflection. Christian education grounded in nuanced, depth and critical perspectives gives content and life to following Jesus.

3. I believe Christianity can partner with people of goodwill in other faith communities to make a difference in our world— to together work for transformation.

First, I have experienced the transforming power of Christian faith in my own life and work. "Following Jesus" has made a profound difference in many people's lives, giving them power, for example, to triumph over addictions. It has redirected people's lives, giving them purpose, hope, and vocation. People individually and collectively have been transformed to work for the care of creation and justice of all. Faith empowers people to be for others, rather than selfishly focused on themselves. Such powerful affirmations stand over against the "fear, reaction, and aggression" of which Marty speaks.

Jesus proclaimed to disciples over and over, "Fear not." At the heart of his affirmation was an experience of God's prevenient grace—of God's grace going before us, calling us children in God's family. As the Apostle Paul so eloquently expressed: "We are God's children. . . . I'm convinced that nothing can separate us from God's love in Christ Jesus our Lord: not death or life, not angels or rulers, not present things or future things, not powers or height or depth, or any other thing that is created" (Rom. 8:16, 38-39).

Paul's witness is powerful considering it was made in a world where tyranny equaled the Roman Empire and suppression was experienced through all of Galilee and Judea. Each day was dependent, it seemed, on the mood of the Roman overlords. Even Jesus had been crucified by the maniacal power of the Roman military demanding absolute obeisance.

How could Paul make this affirmation? How can we? Because Christians have experienced the triumph of Jesus' way over the powers and principalities that sought to silence his message! Because we know that God is a living God engaged with the world, seeking the good of creation! Therefore we can, to use the words of theologian Johannes Metz, "face into the world."[11] "Facing into the world" means we have the confidence to follow God into transforming actions seeking new life and hope. "Facing into the world" means that we can be, as Jesus calls us, partners in the realm of God—loving the world, redeeming people, addressing the suffering of humanity and creation, and creating communities of care. Reaction and aggression are, in contrast, the behaviors of those who need to horde, to hold on to, or to control what they are afraid will be lost—behaviors of those who do not trust God. Since God is living, we are called to follow, knowing God is going before us.

We hear this affirmation in the message Jesus offered to the towns in

Galilee. Even with the oppression of Rome breathing down their throats, he proclaimed: God is present and the realm of God is present in your lives. God is making all things new. As with the young boy who had five loaves and two fish (Mark 6:41), they were multiplied. With God, even meager gifts multiply. The Christian gospel of "following Jesus" is a theology of abundance—thousands are fed (Mark 6, 8). Therefore, "fear not"—risk living with and for others as God commands.

Second, we understand what "following Jesus" means by studying the gospel writers' proclamation of him and his ministry. Our perspectives are extended as we listen to those theological witnesses, historic and present, who tell us how lives have been transformed by following Jesus. Furthermore, today, we have the amazing gifts of historical scholarship to empower education. Over the last fifty years, significant studies of the Roman and Jewish worlds of the time of Jesus have become fuller.[12] New documents and archaeological evidence teach us what the oppression of Rome meant, particularly to the Jewish world. We know more about the parties within Judaism and how they sought to address this Roman threat. Thus, some of our understandings of Jesus and the proclamations of his followers are clearer. We have been gifted with historical and theological resources on which we can draw to understand more fully what following Jesus means.

Our obligation, if we seek to follow a living God, known through Jesus, is to learn and understand. Study and scholarship are essential. That is precisely what Christian religious education is, in the past and today. It is a transforming ministry of God's grace. Through scholarship and practice, we understand how the identity of a people is passed from one generation to the next. As Christians throughout time, we engage in theological reflection seeking to understand what these mean for today. Finally, we discover ways to live redemptively in the world.

Third, I believe that following Jesus empowers us to partner with people of goodwill in other faith communities to address together the issues of the world we share.[13] Within each of the great world religions are those people with public commitments who seek to work with others to build a world of hospitality, mutuality, and care. To make a difference, work for new life must be a cooperative project. Christianity cannot go it alone. We must join with people of hope and goodwill to offer a vision to empower efforts at humanization and social and environmental justice.

We live in a time when political stalemates reflect deep divisions in the nation, where people argue over the resources available to provide health care and to end hunger at the same time that the gap between the wealthy and the poor grows, and when some religious groups fuel divisions by demanding, "Our way or no way." We need new visions to help us build a world that provides opportunities for people and seeks to build communities of hope. I am convinced that those new visions are consistent with Jesus' historic message, pointing to and working for the realm of God emerging in the world.

Christian Religious Education

Thus, this book focuses on the work of Christian religious education in dynamic relationship with scholarship about the way of Jesus. It connects theological and biblical scholarship with Christian education scholarship. Those of us who study and teach have the responsibility to call ourselves and the people of God to faithfulness. How we accomplish this task is the agenda of this book.

We have learned excellent biblical study methods and skills. Theological reflection guides us to study in fulsome and nuanced ways—to seek critically to understand the past of the faith and how it can be carried into the present. We have outstanding educational scholarship about how people learn and about how the community of faith teaches. Without biblical, theological, and educational study, people's faith is naive, rigid, or confused, or, to use Marty's phrases, based on "fear, reaction, and aggression."[14]

Some religious groups hold on to limited perspectives born in the past; others believe they can grow in faith without study; and others teach rigid views that exclude the insights of critical scholarship and study. None of these are adequate to assist Christian faith to seek God's living hope and guidance. They are not consistent with Jesus. They will not help us "face" into the world.

The faith calls us to listen to the vision that guided Jesus' work and his call for abundant life. Teachers and leaders who followed Jesus knew that something was new in the world. Redemptive living and redemptive community were profound gifts he offered. New life is possible as we follow Jesus toward God's renewing of creation.

This book is an affirmation and a proclamation about how Christian faith can be taught in our world. It offers a comprehensive perspective calling the church to expand its expectations, listen to the living God, and follow Jesus into the world with hope and compassion. We engage in theological reflection; we study what we are learning about the way of Jesus; we listen to the people of God as they ask foundational questions about creating the world; and we attend to the practices of teaching and learning. Thus, this book is an exercise in practical theology—a Christology for a teaching and serving church seeking shalom. Churches can become communities of teaching and learning empowered by the realm of God.

As a work of practical theology, the book seeks to integrate historical and biblical research, educational analysis, Christian education scholarship, and congregational experience. Theological reflection ties these together. The first three chapters expand and clarify the call for Christian education. Chapter 1 is a historical and biblical foray into the vocation of following Jesus. Jesus' own call and first proclamation in his hometown (Luke 4) is our guide. The second chapter extends this discussion to the imperative to teach. Why do we need Christian education? What does it mean today? How does it offer us hope for the future? The third chapter looks at how God's people draw on methods of theological reflection and Christian education to understand their identities and vocations—their yearnings.

The second section of the book is a close examination of approaches to Christian religious education. What have scholars in the field of Christian teaching learned? What do they want us to know about how learning takes place and how congregations structure vital teaching ministries? I look at three sets of scholarship, all interrelated, about Christian religious education: (1) community of faith, (2) instruction, and (3) mission. In each case, the strengths and weaknesses of each is assessed by the way of Jesus. Each chapter begins with an illustration from the ministry of Jesus. It moves to a description of a Christian education approach. The approach then is questioned theologically and biblically to define how we follow the ways of Jesus in congregational, personal, and community living.

This book builds on past Christian education scholarship. Thirty years ago, when Donald Miller and I coedited *Contemporary Approaches to Christian Education*, religious instruction, community of faith, faith development, liberation, and interpretation were alternative ways proposed for the field.[15] While there were connections among the approaches, each was emphasized as most important. Religious instruction attended to teaching the content and practices of the faith. Community of faith focused on congregations and how participating in their lives is educational. Faith development assisted people in moving along a sequenced path to grow in the faith. Liberation reclaimed the power of the gospel for social change, to free people from conditions of oppression. Finally, interpretation was a theological task helping people grow as meaning makers. Each was seen as a distinct and separate emphasis.

In 1997, I edited *Mapping Christian Education: Approaches to Congregational Learning*. Four distinct approaches/metaphors were highlighted as starting points for dialogue about Christian religious education: social transformation, faith community, personal formation and growth, and religious instruction.[16] Again, while not unrelated, transformation, community, person, and teaching were distinct metaphors. Each was a starting point. Each connected with profound theological convictions about the nature of the church, the power of ministry and mission, and the role of teaching and learning.

The field of Christian religious education continues to develop. The task of a field of study is not to perpetuate itself; rather, it enhances the holistic manner in which the ministry of the gospel is enacted. The focus is on God's ministry and on our responsibilities as agents of redemption, hope, and justice in the world.

The three emphases on which I focus here are efforts to help faith leaders claim and interweave their responsibilities. Communities of faith and commitment profoundly shape people through practices of learning and living. The scholarship of Maria Harris, Charles Foster, Craig Dykstra, and Mary Elizabeth Moore is illustrative. Knowing the content of the faith and having the wisdom to access it in the midst of decisions, both personal and corporate, is a second emphasis. Here the works of Elizabeth Caldwell, Anne Streaty Wimberly, Dori Grinenko Baker, and Thomas Groome are illustrative. Third, education occurs profoundly through enacting the mission of the gospel. The very work of justice and hope teaches. Here we examine the work of Evelyn L. Parker, Mai-Anh Le Tran, Margaret Ann Crain, Grant Shockley, and Reginald Blount.

In each chapter, Christian education scholarship is put in dialogue with the passionate commitments embedded in the way of Jesus—for rebuilding community when culture is destroying it, explicitly teaching and interpreting the content of the faith in times of cultural stress, and living faithfully the gospel of justice and abundant life. The three perspectives, community of faith, instruction, and mission, are interconnected. They help us see a comprehensive ministry of the church.

The third section of the book is the constructive practical theological proposal for the field of Christian religious education. In summary form, the way of Jesus is clarified. As it has since the first century, the way of Jesus defines the goals for teaching and learning. The final chapter offers examples of how the ministries of the church, in and beyond congregations, teach the way of Jesus. Furthermore, the section reaches out to the church's responsibility for education in culture and for partnering with others in abundant living.

As John records the hope of Jesus, "I came so that they could have life—indeed so they could live life to the fullest" (John 10:10). Living life to the fullest or, as the New Revised Standard Version reads, "have life, and have it abundantly" is a hope of the way of Jesus. Even in the midst of conflict and rejection, of impending death and fear, abundant living is what Jesus proclaimed. Religious people can pull in, raise walls, and strengthen boundaries out of fear, reaction, or aggression. Or, even in the midst of forces of death, they can enter hopefully into the practices of abundant living. That is the imperative and hope of this volume—that we will all learn from Christian religious educators who point us to the practices of abundant living. Let's join the journey.

Section I

Christian Faith in Public Life

This first section, "Christian Faith in Public Life," sets the foundation for the argument of the book. Chapter 1 begins with a foray into the ministry and teaching of Jesus, looking specifically at his own call to ministry and to his first formal teaching in his hometown. That teaching recorded in Luke 4 describes both the reception of his ministry and also the resistance to the new life of the realm of God that he was proclaiming in the midst of a culture bound in the oppression of the Roman Empire. His teaching proclaimed a way of confronting the misery caused by this culture, consistent with the teachings and prophecies of his people, the Jews of Galilee. Jesus' teaching vocation becomes a sign for our own teaching vocations in a new world and a new time.

Chapter 2, on the imperative of Christian education, directs our attention to the work of education in any faith community. Many people have repeated the adage that we are only one generation from losing the commitments and beliefs of a faithful people. Without teaching to the next generation, the faith of committed people ends and its direct impact on the world also ends. Education, all education, is therefore ultimately about the future; about what a people think is of so much value that it must be taught to children and children's children. An example is the biblical witness expressed by the Jewish people. At the heart was a sacred vocation to live the ways of God for all the nations of the earth: "Keep them faithfully because that will show your wisdom and insight to the nations" (Deut. 4:6). To be able to remain close to God and to follow God's expectations, the importance of teaching was proclaimed. To live close to God and be witnesses to others required teaching the expectations of faithfulness to all their ancestors: "Teach them to your children and your grandchildren" (Deut. 4:9). Education thus, for all cultures, is about passing on to the next generation the heritage, the responsibilities, the meanings, and the commitments about how to enter into the world with honor, integrity, and hope. The chapter ends with a definition of the tasks of Christian education, to teach the identity and vocation of the ways of Jesus and to empower people with the resources to live these ways in new days and new times.

Finally, chapter 3 examines how people engage religious faith in their learning and living—how the yearnings of God's people become the context for Christian religious education. The chapter examines the ways the people of God seek to understand their lives and vocations. It focuses on the processes of theological reflection, the resources needed for faiths to be lived in new times and circumstances.

Let's move into this foundation—why do we teach, why do we teach the way of Jesus, and what empowers us to live the faith?

Chapter One
Following Jesus: Naming a Vocation

Jesus returned to his home and was invited to read at the Sabbath gathering (Luke 4).[1] The people had heard news about his miracles of healing. In a world where Roman taxes and the oppression of the Roman military drove people to hide, traditional village patterns built on community sharing and responsibility were breaking down. Spies fueled this division as they traversed villages, searching for people and communities that resisted Roman taxation. When villages were found hiding their little wealth or even bountiful harvests from Roman taxation, they were subdued and punished. In places, crosses of execution lined the roads to provide public examples of the consequences of resistance. In other places, Romans took prisoners and burned villages to the ground, as in Sepphoris. Roman terrorism divided people, forced resistance underground, and caused religious leaders in Jerusalem to compromise so as not to lose what they had left—the ability to worship their God in their own way. Healing was what the people desired. Healing and offers of new life were what they heard this son of a local tradesman was offering.

Jesus taught, as did his followers, amid this context of oppression and social upheaval. For example, the prayer Jesus taught his disciples points to this reality. He pleads, "Give us this day our daily bread [the bread we need]. And forgive us our debts, as we also have forgiven our debtors. And do not bring us to the time of trial" (Matt. 6:11-13 NRSV). The people needed bread, the search for bread and goods divided people from each other, debts piled high, and the time of "trial" was near, seeing much evidence of Rome's retribution. The people hoped for an eschatological time when the banquet of God would replace the present time of terror. The "way of Jesus" attends to this division and poverty:

- People without bread, for whom he seeks the endless bread of the kingdom

- Debtors who have lost all, for whom he prays for restoration

- A culture torn by oppression and subjugation, for which he pleads for release

Teaching the way of Jesus fundamentally points to how we educate for all of life—in families, communities, and the wider public.

Educator Duane Huebner reminds us that all education is fundamentally about "openness" to the future.[2] We teach because we want to affect the ways that people are formed so we can build the world into a home for living together. We teach because together we are creating the future. For Jesus, hope in the future was grounded in his prayer—recognition of the brokenness of life and hope for God's realm.

This chapter begins to explore what scholarship from biblical, historical, and theological sources are teaching us about the way of Jesus. It first offers a summary of the time of Jesus, clarifying the pervasive Roman oppression and the various responses to it in the Jewish community, including that of the Jesus movement. Second, Luke 4 is examined as source pointing to the vocation Jesus chose and the one he offered those who followed him. Last, the chapter points to the vocation of Christian religious education.

The Galilean World: Understanding the Context

Contemporary historical research has taught us much about the time of Jesus and the emergence of the Christian community. The context of Jesus' life and ministry and the spread of the Jesus movement occurred in a world of conflict and crisis. Throughout their history, the Hebrew people had lived at the intersection of great warring nations. Except for a few years here and there, they were subjugated or challenged by external forces—the Egyptians, the Assyrians, the Babylonians, the Greeks, and the Romans. The three hundred years between 165 BCE and 130 CE were a particularly difficult period of oppression, revolt, and messianic dreams.

These events affected the life and ministry of Jesus and the subsequent development of the Jesus movement. The time was one of Roman oppression, diverse groups in Judea and Galilee sought to deal with this oppression, and desire for liberation and self-determination fueled the expectations of many people.

165 BCE to 130 CE: The culmination of this period is 130 CE, the scattering of the Jewish people. A Roman victory in the Roman-Jewish war of the late 60s and early 70s CE resulted in the destruction of the magnificent temple in Jerusalem and intensified conflicts among Jewish groups: on the one hand, rebels, and on the other, those seeking to preserve the nation. The final Roman Jewish war in the 130s CE led by the messianic figure Simon bar Kochba, who even gained the support of the high priest, resulted in the total destruction and depopulation of "Jewish" Judea and Galilee. The people were scattered, and furthermore, the Romans outlawed circumcision in an attempt to excise all Jewish allegiance.

In turn, the year 165 BCE is the beginning of this period of unrest and messianic hopes. In 165 BCE, the Jewish people were led in a successful revolt by the family of the Maccabees (Judas and his brothers) against the cruel rule of Antiochus Epiphanes, the leader of the Seleucid Empire. While for over two hundred years prior to this revolt, Greek ideas and practices had been spreading in Judea, the actions of Antiochus Epiphanes were an abomination to Jews (1 Macc. 1). Seeing internal conflicts between Hellenistic Jews and traditional Jews, Antiochus sought to force the assimilation of the Jewish people. He outlawed circumcision, set a statue of Zeus on the Temple Mount, and demanded an end to Jewish worship practices, including an outlawing of Shabbat worship and Torah reading. As the books of Maccabees describe, through a guerrilla struggle, Antiochus was defeated, the temple was cleansed, and Jewish rule was restored. Such a victory fueled apocalyptic visions of divine intervention. Had not God freed the people from the Egyptians, had not God returned exiles from Babylon and given the people the scrolls of the Torah, and had not God again intervened to free the people from oppression, restoring faithful worship and expectations of just living?

For approximately one hundred years, from 165 to 63 BCE, the dreams of a restored Israel seemed fulfilled. Temple worship expanded and Jewish groups calling for righteous living grew (like the Pharisees). However, incompetence and infighting within the ruling family made few of these years really stable. A final struggle for kingship between two brothers in the 60s BCE resulted in a Roman takeover of Judea and the surrounding territories. The Roman general, Pompey the Great, desecrated the Holy of Holies in the temple and claimed the lands for Rome. Again, the people were enslaved and their traditions violated. With dreams and hopes of freedom from Egypt, Babylon, and Greece in their minds, they lived under the control of the brutal regime of the Roman military.

63 BCE to 130 CE: From 63 BCE until 130 CE, Jewish groups were forced to seek faithfulness in a world controlled by Romans. The Romans defined leaders who would do their bidding and collect their tribute. The family of Herod, partially Jewish, was given control over the lands. In a compromise with religious authorities, the Romans allowed the people to worship their God, yet they demanded the right to determine who would serve as high priest and collect tribute taxes. The Roman military stood in wait to control any expressions of freedom from the people.

The father, Herod the Great, a "great" builder, strengthened the hold of the Romans in Judea and Galilee, and at the same time he directed the expansion of the temple in Jerusalem, making it one of the most beautiful structures in the world (to be completed three decades after his death). He furthermore built other magnificent structures throughout Judea and Galilee, including the port town of Caesarea Maritima (named in honor of the emperor), from which later Pontius Pilate and the bulk of his military forces would control Judea. He cruelly took advantage of the people.

With Herod the Great's death, in approximately 4 BCE, his provinces were divided among his sons. Two are important for our story: Herod Antipas ruled Galilee, and Herod Archelaus ruled Judea. At Herod the Great's death, there were revolts against Rome; one example occurred in Sepphoris in Galilee. These revolts were inspired by hopes of messianic leaders to restore self-rule. The Romans joined "the Herods" in responding brutally, in fact, crucifying many of the rebels and destroying the city of Sepphoris.

In Galilee, Herod Antipas continued his father's practices. He rebuilt Sepphoris into a Roman city, with grandeur and opulence. It was Herod Antipas who encountered the challenges of John the Baptist for purity and return to traditional Jewish values. Herod Antipas brutally put down any challengers to the authority of Rome or himself. Messiahs, prophets, and revolutionary leaders were silenced. Heads rolled, like that of John; others were impaled on spears by the side of the road as symbols of who was in power—Rome.

In Judea, the rule of Herod Archelaus was even too brutal for the Romans. After he sought even more control over temple worship, many Pharisees, Sadducees, and others protested. When a group of Pharisees broke the Roman eagle he had set in the temple, he unleashed a murderous reign of terror, killing more than three thousand people. A delegation of Jewish people met the Roman emperor and pleaded for relief. In response, Roman leaders removed Archelaus and took direct control over Judea (and Samaria and Idumea), installing a Roman prelate to rule.

Compromises still kept Jewish worship flourishing in the temple, as well as the continued construction and expansion of the temple. Many Jewish leaders were very wise in negotiating. They preserved religious traditions and secured a portion of self-determination. Yet the Romans maintained control. A Roman garrison was built beneath the Temple Mount—to guard and control Roman interests. Furthermore, the Romans approved the person appointed to the office of high priest; the vestments of priests were held under Roman control so that priests were always beholden to the Romans, even to perform religious rites; and prayers daily were demanded from the priests for the welfare and life of the Caesar (known as a god by the Romans).[3]

Jerusalem thrived for some, while others were impoverished by taxes to support Roman expansion throughout the world. As historian Seth Schwarz has described, Roman imperialism benefited some in Jerusalem.[4] The temple was one of the most amazing structures in the ancient world. Not only did Jews conduct pilgrimages to it, to fulfill religious rituals, but other worshippers from across the empire visited, awed by its grandeur and religious power. An industry emerged in Jerusalem that funded up to half of the population with religious writing, vendors, and hospitality to support pilgrimages. The surplus income that was earned by many was wisely invested, often to buy plots of land in Galilee taken from their peasant owners for inability to pay taxes. These actions further enraged feelings Galileans had about Judeans. When entrepreneurs combined these plots, estates grew, producing grapes for wine and olives to sell to the Romans. Furthermore, the waters of the Mediterranean and the Sea of Galilee were fished while other industries dried the fish for purchase to feed the Roman war machine.

New Testament scholar John Dominic Crossan calls this social and political scene where some benefited from Roman power and others were impoverished a "domination system."[5] Power is clear. The only response left to the powerless was to comply, hide, or resist. In Galilee, in particular, the domination system worked in the following manner:

1. Military political rulers demanded tribute.

2. Political dependent rulers collected tribute.

3. Aristocracy and priests supported rulers. In fact, the Romans forced the office of the high priest to collect the tribute.

4. Tax collectors and spies were sent to gather the tribute and also to report violations, which would be addressed with swift punishment—from increased tax to crucifixion and to destruction of homes and villages.

5. For peasants, who farmed the fields, taxes increased. Many borrowed to gather seed and to raise crops for family and income. Borrowing, they risked falling into debt and losing their land, the consequences of which were to become renters on land they once owned, or, even worse, to become "day laborers" working at another's largess.

6. Typical village patterns of common sharing and common responsibility were disrupted as people were forced to work as

individualists seeking their own fortunes. In many places this led to the development of an economy of selfishness, hoarding, and secrecy.

7. Great estates were built in Galilee from foreclosed plots of land, and they grew rich and subservient to the Romans.

8. The process was repeated over and over.

This is the world into which Jesus was born and where he lived, ministered, and was ultimately murdered as a threat both to the power of Rome and to the risky compromises in effect in Jerusalem.

Groups Responding to Roman Control: Those in Galilee and Judea developed multiple strategies to live and to deal with Roman colonization. Their responses ranged from despair on the one hand to resistance on the other. Five distinct groups can be identified.

Some were **collaborators** with Roman authority. This describes well the families of Herod and the ruling elites. From both Jewish sources and early Christian sources, we know that some sought wealth and control by serving the Romans.

A second group may have looked like collaborators, but they were merely **compromisers.** To protect deeply held religious practices and to carve out a place for themselves, many of the Sadducee class and the temple priests compromised so as not to lose what little they had left. They sought to be faithful to the letter of the law, but knew they had to still live in Roman-controlled society. Compromises were made when necessary.

The **resistors** were a third group and included the Pharisees. The Pharisees wanted to extend the gifts of God's Torah throughout all of life. Following the Torah was their highest priority. Quietly resisting Roman control, they sought to fulfill the spirit of the law and protect Jewish practices. They avoided as often as they could Roman expectations. Faithful observance was their method of resistance. In their minds, the compromising Sadducees had little faith. On the other hand, the radical groups who challenged Roman control also were problematic, for they risked unleashing the power of the Roman overlords.

Bandits and "guerrilla fighters" were a fourth group. Both thieves who were pushed off the land and rebels who sought to restore and free the lands from the Romans acted similarly. They robbed the wealthy, both Roman and Jewish collaborators; they attacked vulnerable Roman legions; and they sought to establish pockets of freedom in the midst of the Roman domination system. At moments of great change, like Herod the Great's death, or moments of great pain, apocalyptic revolutionary leaders offered visions of the immanent triumph of God over the forces of control. We have two biblical examples bookmarking the Roman era. The book of Daniel, on one end, proclaims that outside political forces, like Greeks, would be defeated. Later, the Revelation of John, on the other, speaks directly of the conflict between the forces of faith and the forces of Rome. An example is the First Jewish-Roman War, when the Sicarii, a Jewish revolutionary group, initiated the war with Rome by killing the priests of the temple, calling them pawns of the Roman Empire. As we know, when revolutionaries were caught, they were killed either by crucifixion or another method. Their supporters were scattered, silenced, or driven underground. The spirit of rebellion was always present in the landscape.

A fifth group were **prophets**, proclaiming God's judgment and God's way. They sought to call the people back to faithfulness—believing that faithfulness, as had been the case in Egyptian times, in Babylonian times, and in Maccabean times, would free the people. Many operated on the fringes of the wider society. One example is very familiar: John the Baptizer called for repentance and turning back again to Jewish values of justice and righteousness. As long as John remained in the wilderness, he was ignored. Yet when he directly challenged the legitimacy of Herod Antipas, the forces of power dealt swiftly and cruelly. There were others like John. Some took to the wilderness and formed communities of hope seeking to live faithfully out of sight of Roman control. This is true of the Qumran, the Essene Dead Sea Scroll community. Two other examples, described by Josephus, the Jewish historian: Jesus son of Hananiah, who prophesied against the temple and the high priest, was stoned; and Bannus the bather, who sought moral purity as a means of hope and repentance, was killed.[6]

Times of conflict and despair resulted in a variety of responses of how to live in the world of Roman military terrorism. To this time, Jesus shared a message of hope, repentance, and new life for a people who were beaten down. The Jesus movement maneuvered among collaborators, compromisers, righteous religious people, bandits and revolutionaries, and prophets.

As we know from the gospels, Jesus began his ministry when John was imprisoned. In fact, John sent his disciples to inquire about the ministry of Jesus, his cousin. Matthew 11:3 records that they asked, "Are you the one who is to come?" Jesus, quoting Isaiah 35 and 61, responded with a hopeful litany about the realm of God.

> "Go, report to John what you hear and see. Those who were blind are able to see. Those who were crippled are walking. People with skin diseases are cleansed. Those who were deaf now hear. Those who were dead are raised up. The poor have good news proclaimed to them." (Matt. 11:4-6)

Without a doubt, Jesus supported John's call for repentance and lauded his work: "No one who has ever been born is greater than John the Baptist" (Matt. 11:11). He compared him to Elijah.

Jesus' ministry emerged in this time of crisis. Competing groups sought to secure a future. Their efforts involved compromise, purification, prophesy, and revolution.

A Vocation to Follow

In Jesus' hometown, people were crying over their losses and the ubiquitous presence of the Roman forces. They were honored by Jesus' return. They were a little curious, wondering if all they had heard about him was true (see Luke 4:14-30). From this interaction, we see Jesus' statement of his own vocation.

At the community religious gathering (the Shabbat, or Sabbath observance), the leader handed Jesus the scroll of Isaiah, probably the *haphtarah* reading (the passage from the Prophets to complement the Torah reading for the day).[7] Jesus took the scroll, opened it to the marked place, and read the words of Isaiah.[8] They were powerful and hopeful, calling the people to faithfulness: "The Spirit of the Lord is upon me, because the Lord has anointed me. He has sent me to preach good news to the poor, to proclaim release to the prisoners and recovery of sight to the blind, to liberate the oppressed, and to proclaim the year of the Lord's favor" (Luke 4:18-19; see also Isa. 61:1).

As the Gospel of Luke tells the story, the people were impressed by Jesus. His reading of Isaiah's hope inspired the people, as did his interpretation of the text. His saying, "Today this scripture has been fulfilled in your hearing" (Luke 4:21 NRSV) did not offend them. In fact, they were delighted: "Everyone was raving about Jesus, so impressed were they by the gracious words flowing from his lips. They said, 'This is Joseph's son, isn't it?'" (Luke 4:22). Did they wonder if Isaiah's message of liberation was to be theirs? Could the world return to a time when villagers cared for one another in a spirit of community and family? Would the Romans leave and their spies be silenced?

Yet, with all of their accolades, the people's pride turned to anger as Jesus challenged them with the text. He pointed to two historical memories: times when the people's unfaithfulness prodded God to extend blessings to strangers, even offensive strangers. Was Jesus accusing them of offending God? They wondered how his words of hope had been turned into a challenge. Their pride then turned to rage, and they wanted to "throw him off the cliff" (Luke 4:29). How dare he act in such a manner!

Many scholars have treated this text (Luke 4) as if it were simply Luke's construction to define and extend the gifts of the kingdom to outsiders. While it is true that Luke gives it his own twist, as do all the Gospel writers, when we probe it, there is much more going on. Could it be a concrete memory of an event in Jesus' hometown? Without a doubt, we know that Jesus was rejected in his hometown (see also Mark 6:1-6; Matt. 13:53-58; John 4:44). Even his family seems to have feared that he was out of his mind (Mark 3:20-21).[9] We ask why these rejections occurred. Moreover, we wonder what they signal about the alternative vocation to which Jesus called followers. He clearly interprets the text he read from Isaiah as pointing to a real and immediate in-breaking of God's realm.

While Luke organized his telling of this passage for his own purposes, the text incorporates a historical memory of Jesus reading one of the Sabbath texts in his hometown, his preaching, and his rejection.[10] Why might Jesus have been rejected in his hometown? Consider the details of the story again. Jesus came home and went to the community Sabbath gathering. Sabbath worship was his practice. He was faithful. His reputation was growing. News of Jesus' healings, exorcisms, and authoritative interpretations were spreading fast. It is therefore not at all strange that Jesus, a child of the community, and a person gaining recognition for his healings and authority, would be invited to read and comment on the prophetic reading. Examining the text closely, the reading does not get Jesus into trouble. Something more was happening here. The people were amazed. They received him as one of their own—as Joseph and Mary's son.

Furthermore, note that the subject of the reading is Isaiah and the Jewish people, not Jesus. He read the expected text, for the day, the prophetic message of Isaiah, and he sat down. They were all happy! What, then, gets Jesus into so much trouble? Isn't he just doing and reading what he was asked to do? He is recognized as a "homeboy," as one of them.

Jesus' "offense" that fills them with rage is the last part of his interpretation. After they have praised him, he seems to turn on them. Remember Jesus was here speaking to people whose lives were fragile and whose patterns of support and kinship were being systematically destroyed. They were oppressed by the Romans, taxed mercilessly by Herod, and used by the temple leaders in Jerusalem (as Galileans were always used by Judeans).

In the midst of this oppression, one of their own proclaims Isaiah's vision that the realm of God is being fulfilled in their time. For this, they are grateful. They need the good news of God's banquet. Yet, he then challenges them by reminding them that when their ancestors rejected God's gifts, then God's abundance was shared with outsiders: the widow at Zarephath in Sidon, who received an endless supply of meal and oil and healing for her son (1 Kings 17), and even the offensive Naaman the Syrian, who was cured of leprosy (2 Kings 5:1-19). Instead of being given Jesus' miraculous healings and exorcisms, his neighbors were challenged.

We do not know exactly why Jesus challenged them. We can only presume. He seems to equate them with the unfaithful on whom God turned God's back. Elijah and Elisha had sought the recovery of faithfulness for Israel and Judah when the powerful used the division of the kingdoms for military and political advantage. In many ways, the parallels to Jesus' time are amazing: Herod, the Romans seeking political advantage, the complicity of some in the Jerusalem hierarchy, and the oppression of the people—all parallel Elijah's and Elisha's times. Furthermore, wasn't Jesus also a healer and miracle worker for all people, particularly for those without power, as were Elijah and Elisha? Didn't he seek the faithful teaching of the Torah? There are many parallels!

13

However, it is not to the powerful that Jesus directs his rebuke; it is to his neighbors. They are called unfaithful. Their needs seem ignored. This sermon is not the typical one a child of the community shares upon returning home. Usually that sermon is an occasion of thanksgiving. That is not what Jesus did! What is going on? Honestly we don't know. But we do know how oppression works. Victims sometimes take on the images of themselves in the eyes of the oppressor. They are thus blinded to all but the oppressors' definitions and expectations. Jesus' neighbors may have lost identity, pride, and "somebodyness." When this occurs, victims turn on other victims. Simply: in times of fear and crisis, people tend to hoard what little they have; believe falsehoods and innuendo; and become desperate, hidden people.

Jesus, in contrast, sees the kingdom of God as a redemptive experience that changes people and re-connects them to community. The miracle of Jesus, told so well in other stories, may be that he was able to take a fearful and oppressed people and reestablish patterns of sharing so that five thousand could be fed from limited supplies and the best wine brought out at a wedding. His miracle was gathering people who were outcast, questionable, and sinners into new life. He helped people see who should be on the invitation list to God's table. He gave birth to the redemptive community in his healings and ministry. The sick were restored to community, the strangers were invited to sit at table, the outcasts were invited back in, and new life was offered to those who were near death. Furthermore, these actions of the redemptive community were patterns that challenged the hierarchy—we can live for each other even when those in power divide and control.

But this did not happen at his hometown. Oppressed, traditional people—fearful and grasping—seemed to want their benefits, their miracles. They refused to see the work of God in their present, the realities and possibilities of which Isaiah proclaimed. They resented that Jesus seemed to hold back the miraculous about which they had heard; and they were hurt that his words challenged their faithfulness. They looked in the wrong place for the miraculous.

They were so angry—angry enough to throw him off a cliff. They rejected the benefits of community, of a meal of new life, and of new relationships that he offered. Jesus was looking for "changed hearts" and renewed commitments to a community of redemption. Matthew and Luke remember a phrase probably used in the early Christian communities, if it was not from Jesus himself: "Woe to you" (NRSV), or in the CEB, "How terrible will it be for you, Chorazin! How terrible will it be for you, Bethsaida!" (Matt. 11:21; Luke 10:13). Lives were not changed and hearts did not repent. "Woe to you" was not a threat; it was a description. In these places, lives did not change, and because they did not, woe and loss continued.

The focus of Jesus' challenge is to people who *think* they are faithful and define themselves as victims—as people without power in the face of Roman domination. He simply reminds them of the promises and responsibilities of the Torah—to remember to whom they belong and from where their hope derives. Can't you hear the comments of his neighbors as he passed through their midst?

- "Doesn't he know the pain in the village?"

- "Doesn't he know that we are the faithful ones who taught him?"

- "What we have heard about him must be true—he is a drunkard and a glutton who associates with the most reviled people."

- "Indeed, he must be crazy. He asks for wine to be shared, for us to forgive enemies, for us to live as if God's realm is being fulfilled."

These comments contrast with what we see as Jesus' message: God is in the present, doing new things. We have a choice: we can live as defeated people hoarding and protecting what we have; or we can live in new ways, being God's light to the world and rebuilding community.

The trouble Jesus gets into in the passage is the same as the good news we see him proclaim elsewhere—God is empowering people to live with hope and new life, to live as a redeemed community, even in the midst of losses and rejections. They (we) can flee and hoard what little we have. Or they (we) can hope and share. We can live

- as if health care is possible for all,

- as if we can end environmental degradation,

- as if all people matter, and

- as if hunger can be eliminated.

This interpretation is further supported by an amazing coincidence. A different section of Isaiah 61 is the *haphtarah* (prophetic reading) listed for each year in Jewish synagogues at the New Year celebration of Rosh Hashanah.[11] The texts combined on that day are Torah (Deut. 29:9–30:20), *haphtarah* (Isa. 61:10–63:9), and song (Ps. 65).

Was Jesus at home for Rosh Hashanah? We don't know. It might be a stretch. Yet the above effort to explain why he was rejected in his hometown and the meaning of the texts are very similar. The Torah portion for that day of Rosh Hashanah coupled with Isaiah 61 is Moses' last discourse to his people. Moses says, "Today we stand in the presence of God": "*For this commandment that I command you this day, it is not too hard for you, neither is it far off*" (Deut. 30:11 Tanakh[12]). The call of both the Torah and the *haphtarah* is to live the covenant. To live the expectations of the *Shema Yisrael*—loving God and loving neighbor! In fact, Jesus might have been reminding his neighbors to follow the vision of Isaiah. God is living in your midst—even in these times. God is calling you to rebuild community and to live for each other. If you don't, the grace of God will not take root in your present, as happened in the time of Elijah and Elisha. His words were descriptive. If you do not live the promise, it will be absent from the community. The new year is a time for reestablishing and recommitting to faithfulness. Were the people in Jesus' hometown able to do this?

A friend from Israel sent me a greeting for Rosh Hashanah. She wrote: "*Shana Tova*—have a good year and may you and your family be inscribed in the Book of Life." An amazing gift and grace! At the heart of her greeting was a wish that we be remembered by God. Identity and vocation are initiated in the grace of God. Knowing we are remembered by God calls us to claim our identity as God's children and to work to rebuild community—to love God and neighbor.

Does this summarize the message of Jesus to his home community? God's grace is present, even when you are defeated. Each day we have a new chance to live by God's grace because we are remembered by God. Yet, how many times do we both subtly and overtly hoard and protect when we could reach out with abundant trust. Is that what his neighbors were doing? Is that the message of hope that following the way of Jesus teaches?

I, of course, think so. This interpretation of the texts for Rosh Hashanah coincides with the message that seems to be at the heart of the memory of Jesus commenting on the text for the day and the people's confusion and rejection. In a world of conflict and crisis, with competing agendas and efforts to respond to Rome's oppression and God's presence, the vocation Jesus proclaimed is simple and clear—a way we will explore in more depth in future chapters. Just like Jesus, his followers are grounded in God's grace, knowing that even in the midst of loss, pain, and political oppression, God's grace is still present. The presence of God's grace inspires the followers to live the covenant, or even more, it expects those who receive God's grace to live it! The vocation of followers is to restore and live community even in a broken world. That is precisely what Jesus saw God's kingdom actions doing.

The text of Moses coupled with Isaiah is "We have turned away from the ways of faithfulness. And God will not avoid seeing that." No wonder the Nazareth villagers would be angry! They were reminded of how far they were from living the covenant. The message of Jesus inserted into his world was that the abundant grace of God is ubiquitous—that is the good news. Such grace calls for a vocation of risky faithfulness!

Teaching for Vocation

We are back at the educational questions about the way of Jesus. What does it mean to live that vocation? Here is a hint of what we will continue to encounter as we explore additional ways of seeking to understand and teach the way of Jesus. Where new life is proclaimed and embodied, redemptive communities are being built—redemptive communities that change individuals and whole towns and public spaces.

Congregations are teaching the ways of Jesus when they point to redemption occurring in their midst. They are teaching that hope, charity, mercy, and justice matter. Congregations (or communities) insulated from the world in "fear, reaction, and aggression" do not engage the gospel.[13] Redemptive mission is central to teaching the way of Jesus. Without teaching redemption and new life, the gospel becomes a facile, polite hope for civility, not the "good news of God" transforming the world.

The vocation we glimpse here is the power of the good news that is developed everywhere in the Gospels and records of the followers of Jesus. Actual people and communities were being transformed even in the midst of Roman oppression. People were healed, crowds fed, the blind given sight, and the possessed released. People were being freed to live and serve as new people with the possibility of life abundant. In fact, as healed people, they were welcomed back into community. Furthermore, awareness of the presence of God became a reality in the lives of people and communities. Intimacy with God (God's claim that they were God's children) freed them to live new lives. The caring for needs led to the celebrating of the love and power of God. This vocation is explicitly the vocation of Christian religious education. Moreover, the task of education is to teach people to live in this transformed, community-building manner. All of its practices and approaches point to this responsibility.

Finally, Jesus' call to vocation gave new possibilities for the building of community where people could live responsibly with and for each other. The miracle of Jesus was that people and communities had the possibility of changing. By faith, people accepted this grace, and new possibilities were present in human living.[14]

How do we teach people to live the way of Jesus? How do we teach the way of Jesus? We should pay more attention to the home community that welcomed Jesus, but resisted his efforts to teach them to renew and live their traditions. Were they so focused on their own needs that they could not hear the radical call for new life in Isaiah's vision of God's presence and call? They were scared and defeated. They took the definitions of the victimizers to heart. They lived as if the powers of the world determined life and meaning. They demanded a miracle, rather than living the joy that was present already in their midst. They focused on the scarcity in their experiences, rather than trusting in the abundance of God's love.

We live the way of Jesus when we follow the vocation Jesus offered, when we seek to translate this vocation in the ministry and mission of the church. The vocation of which Jesus speaks is first of all grounded in

God's grace. When we know we are known by God, we look for God's kingdom emerging in the world. Then we are called to live it: loving God and neighbor, inviting and welcoming strangers to the table of friendship and renewal, resisting powers of the world that would destroy life, and living expectantly and joyfully. Perhaps this is a good start to seeking to understand and live the way of Jesus.[15]

Chapter Two

The Imperative for Christian Education: Following Jesus into Public Life

Acts of the Apostles tells many stories of how early believers taught good news to others—how they told of the signs and wonders they encountered, the goodwill and possessions they shared, and their "gladness and simplicity" (Acts 2:46). Acts tells how the early Jesus movement taught what it meant to follow Jesus. They "demonstrated God's goodness to everyone" (Acts 2:47). Their lives had been transformed. They wanted all who surrounded them to know of the power of the way of Jesus. They taught by the ways they lived.

Is such passion at the heart of the ministry of the church today and of the ministry of Christian education? Building on a story from the Acts tradition, this chapter seeks to define the imperative for Christian education in our day. Why do we teach? What results from our teaching? Teaching what it means to follow the way of Jesus shapes the content and methods of Christian religious education.

One story from Acts focuses on Philip, who began healing, preaching, and teaching in Samaria (Acts 8:26-39). As the story goes, because of a dream, Philip traveled to a desert road between Jerusalem and Gaza. There he encountered a court official in charge of the treasury of the queen of

Ethiopia, who had been worshiping in Jerusalem. The official was reading the scroll of the prophet Isaiah. Philip asked him if he understood what he was reading. The official responded, "Without someone to guide me, how could I [understand]?" (Acts 8:31). That is simply what Philip did. His teaching so convinced the man that he asked to be baptized and left rejoicing.

Details of the story are very skimpy. We have no idea how the man lived his life after returning to Ethiopia, nor do we really learn much about what he was doing in Jerusalem, except that he worshiped. We know that there were many "God-fearing" Gentiles who would gather around Jewish worship and teaching sessions. The "God-fearers" were so impressed with the quality of the teaching and particularly the quality of the living that was evidenced by Jews that they searched Jewish traditions for guides for their own living. Was the Ethiopian in Jerusalem on business and simply encountered Jewish teaching, or did he intentionally go to Jerusalem to learn more about the Jewish community and its ways of living? Either or both are options.

He was a eunuch. We know that many ancient cultures made "eunuchs" for social or religious purposes, thinking they could better be controlled. Probably this was the case with this person because he had an important social and public service in the queen's treasury. However, eunuchs were not allowed to participate in temple rituals in Jerusalem, nor were they allowed as converts to Jewish faith.[1] Nevertheless, the Jewish writings were so important for him that he acquired a copy of the scroll of the prophet Isaiah.

Interestingly, as we know, it was from the scroll of Isaiah that Jesus first read in his hometown (Luke 4; Isa. 61). Also the prophet Isaiah proclaims that eunuchs will be given "a monument and a name better than sons and daughters" (Isa. 56:5). Isaiah expects faithful followers to "act justly and do what is righteous, because my [God's] salvation is coming soon, and my righteousness will be revealed" (Isa. 56:1). Isaiah proclaims that the Jewish community will be a model of righteousness for all humankind. God will bring those excluded, will bring the immigrants, "to my holy mountain, and bring them joy" (Isa. 56:7). Isaiah extends the invitation to God's great banquet of rich wines and wonderful foods to all creation. Isaiah includes, rather than excludes, even eunuchs. Isaiah expects the Jewish community to be an embodied witness for God.

The Ethiopian had listened and learned. Like many before from many places in the world, he probably had been amazed by the beauty of the temple in Jerusalem—its golden surface shone for miles. He was a pilgrim, seeking meaning from the convincing witnesses who lived the faith of Israel. He may have wondered at how the people had succeeded in preserving their religious traditions in a world where Roman overlords typically demanded allegiance to the Roman cult of emperor worship. He may even have been drawn to the ones in the Jewish community, the "eschatological" Jews, who turned to Isaiah, Daniel, Micah, and Zechariah to interpret the "signs of the times" (see Matt. 16:1-4 NRSV and Luke 12:54-59) amid the extraordinary violence with which Rome ruled its controlled lands.

The traditions of the Jewish people were so powerful, intriguing, and hopeful to him that he had acquired a scroll of Isaiah. On the road home, he was reading for understanding and insight. He was attempting to teach himself. Of course, as the writer of Luke and Acts would want to focus, he was reading "suffering servant" texts that early followers of Jesus used to make sense of their own experiences of confusion and rebirth at Jesus' death in Rome's terrorist campaign.[2]

The significance of this simple passage from Acts is often overlooked. Consider the elements that cohere in this story: a powerful and prestigious court official, yet one who has been controlled by his rulers and therefore is limited and defined; a person intrigued by the integrity and witness of Jewish believers, yet excluded from worship; and one who hears through the prophet Isaiah that there is a place for him in God's kingdom, but wonders if the news can be true. His confusion must have been intense. His prestige was challenged, his limitations were redefined, and he was welcomed to be a servant of a new life.

Then he met a teacher; Philip told him that he was a child of God. Philip witnessed to the good news of new life that Philip had himself experienced. Philip interpreted the traditions of Isaiah for him in a way that offered a transformative understanding of himself and his future. Again, we do not ultimately know what happened to him, yet this event was socially and personally transforming, triumphing over all the limitations and definitions that the world had placed on him. The teaching communicated the hope that Isaiah offered and gave him a place at the table. The message of the good news makes a difference. It challenges personal and social definitions. By teaching and guiding, Philip offered hope that was convincing and transforming.

For those for whom the way of Jesus is a transforming gift of identity and vocation, teaching is the primary means of sharing how to live with integrity and vitality. Teaching is personally and socially transforming. The vocation of the Christian religious educator is to teach this convincing and transforming way.

Yet, without a robust understanding of the texts and traditions, followers of Jesus can themselves be potential victims of misunderstanding and deception. For example, theologian Edward Farley has asked:

> Why is it that the vast majority of Christian believers remain largely un-exposed to Christian learning—to historical-critical studies of the Bible, to the content and structure of the great doctrines, to two thousand years of classic works on the Christian life, to the basic disciplines of theology, biblical languages, and Christian ethics? Why do bankers, lawyers, farmers, physicians, homemakers, scientists, salespeople, managers of all sorts, people who carry out all kinds of complicated task in their work and home, remain at a literalist, elementary school-level in their religious understanding?[3]

For many believers, isn't Farley's description true?

We all know believers who are very well informed and engage in mature, critical theological reflection. We know people who work to interpret what the way of Jesus means for daily living. Personally transforming interpretations help them know what it means to be a child of God and live, as Isaiah hoped, as righteous witnesses for God in the world. Socially transforming interpretations call them to challenge the definitions, exclusions, and name-calling that are part of the cultures in which we live.

Yet, we also know Christian believers who remain immature in their faith lives and can be easily misled. We know that many congregations fail adequately to teach children, youth, and adults the multiple Christian traditions that have emerged throughout history as well as the failures and successes of the church throughout history to live faithfully the ways of Jesus. We know some biblical content is taught, but wonder if people ever engage in historical biblical study? Moreover, do we assist people with the difficult, yet crucial tasks of engaging in theological reflection on their lives and ethical decisions? Do we help people practice the methods of theological study and interpretation?

Without continuing study, doctors, therapists, engineers, or public servants would not be able to fulfill their service for the human community. Parallel in the church, without knowledge and continuing study, those who call themselves disciples of the way of Jesus cannot fulfill their service to the human community.

The Ethiopian court official asked Philip, "Without someone to guide me, how could I [understand]?" The same is true of us. Without someone to teach us to understand the texts, traditions, interpretations, and expectations of the community, how can we be faithful to the identity that we claim and fulfill our vocation in the world—to follow the way of Jesus?

As we move through this chapter, I will explore more the power of a guide, a teacher. I will clarify the need of a teacher for the faithful and ask how we are called to teach even those who are strangers to this Jesus movement. Finally, I will end with a definition of education and Christian religious education.

Someone to Teach Us, Someone to Guide Us

Without a doubt, the questions of meaning asked by the Ethiopian official are similar to questions many of us ask every day: What is my vocation? What is our vocation as a nation or as a people? How do we live with our neighbors? How can we build just human communities? How do we find hope in the midst of loss and despair?[4] Daily we ask these and similar queries about how we should live our lives and build our communities. Drawing on the richness of the tradition, we address these questions, clarifying how we follow Jesus. These are the tasks of Christian religious education. What does it mean to teach and guide others?

Families are where we are taught some of our most enduring meanings. That is where I learned about teachers and guides for learning. I grew up with a grandmother and aunt living next door. Many a day after school, I would go to my grandmother's house. Of course, she always offered a snack, but she offered so much more. She included me in her activities, she invited me to meet her friends, and she let me listen as they negotiated problems and sought to care for others. By simply being with her, I learned so much. My grandmother's home was open to friends and those in need. She had taken in family members when they were sick or lost. For example, her brother lived with them, damaged by the carnage of World War I.

Seeing these interactions was very meaningful for my formation. She would talk with me about disagreements I had with my parents, she would encourage me, and she let me know that she had expectations for me. One of the most important was to be a "Seymour"—to live the values of the family. I was named after my grandfather, her husband, who had died when I was only five. I was his namesake. From a simple beginning, few years of school, and a first job gathering rocks in farmers' fields, my grandfather had overcome hardships. Early in his adult life he had a serious illness. It became an opportunity. From his sickbed, he studied and read, earning the equivalent of a high school degree and additional technical instruction from mentors in the Detroit automobile complex. He eventually became the assistant manager and then manager of a foundry that built auto parts. Being "Jack," I was given his watch and knife after his death. My grandmother let me know I was to fulfill the hopes Grandpa had for me. She was amazingly truthful about his strengths and weaknesses, his triumphs and failings, both professional and personal. For her, his life guided expectations for my brother and me.

As we would sit in her living room or on her front porch, she would tell family stories about her folks. Woven through many stories were the values and perspectives of the family: hard work, steadfastness, humility, openness to others, caring, and faithfulness. Clearly she was a guide to a way of life. Simple roots demanded resisting ostentation. Having opportunities demanded openness to strangers and caring. Overcoming demanded steadfastness. Hard work demanded learning to use one's hands and mind for the good of others. Loving God meant attending church and seeking to live the faith.

Of course, she wasn't the only mentor, but other mentors, from parents to classmates to teachers to religious leaders, taught what it meant to live faithfully each day. Without a teacher and guide, how will we know? Without a teacher and guide, how can we understand and claim our calling?

A Teacher for the Faithful

We all know that teaching occurs in the daily rhythms of life. Our inheritance is interpreted and then is revised as family members meet new situations and new realities. Similarly, the task of Christian education is to teach the inheritance of the faith, to interpret it for new times, and to guide believers into faithfulness.

We expect those who are active in a Christian community to know the faith well. While this is of course true for many, it is not true for all. Popular piety, community expectations, and civil religion too often triumph. We live in a "consumer society," defined by media representations of ever-new products and styles to make life better. The messages of a consumer culture, of how to succeed, of how to acquire the latest and, of course, the best, are communicated through the news media. Everyday culture teaches powerfully.

This context for contemporary learning is much like the ubiquitous presence of Roman culture in Jesus' day. Roman expectations of who was good and of value profoundly affected all, even those whose religious faith and cultural expectations were themselves very different. In fact, even though Jewish leaders had won the right to practice their own religious traditions, the high priests in the temple in Jerusalem had to pray daily for the emperor. Who was in charge was clear and who could be pushed aside was also clear. In similar ways, the cultural realities that surround young people today tell who is of value, who is good, and what is important. Christian education seeks to teach the way of faith in the midst of that world—sometimes challenging the world and other times directing how people live and relate to others.

Many do study and grow in faith and theological wisdom. Many are able to explain how faith convictions and even creedal formulas were constructed. Many are able to draw deeply and critically from faith meanings and traditions to understand how to live and for what to advocate. Yet, others cannot find books in the Bible and conflate biblical aphorisms with cultural sayings. How many believe that Ben Franklin's "To err is human, to repent divine, to persist devilish" is a biblical quotation? How many are convinced that the statements of some media preachers actually define the complexity and depth of Christian faith?

Teaching the faith is an imperative for believers. It is a complicated business of learning traditions, of learning a history, of learning biblical study methods, and of learning how to think theologically. A rich young man ran up to Jesus and asked, "Good Teacher, what must I do to obtain eternal life?" (Luke 18:18). Jesus answered reminding him of the commandments shared by Moses. The man acknowledged he knew them: "I've kept all of these things since I was a boy" (Luke 18:21). Yet, Jesus, as the historic prophets of Judaism, challenged the man's riches because they blocked him from living fully his faith (Matt. 19:16-22; Mark 10:17-22; Luke 18:18-24). This "faithful" believer was challenged by the deepest meanings of the faith story. Jesus was a guide and teacher, drawing on and reinterpreting the traditions.

Or, a similar incident, an expert in the law, asked Jesus, "Which commandment is the most important of all?" (Mark 12:28). Jesus' answer pointed him to the most important of all understandings of Judaism, to the Shema Israel (defined in Deut. 6; 11; and Num. 15), to be recited in worship and in prayers, even today, twice daily. The legal expert affirmed Jesus' words. Yet, Jesus added, as did many prophets and rabbis, that loving God and neighbor are more important than "burnt offerings and sacrifices" (Mark 12:33). Furthermore, as the story is recorded in Luke, Jesus tells a story, the parable of the good Samaritan, to interpret the call of the Shema (Luke 10:25-37). Teaching and interpreting the meanings of the faith are practices of Jesus. They involve nuanced, critical reflection, and depth theological reflection.

Without adequate theological knowledge and study, we are at a loss, becoming alienated from the very faith we express. How do we deal with the conflicts found in the biblical text? How do we decide among differing interpretations of ethical decisions advocated by religious leaders?

Diana Butler Bass, who has been studying congregational vitality in the United States, has discovered that vital congregations are connected to the Christian tradition, committed to Christian spiritual practices, and concerned to live "God's dream" for individuals and the wider world.[5] They help people practice theological reflection. In other words, vital congregations provide places for people to know more about the Christian story and tradition; to learn from, practice, and engage Christian practices as a way of focusing one's attention; and finally, to empower people to consider how the grace of God is transforming and renewing living. Vital churches are teaching churches. She concludes:

Some Christians, from pews, pulpits, and classrooms are asking the right questions—and are working toward a spiritually renewed and intellectually credible Christianity. . . [They have been] listening to the grassroots questions of American religious life, and constructing new patterns and practices of faith. For them, the questions are becoming clear—and some answers are emerging. Three deceptively simple questions are at the heart of a spiritually vibrant Christianity—questions of believing, behaving, and belonging.[6]

She argues that believing, behaving, and belonging are traditional questions for religious people, yet she argues that they are being asked in a more nuanced and critical manner today. Believers are not looking only for content and rules, but processes of theological interpretation. They need, as did the Ethiopian who met Philip, a guide.

An example: How does a person answer the questions proposed at a child's baptism without fulsome guidance and interpretation? Baptism is the rite of inclusion of those who believe and desire to be faithful.[7] While the questions may have been answered for a person, in some traditions, by one's parents, each time one hears the questions asked, one is called to answer them again.

The questions parents are asked in the United Methodist liturgy is an illustration of concerns shared ecumenically across many Christian communities:

- Do you renounce the spiritual forces of wickedness, reject the evil powers of this world, and repent of your sin?

- Do you accept the freedom and power God gives you to resist evil, injustice, and oppression in whatever forms they present themselves?

- Do you confess Jesus Christ as your Savior, put your whole trust in his grace, and promise to serve him as your Lord, in union with the church which Christ has opened to all people of all ages, nations, and races?

- According to the grace given you, will you remain faithful members of Christ's holy church and serve as Christ's representatives in the world?[8]

29

How does one even attempt to answer these questions with meaning and purpose without serious study?

Question one recognizes that the world in which we live is one where wickedness and injustice often rule. Wealth grows as poverty grows. Life chances of some improve while life chances of others decline. Power is used for gain, rather than community. Responsibility is shirked in favor of personal fulfillment. Concomitantly the environment is daily destroyed by thoughtless choices. Realizing that none of us can address these issues fully, and that we too often are guilty of actions that further wickedness, do we have a desire to repent? Question one is a political question: With the grace of God, with God's help, do we seek to be representatives of hope and new life?

The second question is clear that many of our choices are complicit with division and hurt of others, yet we can live differently. We can seek to change our actions and build a world where hope and justice emerge.[9] Finally, to whom do we give allegiance—the nation, ourselves, our professions?—or do we seek to follow Jesus as a guide to "God's hope for the world"? Do we, indeed, accept the freedom to resist evil, injustice, and oppression?

The fact is that theological study is difficult, as is child rearing, fulfilling the requirements of our work life, or learning the intricacies of a hobby. There are ways of learning to interpret scripture, of knowing the faith, of assessing our community's convictions, and of making ethical decisions guided by those commitments. In fact, for many of us, we simply ignore conflicts. As such, we wonder if faith can really make a difference in how we live, raise children, hope, and seek to contribute and serve others. Secularism, consumerism, and culture subtly control our decision making.

This does not need to be the case. We care about how we raise our children, and we study and seek to improve that. We care about our jobs and the ways we serve others; we are constantly learning. We care about our hobbies, and we learn, study, and experiment. The same can be true of our faith lives. As with Philip and the Ethiopian, study transforms our lives and the ways we interact with others. Our identities and vocations are shifted.

The good news of the way of Jesus is profoundly transforming—personally and socially. We live knowing that God calls us God's children.

We seek to build community knowing that God cares about the world in which we live. We seek to live in ways that make a difference because God's redemptive presence is alive in our world. All of these are dependent on engaging in serious, systematic, and sustained theological interpretation. We seek to teach and to educate.

Back to Bass's questions, which are central to religious life. Knowing how to believe, seeking to make a difference, and finding a community of hope guiding others into a fuller life—the realm of God—is precisely the motivation for believers to grow in faith and to deepen their understandings and practices. Frankly, such action is empowering—we experience new life as we seek to be part of a people following Jesus. Theological reflection is a life practice for Christians.

Christian Education: A Guide for Public Life

Christian education teaches believers. Their lives affect their worlds. Moreover, we must ask: What role does Christian education have to play in public dialogue? The United States is one of the world's most diverse societies, and that diversity is increasing. If it were ever the case, the Christian faith is not the only player in public dialogue. A task of Christian educators is to help the faithful know what it means to be Christian amid this diversity. In addition, the task of Christian educators is to teach and interpret to the wider world its meanings. Just as Jewish educators and Islamic educators are teaching the faithful the meanings of their traditions, they are also interpreting the impact of their traditions on our wider shared world. We seek partnerships in a diverse world.

At one time, Christians thought their meanings and values were being taught everywhere in the public square. There was a time when communities published Bible lessons in Saturday papers so readers could prepare for Sunday school, which is no longer the case. At one time many public school classes began with prayers and Bible readings. As I grew up in northern Indiana in the 1950s, Bible verses from the King James Version were often read. In third grade, all of us were asked to pick a Bible passage to read at the beginning of school with a brief devotion. In fourth grade, my school had "released-time" instruction where, with parents' permission, we students walked two blocks to the basement of a nearby Free Methodist Church for religious instruction provided by the Howard

County Council of Churches (nonsectarian and Protestant). The town also had Sunday "blue laws" where businesses were closed so families could spend a day in church and family activities. My dad always filled up his car on Saturday at the local Marathon Oil station so that he would have plenty of gas for Sunday activities. Religion—a kind of lowest-common-denominator Protestantism—was present in much of public conversation. We knew there was a local synagogue near the public park, and we knew the two local Catholic churches provided grade schools. Only occasionally was the local rabbi or priest involved in public prayers. Finally, all the local public officials listed their church affiliations as they ran for public office—who would vote for one without it?

However, even this low-level "religious atmosphere" did not really provide a public education in religion. With increased US religious diversity, including even active nonreligious perspectives, religious participation in public life is starkly different. Clearly, religions still affect public life, but in a more complicated fashion. In fact, the news tends to focus on the "sound bite." News has to entice since news programs survive on ratings. Therefore, the extreme religious stories become public. Religion is an aspect of public conversation. It affects how people think about their world.

How are the perspectives of Christian faith, in a complex and nuanced way—in an educated way—made part of these conversations? It takes much longer to tell a religious story or to clarify a faith position than is allowed on news programming. Current stories about the requirements of the US health care legislation, about family planning, and about creationism in public schools, as well as stories about clergy abuse, clearly raise the importance of religion in the public sphere. Many public issues are at their heart religious issues. Health care, for example, is about how we care for those who are excluded. How do we create health care legislation that provides enhanced standards of care for all? The present controversy over "entitlements" or government guarantees through Social Security and Medicare is again an issue of care and health. What is our obligation to those who are the "least of these"? The federal budget itself is a religious statement defining how we think about the meaning of community and our responsibility to one another. Ideas of equality and equal opportunity have been at the heart of the American dream. Dr. Martin Luther King Jr. drew on these images of what the United States could be in his call for dismantling racism. For example, Dr. King, in his "Letter from Birmingham

Jail," wrote, "So here we are . . . with a religious community largely adjusted to the status quo, standing as a tail-light behind other community agencies rather than a headlight leading men to higher levels of justice."[10]

Moreover, if contemporary research is true, this dream is getting farther and farther from a reality. Economist and Nobel Prize winner Joseph Stiglitz has argued that public policies over the last thirty years have in fact muted equality of opportunity. While the top 1 percent enjoys the privileges of health care, education, and wealth, these are increasingly out of reach for the vast majority. A child born into poverty with limited life chances remains with limited life chances.[11]

Indeed the questions of poverty and life chances are religious questions of how opportunity should be shared throughout the public. Who is of value and who is not, or in other words, who is a child of God? Furthermore, many have suggested that childhood diseases and even hunger itself could be eliminated with the appropriate priorities for public action.[12] Such powerful and important questions about the kind of world we want to live in and the value of people are at their heart religious questions.

While there is not clear evidence of how and if Jesus directly addressed Roman public officials of his day, it is clear that he held to the high standards for justice of the biblical prophets. In villages desperately affected by the exorbitant taxation of court and Roman officials, Jesus called them back to patterns of care and support for one's neighbors. Moreover, in one incident in the Gentile territory of the Gerasenes, where he freed a demoniac of his powers, the demons are explicitly named Legion, and Jesus drives them out of the country (Mark 5:1-20; Matt. 8:28-34; Luke 8:26-39). Legion is clearly the name of the Roman army, and the people were afraid that Jesus' actions would have negative repercussions for them, as so often happened with the military might of Rome, destroying rebellious cities and crucifying rebels on the sides of the road. We also know that Jesus was precisely crucified himself as an agent of sedition—named on his cross as "King of the Jews." All of these confirm a direct connection of "following Jesus" and public impact.

Without intentional effort of Christian education of the public, the general understanding of Christian religion is dominated by the extreme media example and the most recent protest or scandal.

In the last decade, the word "religion" has become equated with institutional or organized religion. Because of crises such as the Sept. 11 terrorist attacks and the Roman Catholic abuse scandal, Americans now define "religion" in almost exclusively negative terms. These larger events, especially when combined with increasing irrelevance of too much of organized religion, contributed to an overall decline in church membership, and an overall decline of the numbers of Christians, in the United States.[13]

The public conversation then often focuses only on the controversies and does it with such little ambiguity and nuance. This raises a profound challenge for those who seek to engage public life out of a religious perspective.

A story: in a recent report about the life and work of Sargent Shriver, cousin to President John F. Kennedy and director of the War on Poverty and Peace Corps, his children spoke about how his faith helped him find "peace and purpose." His deep Catholic faith empowered his desire to help discover ways that poverty could be eliminated and peace advanced. Mark, one of his sons, commented, "He wanted to be with you because he really felt you were a gift from God. It didn't matter whether you were a big shot or a regular person."[14] In turn, many public leaders have spoken about how religious convictions empower decision making. Religion makes a difference in the official corridors of public decision making.

Christian education enhances and contributes to public conversation. Religions guide how decisions are framed and discussed. Religions also guide how individuals enter the public realm. That requires depth, critical analysis. An example is the Protestants for the Common Good (PCG) in Chicago. An advocacy group, PCG seeks to educate the public and provide resources to church groups to explore contemporary public issues. Their explicit purpose, referring to Micah 6:8, is stated as follows:

> The prophet Micah proclaims that faithful living encompasses three distinct, but inter-connected, dimensions of faithful living. The call to "do justice" points out the social, or public, dimension while the mandate to "love kindness" focuses on the personal and interpersonal. In both, we are to "walk humbly with God," i.e., accept God's guidance for both the public and personal aspects of our lives.[15]

Education about social justice concerns is their work. Many other such groups could also be described.[16] Their public conversation serves as a guide for public religion.

Christian Education for Those Who Have Never Heard

We understand the imperative for education for believers—otherwise they will not continue to grow in faith and robustly participate within their religious communities. In addition, we clearly can argue that the Christian religious education of the public empowers the "followers of Jesus" to participate in discussions about the kind of society we want to build. Yet, what about those who eschew religion or do not show interest in claiming a religious faith? How is Christian religious education an influence?

Diana Butler Bass again offers an interpretation of a potential group who has never heard. While documenting the decline of religious institutional participation, she identifies two categories of people outside congregations who are interested in faith issues: popularly called the "nones," these two groups are the "spiritual but not religious" and the "spiritual and religious." They represent a significant part of the population. In fact, the "nones" are not interested in churches because they do not want to be "caught up in political intrigue, rigid rules and prohibitions, institutional maintenance, unresponsive authorities, and inflexible dogma." Rather they are looking for places that address their "spiritual longings" that "offer pathways of life-giving spiritual experience, connection, meaning, vocation, and doing justice in the world."[17] How does Christian education respond to these realities?

Theologian Linda Mercandante and Christian educator John Roberto also echo Bass's conclusions. They offer us a way to understand the tasks of Christian religious education. Mercandante, for example, has conducted sustained interviews with the "spiritual but not religious" group (SBNR). She concludes:

> It's tempting to dismiss SBNRs as salad-bar spiritualists concerned primarily with themselves. But for both demographic and theological reasons it is important to think more deeply about the people who invoke that description. They represent a profound challenge and an opportunity for religious groups today.[18]

She has discovered their amazing diversity. Many speak wistfully about "community and sense of purpose." Many of them reject positions they think that the Christian faith holds, yet the fact is that they have been misinformed by much of the public conversation and media hype about religion. They speak of spirituality as the "core of faith" while religion is the "institutionalized shell."

While many oversimplify the relationship of religious belief and its cultural forms, they in fact long for serious conversation about theological questions of God, the future, sin, and hope for the world. Many claim no one ever gives them a chance; they have not experienced many religious people or churches open "to learn and dialogue" with them "about theological concerns." Mercandante argues that churches need to develop ways of engaging these people theologically. She writes:

> Unless the church takes seriously the theological reasons that they give for staying away from organized religion, any efforts to engage this population will be hampered. SBNRs represent an opportunity for churches to reinvigorate their ability to speak and think theologically.[19]

Note Mercandante's focus on theological reflection. On the whole, this group is hungry for theological conversation and theological education.

Roberto agrees. His research names the same factors affecting decline of religious institutions: increasing individualism; declining participation in social groups, including the church; more people identifying themselves as spiritual-but-not-religious; increased pluralism in society; changing patterns of family religious socialization; and increased impact of digital technology and media. His research points to four scenarios of how people relate to the church.[20] The first is the believer and active participant group. These people with vibrant faith and active engagement fully participate in the life and ministries of congregations. They are the ones for whom we tend to plan educational programming. In fact, for this group, traditional Christian education and program planning have been successful.

A second group participates in the church, but not actively. They enter the congregation for major liturgical events and high holy seasons. Some may have a faith community, attending irregularly; others do not have regular community but are willing to attend for a major life transition, like a marriage or a baptism. When these people attend, it is not so much out of a spiritual need but out of a need to belong and connect with friends and family at key events or offer children a chance to belong. For this group, Roberto argues, an opening for Christian religious education is building on the ritual moments and the desire to find a place to belong—to be understood and accepted. Enriching theological articulation about holy days, enhancing the meaning and depth of the ritual events, and helping people make meaningful connections are all agenda to potentially deepen participation and understanding.

A third group may be hostile to religion. This group includes people who have been hurt by faith communities or in contrast are third- and fourth-generation members of families who never darkened the door of a congregation. They are "unaffiliated and uninterested." Roberto argues that planting a hospitable presence in the midst of the places where they associate is one way to reach out or provide welcome. Presence also offers a glimpse of meaning and potential in moments of questioning and challenge. For example, a growing congregation in Chicago, Urban Village Church, sent several members, after instruction, to provide "ashes" for anyone who wanted them on the street corners downtown on Ash Wednesday. Many people had no idea of the liturgical or theological meaning of this symbol; others knew very well what they meant. But the fact was that many asked for ashes. Some took literature of welcome and hospitality. Others risked attending a gathering of the congregation to see what this church was about. They were drawn by its open acknowledgment of brokenness and the offer of hope and new life.

A final group is the "spiritual, but not religious." Like Mercandante, Roberto challenges congregations to listen to the theological questions of these individuals and engage in thoughtful conversations. In fact, Roberto is a believer in Internet outreach where congregations provide and point to Internet resources engaging theological issues. He recognizes that much of what is on the Internet about religion is not helpful, is authoritarian, is wrong, and may be harmful. What if a church found a way to engage in critical, nuanced resourcing of spiritual concerns and theological questions at the heart of living? What if we work to provide the kind of depth theological reflection possible in a critical theological community that honors biblical criticism and theological reflection? What if we provide the quality of theological education that could make a difference? This is impossible without listening to people's questions and concerns; otherwise one would provide answers for questions not being asked. Two of my colleagues at Garrett-Evangelical, Jim Papandrea, a church historian, and Brooke Lester, a Hebrew Bible scholar, have regular Facebook and blog entries responding to questions and offering wisdom. Papandrea also has written a new book on the earliest church leaders. Through the Internet, he offers his scholarship demonstrating how Christian faith is open, critical, nuanced, and addressing the most important practices of daily living. Lester provides resources for people to study the Bible.[21]

How are we guides for those who have not heard—for those who are "spiritual but not religious?" Isn't the advice that Mercandante, Roberto, and Bass provide much like some of the ministry of Jesus? He stopped by a well in Samaria, a land where many Jewish leaders like himself rarely went. While there, he met a woman who was drawing water (John 4:1-42). They engaged in a conversation at the well, he listened to her, he accepted her surprise at his openness, and he offered her the gift of "living water." The depth and truthfulness of their conversation amazed her. Jesus accepted her, even as he was being challenged by his disciples. He offered her the promise at the heart of Judaism—that by living as "light for the people," as children and witnesses for God, all humankind would be brought together to celebrate at the feast in the kingdom of God (Isa. 49). Because of his engaging, his hospitality, and his challenge, she went to her people and drew others to him. We can name many other places in the New Testament witness where welcome and faith are offered in ways that transform. That is the heart of Christian education that guides those who do not yet believe or know.

At the Heart of Christian Education

We have seen that Christian education is crucial for assisting believers in understanding how to follow the way of Jesus into the world. Christian education teaches people the depth of the faith and provides resources on how to live in the midst of a diverse public world. Furthermore, Christian education has a responsibility to offer options to those who have never heard, to the public. Christian education deeply cares about the kind of world in which we live. The vocation of those who follow Jesus, acknowledging God's grace and seeking for abundant living, healing, and justice for the world, is fulfilled when we teach the faith and openly share its hopes and visions with the public.

Let us move from these convictions to look more closely at education and Christian religious education.[22] At the heart of all education are identity, vocation, and resources. Lawrence Cremin, former professor and president of Teachers College in New York City, has defined education as "the deliberate, systematic and sustained effort to transmit or evoke knowledge, attitudes, values, skills, and sensibilities."[23] He shows in his monumental, Pulitzer-winning, three-volume *American Education* (*The Colonial Experience 1607–1783*; *The National Experience 1783–1876*; and *The Metropolitan Experience, 1876–1980*) that education is fundamentally about passing on a heritage, a way of being, to another. Just as families seek to pass on a heritage, cultures are passed on through explicit teaching and through storytelling, artifacts, and rituals. Just as my grandmother explained to me over and over, time and again, what it meant to be a "Seymour." She wanted me to carry on family values. To use Cremin's words, she deliberately, systematically, and in a sustained effort sought to transmit to or evoke in me a way of living that was consistent with and that honored the values for which the family stood.

Education, at its heart, involves efforts to pass on a heritage or a way of living in a new time and place. While, of course, the passing on will be challenged by new circumstances and encountering people who are different, it is a foundation from which an identity is built. We need to know that heritage and be able to interpret it in a new day and time for it to be a vital way of life. Psychologist and educator Dan McAdams describes the "stories we live by"—how each of us weaves from the threads of our childhoods, our experiences, our mentors, or our guides a story that gives us an identity and meaning of self.[24] Education is fundamentally about who we are in a way of life that surrounds and defines us—an identity. This understanding of education is fully consistent with Cremin's picture of what American educators sought as they passed on meaning, values, myths, and an identity that sought to help a person know himself or herself.

Second, education is about vocation. In a later book, *The Redemptive Self*, written from ten years of research, McAdams discovers not only how people know themselves, how they respond to crises and challenges, but also how they define what they are called to do—a vocation.[25] Education is about our commitments to ourselves, our families, and our communities.

My grandmother did not require that I become interested in manufacturing of automobile parts to fulfill the hopes embodied in my life, yet she did encourage me to enroll in higher education. She expected me to live out the gifts I had been given in ways that addressed human need.

Finding a calling or a way to fulfill an identity is exactly what happened with the woman at the well. Knowing she was accepted, hearing a renewed identity, she went into the village as a witness, proclaiming the person and work of this Jesus she had met. Her identity called for a new vocation. She could not have had a major role in the village before her encounter at the well, but after it she claimed a vocation of responsibility for others.

Third, education is about providing the resources and skills necessary for us to live out our vocations. A career as a medical professional means the development of skills to fulfill the vocation. Teachers seek to understand the teaching/learning process, grasp practices of assessing learners, set learning goals, and develop design skills for organizing teaching and learning so students can learn. We could describe how providing the resources and skills is true for a number of other professions and tasks. They are essential to the fulfillment of a vocation and identity.

Christians have an identity. They are followers of the way of Jesus. They know what it means to experience the acceptance and grace of God that calls for new life. They know they are children of God. As Paul says, they put on Christ; they "dress" themselves in Christ (Rom. 13:14). As Peter proclaims, "You are a chosen race, a royal priesthood, a holy nation, a people who are God's own possession. . . . Once you weren't a people, but now you are God's people" (1 Pet. 2:9, 10).

This identity gives Christians a vocation. Just as Jesus sent the disciples out "to proclaim God's kingdom and to heal the sick" (Luke 9:2; see also Matt. 10:1-14; Mark 6:6b–13), we are sent out to tell the good news and heal sickness as followers of Jesus. Of course, the particular faithful vocation of each of us will connect with our abilities and strengths; our vocations connect so that in daily life our actions may fulfill our call as followers.

Finally, we will need skills for the work of living, proclaiming, and healing. They will be:

- skills of faithfulness in our daily lives and tasks,

- skills of theological wisdom and reflection so we continue to struggle with what it means to follow Jesus,

- skills of listening to ourselves, the community, and others so we know how to engage and respond to others,

- skills of leadership and coalition so we can work across boundaries to seek to fulfill the hopes of God's good news,

- skills of continually praising and seeking God for grace, and

- skills in learning what it means to walk in the way of the followers of Jesus.

A Challenge to Christian Religious Education

The Ethiopian court official that Philip met on the road was reading a scroll of Isaiah. It was not the literature he usually read. Its words and meanings captured his imagination, but he was not sure he understood. Isaiah seemed to be offering hope. Philip appeared with confidence; he was clear about his identity and his vocation. The court official drew on his skills to ask if he would be a guide. "Without a guide," he said, "how will we learn?" How will we claim a new identity, a new vocation, and grow in the resources to fulfill it?

Such indeed is the challenge of Christian religious education. Are we fulfilling our vocation? Do we assist believers in growing in wisdom? Do we provide the resources for growing identity development and ability as followers of Jesus? Do we help people learn the skills and processes of biblical interpretation and theological reflection? In what ways are we helping the public see the powerful commitments and hopes that followers of Jesus can offer to public conversation? Does the public have any sense of the joy of God's promised banquet or God's call to renew and heal creation? Do they understand what it means to care for the least of these, creating a world of life chances and health, rather than rewarding those with standing, wealth, and power? Do they know that Christians are open to learn—to grow, to engage in biblical criticism and study, to seek to discern God's hope for humanity and the world, to listen to the voices of science and care, and to live theologically reflective and growing lives? Finally, how are we helping those who have not heard to know the resources of a respectful position of Christian faith? Are we witnessing that life can indeed be different and community can be built and meaning can be found that renews and builds community respectfully across differences?

A recent study of mainline churches by David Hollinger, the president of the Organization of American Historians, notes some of their important accomplishments. He argues that they have influenced US public life with hope, justice, openness, and a sense of community and responsibility. They helped give birth to legislation that sought to advance life chances, expect mutuality and responsibility, and provide care for all. They communicated a public vision.

> They led millions of American Protestants in directions demanded by the changing circumstances of the times and by their own theological tradition. These ecumenical leaders took a series of risks, asking their constituency to follow them in antiracist, anti-imperialist, feminist and multicultural directions.[26]

These public churches gave birth to the spirit that inspired the war on poverty and the Peace Corps. They participated in the assault on the racism that has been institutionalized in US history; they sought a world of partnership, rather than conquest; and they reached out to those who were different to build coalitions for community and the healing of creation.

Yet, Hollinger added, that today they seem to have given up on these public tasks, failing "to persuade many of their own progeny that churches remain essential institutions in the advancement of these values."[27] However, he argues, this failure can be traced to expecting people to follow, rather than continuing to educate them in an open, critical theological wisdom. They knew the power of biblical scholarship, they sought to understand the contributions of social science and critical thinking to faith, they listened to truth from other peoples and worldviews, but too often they failed to fully educate their own people or to fully communicate to the public what it means to think theologically about every life and decision.

Another historian, James Carroll, argues that a wrong-headed reading of the separation of church and state caused this educational attitude. As

Carroll comments, we expected our politicians to show "public devoted-ness," but thought deep religious convictions should be kept in private so as to not violate others. "Public Christians" have failed to fully communicate their religious convictions. In a rather extreme manner, with a lot of truth, Carroll concludes:

> Because matters of religion would be kept in a realm apart, the zone designated as private, the kinds of human development nurtured in the public square would not find a hospitable niche in religion. . . . Church-sponsored religious education—Sunday school—would be overwhelmingly focused on children, resulting in an infantilization of belief. Bible stories yes, biblical criticism no. This would lead to a widespread religious illiteracy. . . . Relatively few American believers would ever be offered significant religious instruction by their faith institutions. . . . The result of all of this would be a population that takes for granted the methods of historical and critical thinking in all other areas of life while remaining intellectually immature when it comes to religion.[28]

For one who has spent his life in Christian religious education and sought to educate future pastors and educators, these words seem very harsh and hurtful. Yet, there is too much truth in them to ignore them. Out of a fear of offending public conversation, many public Christians have abandoned the public stage to more narrow and rigid forms of religious understanding. Frankly, we have acted as if we were superior.

Moreover, while we have sometimes done a great job of providing educational materials with critical and historical perspectives, we have failed to proclaim in churches the importance of continuing study and education. Frankly, we have celebrated the liberation and empowerment of these methods, but have feared to fully teach them to those with whom we worked. We knew that a nuanced and ambiguous set of conclusions was hard work. We have tinkered with institutional reorganization, rather than simply honoring the channels for education and engagement that were present. We have followed publishing trends, "glossing over" excellent curriculum materials.

We have provided instruction for some of the believers that Roberto calls *those with vibrant faith and active engagement*, but we have failed to hold others accountable to the responsibilities and rigors needed for following Jesus. In fact, we have acted as if providing a felicitous community in a congregation would empower believers to make significant public changes. Maintenance has too often replaced prophecy.

Again, I celebrate the many places where education has occurred in depth. We have individuals in the congregation I attend who know the faith traditions, who have engaged in deep and critical Bible study, and who engage faith and tradition with the same critical skills they engage medicine, teaching, law, or social service. Yet even this congregation, until a few years ago, had abandoned adult education. Without a culture of theological reflection, without a call for responsible belief, without a regular effort to listen and engage the issues people bring to faith, and without membership vows that mean something, education is limited and its power muted. Carroll is then correct.

Moreover, the failure of our actions to communicate with and challenge our public world has meant that we have ignored the "spiritual but not religious." Our fear of looking too much like the extreme Christians who do get the news bite has meant we have not provided an alternative for the "uninformed and uninterested." Without this, and without genuine partnership with other religious people from other religious traditions to seek to work for new life in the world we share, we have even driven some serious believers away from the congregation because they have become tired of the same old surface, repeated study.

Cremin, the educational historian, himself an American Jew, told his Protestant and Catholic students to study and reclaim the heritage and contributions their publicly committed and intellectually open ancestors had contributed to hope and community in the United States. Hollinger offers similar advice when he argues that the "faith-affirming voices" of ecumenical Christians can vigorously return to the public conversation. They can, if they focus. They can be an articulate and educated "prophetic minority."[29]

In turn, Cremin argues that an essential role of good education is "prophesy, or the artistic linking of tradition and aspiration."[30] Education "prophetically" calls a people back to their deepest and most important values. Education helps contemporary people to "artistically" connect current experience with these values. Therefore, educators examine the variety of social procedures that teach, their interrelationships, and their outcomes. The educator then "problematizes" the findings so that people can question—exploring the deepest meanings in their traditions and the hopes that guide their living with the realities they encounter. Education is thus an arena of controversy and public decision making. Christian education calls a people to seek to understand a tradition, claim the hope at the heart of a faith, and provide occasions for the people of God to engage these in ways that help them "follow Jesus." Thus Christian religious education is an imperative so that faithful people can follow Jesus into public living.

Chapter Three

The People of God as Theologians: Seeking the Ways of Jesus

One of the most puzzling stories in the New Testament is Jesus' encounter with a Canaanite woman in the Gentile regions of Tyre and Sidon (Matt. 15; Mark 7:24-30).[1] As soon as Jesus enters the region, a woman shouts out, "Show me mercy, Son of David" (Matt. 15:22). Her daughter is ill. In what seems to be an uncharacteristic manner, he completely ignores her. Of course, she is a foreigner and not of his faith. She persists, shouting after Jesus and the disciples, so much so that the disciples advise him to send her away.

In an exclusivist posture, he tells her, "I've been sent only to the lost sheep, the people of Israel" (Matt. 15:24). When she persists and begs, he responds, even more offensively, "It is not good to take the children's bread and toss it to dogs" (v. 26). His ethnocentrism shows; he and his disciples are offended. Is it her continual pleading, her nationality, or her gender?

There are other stories in the Gospels of Jesus healing Gentiles. Why did he refuse her? Moreover, Tyre and Sidon were Roman port cities. One would expect to meet a great diversity of people there. Immediately northwest of Galilee on the trade routes, they were considered pagan and filled with non-Israelites. In fact, Jesus notes this pagan status when he compares Chorazin and Bethsaida to them, celebrating the ways that people in Tyre respond to his teaching and healing (Matt. 11:21-24). Frankly, if one's ministry was to the "people of Israel," why spend time here? Certainly he would have ignored and rejected her, if she had not continued, "But even the dogs eat the crumbs that fall off their masters' table" (Matt. 15:27).

In this story, we see Jesus change his mind. We see a transformation. In fact, she may be one of the reasons he later praises Tyre. "Woman, you have great faith. It will be just as you wish" (Matt. 15:28). The daughter was healed. In turn, Jesus is challenged and rethinks some of his expectations about his vocation.

Learning begins with our experiences. Learning also begins as we seek to live our traditions. Experiences confirm or challenge accepted patterns of meaning. If the patterns are confirmed, they are reinforced; we then believe them even more firmly. If challenged, we ask, what is wrong with our perception? Ordinary meanings are tremendously stable. We expect them. For example, a person who is always healthy visits the doctor and is told that all is well. The expectation of health is reinforced. Yet, on the day that a doctor raises a question about a test and sends one for further scrutiny or to a specialist, profound questions are raised. Was the test wrong? Am I seriously ill? In fact, fear and depression can result because everyday expectations are challenged. Schedules are shifted. If the new results come back saying there was simply an anomaly, life continues as is; organized meanings and expectations are renewed. If, however, something serious is discovered, the result can be anxiety, fear, and a total upset of expectations. We ask: How will my life be different? What can I count on? What's next?

Did Jesus expect those in his hometown of Nazareth to respond like those he had healed, fed, or saved? On the road, he had become quite a celebrity, so much so that he was exhausted. What did it mean when he saw his neighbors' lack of hospitality to each other and their demand for him to perform? What did it tell him about his vocation and his ministry? Furthermore, what happened when those who were culturally strangers, and expected to reject his gifts, requested them? We know that he was surprised. He did not think the Canaanite woman would be able to see the new life he offered—her people never did. His disciples sought to hold him to the tradition and send this noisy woman away. Yet, in her need to care for her daughter, she violated the conventions of the day and pleaded with him. Not even being offended when referred to as a "dog," she evidently knew her place. All the same, she teaches him that her daughter's illness transcends what he expects. Even though Jesus had little status, being from Galilee, he had more than she did. Just as she reached beyond her comfort zone, pleading and shouting for respect from this miraculous stranger, he, too, reached beyond his. The fate of her daughter drove her to risk boundaries. Her plight and her intensity, in turn, challenged Jesus' expectations. We so clearly see the learning: from "You are not my vocation; your people are not as worthy," to "I have a fuller vocation!"

Here we see Jesus learning. He drew on the traditions of his faith community. He engaged his experiences, particularly the faithfulness of this outsider. He questioned what he thought was his identity. He expanded his vocation. The resources that assisted him in making these decisions were the processes of meaning and interpretation that had been taught to him by his faith community, its experiences with making sense of new realities, and his prayerful intimacy with God and God's realm.

As we discussed in the last chapter, teaching regularly focuses on understanding the traditions that organize our worlds. Teaching assists us toward knowing these traditions, their meanings and expectations, and learning to fulfill them. Yet, teaching also deals with the limits of those traditions. Teaching shapes our identities and vocations and gives us the resources to understand and revise them.

A stark example: in the late 1700s, the newly formed United States spoke about equality and opportunity, yet African Americans, living as slaves, were only counted as three-fifths human, and women were excluded from the vote. The gentry were highlighted as those best able to manage democratic government. Education took on the agenda of assisting people to become citizens in the new democratic republic—to learn to contribute to democratic values and to make wise political decisions. This was not easy. Politicians in Andrew Jackson's time made fun of those he drew to his campaign—calling them uneducated and uncouth country bumpkins. Yet as education was extended, the compromises within the US tradition could no longer stand. After many years of inhumanity, when every other civilized nation had outlawed slavery, the Emancipation Proclamation was finally issued on January 1, 1863. It then took more than a hundred years for full political rights to be added. The same is true of women's suffrage. Access to education was limited; at first, "finishing schools" were the best option. Women were excluded from public office and even from pastoral work, so much so that alternative careers in missions, teaching, and caring were born. Only after much conflict and with a close vote were voting rights allowed. Furthermore, many denominations, even the mainline ones, blocked women's ordination until the middle of the twentieth century.

Just as education affirms and reinforces the traditions on which we draw to live, education also helps us deal with the conflicts we experience and find new patterns of living and serving. For Jesus the conversation with the Canaanite woman was a transforming moment, where his traditional expectations about who was of value and with whom he was to work were challenged. Christian religious education offers us the resources to make sense of our contexts, our experiences, and our realities. These processes are called in the Christian community, *theological reflection*.

Personal questions and concerns as well as public ones fuel our search for meaning and purpose—issues much like those in Jesus' time. For example, how do we as Christians deal with the reality of the wealth and increasing poverty in the United States?[2] The gap between wealthy and poor continues to grow and widen. Differing traditions profoundly affect how people see these gaps and think about addressing them.

Turn back two thousand years and ask similar questions: How was the gospel Jesus taught and the faithfulness he expected received? How was good news taught in a world of massive divisions where the wealthy controlled decision making, commerce, and the military? Poverty and landlessness grew as shrewd leaders built orchards and vineyards to feed the armies of control. The majority of people lived at a subsistence level. Voices crying in the wilderness—crying for justice—were systematically silenced. Intimidation was the primary means of social control. Religious leaders compromised with power—sometimes truncating prophetic faith to rituals. Of course, the times are radically different, yet the similarities are amazing. How do we teach the faith? How do we address the cries of people? Theological reflection is the means by which we seek to interpret our identities and vocations in a new day, faithful to the expectations and aspirations of our ancestors. Theological reflection is the essential practice of teaching.

Yearnings of the People of God

Education is prophetic connecting of the deepest meanings of our communities with contemporary realities. Theological reflection is the way we Christians seek to understand the ways of Jesus. Just as Jesus learned from the concrete experience of the yearnings of the Canaanite woman, our yearnings push us into theological reflection using the resources of the faith to understand and live our identities and vocations. In the following, we will examine and illustrate this essential theological process of teaching and learning.

In my home, Chicago, the last few years have seen a significant increase in the death rate of urban youth. Several have died in inter-gang warfare; many others have been innocent victims of this fighting—infants shot by bullets piercing the walls of homes. The news is filled with cries of anguish from the families and their cries for meaning.

Evelyn Parker, in her important book *Trouble Don't Last Always*, points to the anguish of youth caught in the spiral of racism.

> A lot of black teens are just angry. There is so much complication and pain in their lives that they are angry. They are helpless to address things that give them pain. . . . It comes out in a variety of ways. At worst, it results in fighting or gun violence. . . . expressions of the rage they feel deep inside.[3]

Furthermore, she asks, why do even churched youth seem to believe that God is impotent to address the results of racism? In her research, she discovered: "Surprisingly, the teens most active in worship, Sunday school, and youth groups and most articulate about their Christian beliefs and practices were the ones who poignantly talked about racism never ending."[4] To her surprise, these youth, taught about God's grace in their churches, did not believe that God could initiate significant social change. She asks what is wrong with Christian education. How can Christian education empower a more comprehensive vision?

Another story, of a woman in the midst of a personal crisis: Julia asks:

> I'm not meshing with the world that I see out there. I see it as muck. I don't know how to bring a light into it. . . . There's a lot of grit, anger, and hostility. I don't know how [to respond], besides prayers. I wish there were ways that I could. And I hope the Lord will show me.[5]

Her words are filled with anguish. Anguish drives her to prayer. The cry for hope and justice literally drives people to the church. Yet, how do we answer whether and how God responds to the muck and the violence? Isn't that a central question for theology? Julia is tormented by the experiences she has encountered. She does, however, have some light, found through the support of a group of women at her church. Finding grace and challenge, she now teaches English as a Second Language classes to new immigrants. She has found a vocation. Their sense of community and their hope in the midst of her struggles have empowered her. She has adopted Mother Teresa's motto for her teaching: "I don't do great things. I do small things with great love."[6]

Over the last few years, Margaret Ann Crain and I have interviewed laity, seeking to understand the ways that they make sense of their lives. A study of these reflections was published in *Yearning for God: Reflections of Faithful Lives*.[7] We were impressed with individuals in several congregations who led us in seeking to understand how ordinary, faithful people—who, frankly, we discovered were quite extraordinary—used the resources of the faith. We examined how they learned and lived the faith. We met amazing people: from a young woman who helped in the King home for several days after Dr. King's murder, to a "grandmother in tennis shoes" who was arrested for protesting at the School of the Americas in Georgia, to a youth leader with a near-death experience, to an American immigrant who at fourteen had been drafted into the German army during World War II, and to a school administrator battling cancer. We have spoken with farmers, teachers, engineers, homemakers, lawyers, students, church leaders, social justice leaders, administrators, physicians, factory workers, and even a young man who designed the phone system for a Pacific island.

Their stories are rich and varied. These ordinary faithful people are present in every congregation. Yet, they told us that while they were active in churches, they were often frustrated at the church's lack of openness or seriousness. Too often, specific issues were ruled as unworthy of church conversation and too often the resources for faithful study were ignored. Nevertheless, their yearnings were so strong that they continued to search. Furthermore, they challenged the church because they saw it as the one institution, even with its failures, that could provide places to address important questions in light of God.

We named some of the yearnings that spurred them to theological reflection as the yearning for vocation, the yearning for justice, the yearning for grace, the yearning for healing, the yearning for hope, and the yearning for new creation. Uniformly, we found people asking deep questions about faith, particularly about claiming their identities as children of God and about living into their vocations as faithful disciples of the way of Jesus.[8]

One of the most articulate was Frederick. He was nearing ninety when we interviewed him. He had just come from exercising. While he had been taught that the "elderly" were frail, he challenged that teaching. He countered, knowing that exercise empowered vitality. Learning and growing were passions for him. He told us about his Sunday school class that he had been teaching for over fifty years—once it was a vital class of couples; now eight single or widowed women remained. "I try to get them to question," he said. "And try to make sense of what we are supposed to do." He added, "I'm not afraid of questions. We search the scriptures, we explore the faith, and together we learn to live the faith."

Lamenting, he said, "*Somehow we have not made it possible or easy for people to be theological in their everyday lives.*"[9] He followed with a story about a friend's retirement. At the gathering, the coworker declared "that one of the strongest influences on his life had been his relationship with Jesus." Frederick continued:

> I told him. "I didn't know that." . . . I thought: We were two fellows working closely together, and we never communicated our faith to each other. I'm still puzzled that we didn't do that. There is some element of privacy—you don't want to sound sanctimonious, or you feel that the business place is not the place for religion . . . People don't talk about [their faith] except on Sunday or in Sunday school. And yet it's the dominant element of so many of our lives. Why aren't we able to communicate it?[10]

Responding to his own question, Frederick names the aim of his teaching as "trying to get this subject into communications, where we can talk . . . theology, about our relationship with God."[11]

"*Somehow we have not made it possible or easy for people to be theological in their everyday lives*"—to have the interpretive and biblical skills to make theological decisions for daily living. Frederick wants some help. He is on target: education and ministry are to assist people in nuanced theological reflection that helps people understand, address the brokenness in life, make decisions, and live faithfully.

Frederick thinks being "theological" begins with questioning. He pointed to his own struggle to understand. At the moment we interviewed him, Mary, his wife of over fifty years, lay in their living room in a hospital bed in a coma. She had been that way for over eighteen months. Prior to entering the coma, she had increasingly been a victim of Alzheimer's. One day, she found the keys, took the car, and crashed into a tree. When she was found, her vitals were fine, but she was in a coma. A brash, young doctor told Frederick, "It will just be temporary. If we put a feeding tube in, she'll come out of it in no time." She did not come out of the coma, and legally it now took court action to take her off the feeding tube. Her care was taxing Frederick and the children. Frederick asked, "What has God planned for Mary; why hasn't He let her go?" Frederick focused on being faithful in a traumatic personal time.

Another person we interviewed, Delia, also a Sunday school teacher for fifty years, told us about attending a district workshop on biblical exegesis, and returning home angry and irritated. She said, "Why did it take so long for them to tell me the truth? Why has no one trusted me with the truth?" The moment of that revelation, her life changed. Since then, for the past fifteen years, she has chaired her denomination's regional peace committee. At sixty-eight, she was arrested at a demonstration at the US School of the Americas in Georgia. She continued:

> There is so much fear out there. We need to help people make a connection between their lives and the faith that gives us life. Fear makes people do strange things: they close up, they get angry, and they reject difference. . . . Why has the Christian church been so slow to change? Why do we seem so afraid of asking questions and listening for the voice of God? We preach resurrection, don't we? We preach a God who is living and seeking to redeem people and the world. Well, I've found some wonderful church people to help me struggle to be faithful. And, too often, I've found some others who reject the idea of questioning. I just tell them, that God is living, whether they are or not![12]

"Somehow we have not made it possible or easy for people to be theological in their everyday lives."[13] That is what Frederick called it. Or as Delia termed it, "We seem so afraid of asking questions and listening for the voice of God."

Learning to Be Theological

"Being theological" is a complex task, yet it is imperative for Christian religious education. Only through this process can we understand the connections of the ways of Jesus formed in a particular time and place with our present time and place. There are, of course, enduring themes and meanings, but just as Jesus struggled to understand (to interpret, to be theological) and be faithful as he sought to respond to the real yearnings of the Canaanite woman and her sick child, we, too, draw on that process to continue to live the way of Jesus. Being theological helps people name and claim their vocations as children of God and disciples of Jesus. It means growing in understanding about the content of the faith, its nuances, and methods of study—biblical, historical, and theological

In addition to listening to the people, we sought to analyze the ways they drew on the faith in making decisions about identity and vocation. Clear steps were not always present, yet there were patterns on which we could draw. Take for example Julia: She spoke to us about a moment when her world seemed to be coming apart. (Of course, when she was telling us her story, she was already through the crisis and was reflecting back on what had happened.) She had been particularly worried about her daughter. Life presented her with immense complications—she stewed and fretted; she shared and talked with friends; she read everything she could possibly find to help her understand what was happening to her daughter; and she met with a covenant group at church.

One afternoon, as she remembers it, an insight began to offer her directions, to offer her hope. She told us that she felt "dry." In fact, there was a drought in her community: "The summer sun had beaten the ground to death. The ground was like cement."[14] As she looked out a window, she saw her husband pulling weeds.

> They were tough, like iron. He took and pulled one. He kept pulling and pulling . . . and there was the root, with a tiny bit of green. . . . He brought it to me. . . . As I looked at this plant and knew I was going to survive [sic]. It was right out by the road where the sun baked the soil. There had been no water out there. . . . As I looked at it, I thought, "My God, that's me. You've done it. Lord; you're here!" I had held on long enough. I knew with God's help, I would survive.[15]

She further described to us how she took these insights to her therapist, to her friends, and to those at church. Slowly and carefully she considered her worries. She continued to read, to pray, and to think about what God was asking of her. She decided to take action, to reach out to others and her world in particular ways. She felt empowered to move and to engage.

Look more closely at what Julia told us about her decision making. She encountered an experience that challenged her ordinary, taken-for-granted reality. She could no longer simply go ahead as usual and assume that patterns of daily life and problem solving would work. She scanned, looking for insight. Using the help of friends, of her reading, and of her faith, she widely explored looking for meaning and possibility. It did not come easy; it was not a clear direction. The scanning led her in multiple directions. Then, in the midst of scanning, an insight came as she watched the taproot of a weed being pulled from the ground. The insight gave her energy and direction—energy and direction that she confirmed and tested with others. As she reports, she had a new way of looking at the world. She engaged in a learning process, which for her was a theological process, of finding hope and life in the midst of dryness and desert. In fact, she witnessed that it felt like a revelation from God.

What Julia has narrated is described by theologian and educator James Loder as a "transforming moment." Loder told of his personal crisis, an accident and near-death experience, that gave birth to a renewed faith and a new vocation. He defined the processes of transformative learning in the following stages:

1. Conflict in experience (a conflict in our accepted ways of being)

2. An interlude for scanning (scanning the resources we have at our disposal—public ideas, scholarship, the theological and biblical tradition as we know it, the opinions of others, and so on.)

3. Dialogue (The ideas and feelings we touch in our scanning are put in creative tension and dialogue with each other.)

4. Insight (a moment when a way of putting things together or moving forward almost seems to come from afar with an amazing sense of release and empowerment)

5. Testing (Through interpretation and verification, we share the insights and new direction with others. The insight is tested and its adequacy explored.)[16]

Loder uses a biblical example to illustrate transforming moments of learning—the same we saw in Julia's story of worry, scanning, dialogue, insight, and witnessing. Two disciples were walking on the road to Emmaus. They were leaving behind Jerusalem and returning to careers they had left to follow Jesus. The depth of their despair is seen when they recite to a stranger (Jesus): "We *had hoped* he was the one who would redeem Israel" (Luke 24:21; emphasis added). Even though they had experienced him as a prophet and women colleagues had already told them that his tomb was empty, they were confused and in pain. They left Jerusalem and the site of his crucifixion behind. Their ordinary world of meanings and hopes was upset (1. Conflict). Along the road, they talked to each other (2. Scanning) and listened to his content, "starting with Moses and going through all the Prophets" (Luke 24:27). They talked back to him and shared with him (3. Dialogue). And yet, that was not enough. Content by itself did not answer their questions. As he broke bread with them, suddenly they understood (4. Insight). They were empowered with the power of release, as they ran back the seven miles to Jerusalem in the dark—possibly facing animals on the road, the twists and turns of the road, and the risk of bandits in the dark. The insight and release were the products of an amazing transforming moment when new directions were offered to them. With the return to Jerusalem and the disciples, they shared their story and listened to the stories of others—receiving confirmation (5. Testing).

We saw similar processes with many of those we interviewed—processes of theological reflection and learning. People were faced with an experience. Some were confirmations of ordinary patterns. When this occurred, the motivation to explore was not as powerful. People simply, yet profoundly, confirmed directions and acted in ways consistent with ordinary patterns of meaning and value. Yet, when there was a disruption that did not fit, people were pushed to scan. Scanning involved talking to others, exploring cultural wisdom, reading scholarship that addressed their concerns, exploring the biblical and theological tradition and its heritage, and simple mulling over ideas and considering them. Sometimes this was a long and hard process with little progress. In the midst of the scanning, for many, a moment of insight occurred that indeed felt like release, giving a new sense of direction. Nonetheless, even with this energy and insight, they still tested it with others and/or in light of faith commitments. Insight resulted in action.

The theological reflection we heard in the people we interviewed looked very similar to what Loder described. We saw it as a decision-making process about identity and vocation:

1. Clarifying and considering an issue or concern

2. Critically exploring the content of the biblical and theological tradition

3. Engaging in dialogue with oneself, others, and the tradition

4. Discerning a considered decision

5. Acting on the decision

6. Continuing to reflect on and test the decision and its adequacy[17]

To us, this process pointed to the dimensions of Christian education.

People were better able to draw on the theological tradition if they had been schooled in it and if they had been taught and had practiced the methods of theological reflection. We enhance people's ability to do this natural process of theological reflection with systematic and sustained teaching of the faith. Christian education involves three key elements:

1. Knowing the Christian story and tradition

2. Learning and practicing theological reflection for everyday living

3. Critical appropriation

We found all three in the persons we interviewed. For some, the church too often made it difficult to learn, reflect, and particularly to challenge. They all called for the church to become a new creation—a place of discipling and of mission. Yet, all of them knew that without the church's education, they would have to search on their own, drawing on whatever resources they had at hand. Usually that would be the consumer culture in which we live, with its messages of success and progress, or it would have been popular piety, with its images of therapeutic relief.

Knowing or (Even Better) Cherishing the Story. We need to be serious about teaching the Christian story. We need to do this in a way that honors the diversity within the tradition and tells the truth about the gaps, failings, and sins in the church's history. The people of God expect high-quality instruction. For example, I teach in churches often. Each year, at one congregation, I lead a monthlong series called "Studying the Gospel of Matthew, Mark, or Luke," depending on the lectionary readings for that year. This year the congregation is also beginning a historical study of the developments in the faith. Another church I know has created a three-year church's teachings series for new members, combining study of the tradition, biblical study, and ethical decision making with ministry and leadership skills.

Theological Reflection. The process of theological reflection occurs daily in the lives of the people of God. Yet, too often it is a process that is not guided or enhanced. We all know that new learning is rooted in older learning—the sets of concepts and convictions we hold. Sometimes older learning can be a rich foundation. In contrast, sometimes older learnings are hindrances to new learning. How many times have you been challenged by someone who uses a cultural aphorism as if it were theological truth? The process of theological reflection involves clarifying experience, drawing on the understandings and knowledge we have, and drawing deeply from scripture and the tradition.

A study of children completed a few years ago sought to examine children's views of God.[18] As you might guess, images of divine parent, judge and rule maker, and even clock maker were present. More dangerously, some children referred to God as the "capricious one" who constantly got what God wanted and always changed the rules. From where did that come? Finally, some children spoke of God as the suffering one, who joins us in our troubles. Not surprisingly, these were Jewish and African American children who knew suffering. Real theological reflection occurs in the community as we help people connect the tradition with their lives and experiences. Sometimes it challenges those experiences, sometimes it opens them to new insights, yet all of the time, people are enhancing the ways they go about reflecting on living and connecting it with their faiths.

Critical Appropriation. One of my colleagues, Reginald Blount, defines the task of Christian education as traditioning, transforming, and transgressing.[19] We need to challenge (to transgress) when systems, even churches, teach us that we are less than children of God. Racism, classism, sexism, and heterosexism are just of few of the ways that the tradition is manipulated to deny to some of our brothers and sisters full life chances and their due status as children and heirs of God.

In communities of faith, we are called to critically challenge and to appropriate so ministry is faithful. This, too, was a significant need expressed by those we interviewed—freedom in community to respond to the living God who yet has new things for a new creation. Congregations teach by their practices and actions. I recently attended the "Carefest" at the congregation that Dr. Blount pastors in Waukegan, Illinois. For the last several years, Trinity AME has provided a celebration for children as public school begins. The church first began by collecting backpacks for entering public school students who could not afford to buy the supplies necessary for school. Within five years, this little church of 130 members has moved from collecting a few to gathering many backpacks for neighborhood youth. The festival now includes games and prizes; music and disc jockeys; health screenings and education, including for HIV; and financial counseling. The "carefest" has made a profound difference at Trinity. The people are proud of the impact they make on the community. They have opened their doors to the diversity in the community. They ask themselves more deeply about their own identity as a community of faith and setting for theological knowing, reflecting, and acting.

This congregation is engaging its members in theological reflection to address the real issues of poverty and joblessness. All of the critical resources of analyzing experience, of sharing the Christian story and vision, of scanning, of considering ideas together in dialogue, and of deciding are present in their ministries and their processes of acting faithfully.

What does it mean to follow Jesus and confront the powers of evil in the world? It takes churches who engage in what Frederick requested: making it possible for people to be faithful in their everyday lives. The best answers to this call are congregations who at their heart invite the questions, seek to draw on the traditions of the faith and scripture, and name and claim their vocations, or a shorthand definition, *missional congregations seeking to follow Jesus.*

Educating Congregations

We learned from our interviews that the church can be a setting for faithful theological education. Christian religious education is the process of theological reflection that directs the people of God into their identities and mission in the world. Just as Jesus expanded his identity to include responding to the Canaanite woman and then refined his vocation, we, too, need support as we explore our identities and vocations. This is what educating congregations do for us.

Educating churches guide people on the journey of life, unapologetically witnessing that being disciples makes a profound difference. Like the early Christians, we need communities of support in which we learn to grow in the faith and test our lives. Openness, freedom to share, and a safe and challenging environment are essential to the educational support needed to assist people in engaging the risky behaviors of challenging lifestyles, questioning the tradition, and deciding to be faithful. Following Jesus means offering people the chance to restore the image of God within their lives and within their communities.

Remember the description of the time of Jesus that was offered in chapter 1. The Holy Land was oppressed; Romans knew how to oppress: They were a highly advanced technological civilization. Yet, their advances were built on the "backs" of people. When they conquered Israel, the demands were significant. They knew how to divide and conquer— how to co-opt people to do their bidding. In Galilee, the interconnected economic network of families who nurtured and supported each other was disrupted. People hoarded meager possessions; families turned against families.

Into this world came Jesus, preaching the activity of the Holy God—reminding people that life was a gift from God and that God sought for them to live abundantly in community. As he entered villages and preached, some villages and groups of people accepted his message. They were restored to one another, hoarding ended, and hope and sharing were reborn. Neighbors scheduled banquets of joy, prefiguring the Great Banquet promised by Isaiah (Isa. 25), and lives were transformed. The best wine was served, and a child's simple act of offering his loaves and fishes was multiplied until many bystanders were fed. Where Jesus' message was accepted, there were miracles—hospitality and hope restored community.

These same miracles of hospitality and hope permeated early Christian communities, which were populated by a wondrous collection of wealthy patron women, slaves, urban employees, faithful Jews, and Gentile onlookers accepting the Jewish promises of Sabbath and the Great Banquet. In Matthew's Antioch, James's Jerusalem, and throughout the empire touched by Paul, communities of Jesus' followers shared hope and hospitality. They lived and worshiped together in urban housing. In fact, often, they collected money so the indentured slaves in their midst could be freed. Here is missional living—spreading the vision and reality of God's kingdom—of hospitality and hope.

To answer Frederick, Delia, and others, we need to be theological in our everyday lives. We need to ask hard questions about faithfulness and listen for the voice of God. We need a comprehensive form of education that helps people connect faith and life and empower the ministries of congregations. We need to share our convictions of faith and processes of theological reflection with passion.

An advertisement I saw on the lawn of a vital Jewish congregation summarizes well the work of a teaching congregation—synagogue, temple, mosque, or church. We all realize that our Jewish colleagues have had to learn and speak the language of their faith at the same time they have learned how to live in a land—this land and many, many before—that was dependent on a totally different set of meanings and values. The synagogue sign read, "Join us. Renew your faith through community, prayer, study, and service. Serve God." Using that advertisement, let's look at how religious education can assist us in relating faith to life.[20]

1. Community and prayer. We learn as we live and participate in a culture and its practices—in a time and place. The basic syntax of language and much of the basic vocabulary we will use for the rest of our lives is learned by simply growing up. A silly example: I grew up in Indiana and learned that basketball is indeed the only sport. My high school, Kokomo High School, had a bigger gymnasium than does Northwestern University. Friends from Texas, in turn, tell us that it is not basketball that is THE sport, but rather, football—a different culture and different practices.

The same is true with faith. The community that supports us teaches us the basic values and meanings by which life is lived. Community nurtures faith. But it is not simply an affable community of friends; rather, it is a group of people who study and share with one another because life demands that we seek to understand how the gifts of God shape our lives.

Practices of the community seek to connect us to God's ways. Listening for the voice of God; sharing the deepest meanings of our lives. Every faith tradition has essential practices by which the faithful are reminded of who they are. Methodists have called these practices "means of grace" because by them we experience God's grace. John Wesley spoke of the means of grace as frequent Eucharist, Bible study, worship and prayer, participation in a small covenant group, and acts of charity. For Jews, for example, being kosher is not so much about good and bad food. We all know that pork and shellfish can be safely eaten. Rather as one practices kosher, one reminds oneself every day, and at every meal, that life is lived in light of the expectations of God.

2. Study. Prayer and community expand into study. In fact, in the Jewish perspective, the observance of prayer and community—faithfully honoring God by seeking to build faithful and just communities—is study. Studying the Torah is following the way of God. That is what Jesus sought to do. In turn, we Christians seek to faithfully follow God by following Jesus.

We live in a culture that paradoxically is filled with the noise of faith, but in which little serious study of the depth of faith takes place. Do we regularly study the Bible, share the history of the church, and learn about the shifts in theology throughout the years? We need to emphasize the importance of guided study—of ordered learning. None of us would think

63

about practicing our jobs without in-service training, without reading, and without growing.

3. Service. Service is at the heart of Trinity AME. Through service, people have been able to challenge the taken-for-granted patterns in their community. For example, the community is located in a "food desert," no grocery shopping anywhere close. Therefore, working with local farmers, Trinity has added a weekly free farmer's market in the summer. People are welcome to take what they need. They are trusted.

Service becomes an educational project of discovering the world around our congregations. Moreover, such service learning is a way of asking questions and empowering people to seek new life. Service coupled with education can push a congregation to question the very structure of things and ask how faith empowers action for others—how to follow the way of Jesus.

Conclusion

The sign on the synagogue read, "Join us. Renew your faith through community, prayer, study, and service. Serve God." Serve God. That is being faithful and missional. Isn't that what education in the faith is all about? Frederick asked, "Why are we so afraid to be theological in our everyday lives?" We answer: the focus of our education is to empower us to be faithful in our everyday lives. Learning occurs through the ministries of prayer and community; through direct teaching and study; and through witnessing to the public world. Let us now examine these three—community, instruction, and service—as approaches to Christian religious education.

Section II
Approaches to Christian Learning

How do we teach the way of Jesus? In this section, we focus directly on the discipline of Christian religious education. Scholars and practitioners in the field offer options for how the Christian faith is taught so that it can be understood and lived. As we discussed in chapter 2, Christian education attends to identity, vocation, and resources. How are people formed and know themselves as Christians, how do they name and claim their vocations as followers of the way of Jesus, and how do they acquire the resources to make decisions and live as Christians in the world?

We will directly examine three approaches to the field: community of faith, religious instruction, and mission, or as I suggested at the end of chapter 3: community and prayer, study, and service. The community-of-faith approach examines the character and dynamics of the congregation as a setting for learning. How do the various dimensions of a congregation's life interact to teach Christian people? Religious instruction focuses on how people are taught the content and practices of the faith community. Mission addresses how people learn as they live and embody the faith in the wider world.

As we examine each approach to teaching and learning, we will assess its strengths in relationship to scholarship about the way of Jesus. The goal is to help those of us who call ourselves Christians to faithfully embody and live the way of Jesus. Each chapter will follow a similar form: beginning with a story illustrating the dynamics of community, instruction, or mission in the life and times of Jesus, it moves to a description of an approach to Christian religious education, noting goals and processes. This approach is then assessed and reframed in light of Christian theology and the scholarship about the way of Jesus.

Note the argument of the book to this point. The teaching and ministry of Jesus were so compelling that they drew people into his sphere of influence. Jesus taught an identity and vocation empowered by the grace of a living and transforming God in the midst of the harsh domination of the Romans. Those he taught were so enlivened and transformed that they formed communities of people who sought to live and understand the ways of Jesus in their contexts and times. These communities witnessed and taught the ways of Jesus in their wider world, drawing others into this way. This teaching has continued from this early time to the present.

Through the history of the Christian church, faithful leaders and people had to consider how the way of Jesus impacted their own times and circumstances—sometimes very different from the original context. Theological reflection was and still is the primary means of seeking to make these faithful decisions. Today, Christian education teaches the discipline of theological reflection and addresses the practices that teach this way.

Therefore, just as those whose lives were transformed by Jesus sought to teach his way to their contemporaries and to enliven it in new times, we, too, are obligated to teach and enliven that way in our world—one of diversity, global connectivity, violence, and increasing stratification of wealth. It is our task as Christian educators to extend the practice of teaching the way of Jesus, as has been done since Jesus first taught his way in ancient Palestine.

Chapter Four

Community and Prayer: Community-of-Faith Approach to Christian Education

Jesus experienced the power of the community to educate. He was a member of a Galilean Jewish community where he learned a way of faith by simply participating in the community's practices. On day eight of his life, he was blessed as a child of the covenant at his circumcision. We know he kept Sabbath, returning to participate in the synagogue gathering in his hometown; thus he was weekly reminded that God created the world and the world was God's. The last act of his public life before his trial and crucifixion was celebrating Passover with his disciples, again reminding him of the liberating action of God in freeing the Hebrew people from slavery in Egypt. The words of the Shema Israel were on his lips as he spoke with the "rich young ruler"; he knew well God's commandments to love God and neighbor. Furthermore, he wore his prayer shawl with the fringes and knots, and he kept kosher, reminding him and faithful Jews that their loyalty was to God.[1] Finally, the words of the Torah and the prophets, particularly Isaiah, were on his lips as he spoke to the people. The prophets' expectations for faithfulness and justice and their hope for God's realm were realities to him. He was formed within the matrix of a faithful Galilean Jewish community.

In the midst of a world where Roman law and military authority defined and disrupted every other pattern, the Jews of Judea and Galilee sought to remain faithful to their traditions and the expectations of the Torah. The high priest of the temple in Jerusalem, while appointed by the Roman authorities, sought to serve his people. He walked a thin line between communicating the traditions of the faith and satisfying the Roman expectations for compliance. As some of the high priests took advantage of this relationship, others risked life to preserve the practices of faith, even challenging the Romans when they demanded that the sign of the eagle (the sign of the Roman gods) be erected on the temple. While Romans controlled their vestments and thus the priests' ability to fulfill their ritual prayer obligations, God's priests still found ways to pray.

The life Jesus knew was one of conflict among Jewish parties over faithfulness. Galilean Jews were often furious at the "liberties" taken by powerful Judeans, their investments in Galilean lands, and the political hierarchies that always put them on top. Yet, they shared a *way of life*, remembering their dependence on the God who had chosen them and freed them from captivity. They lived so that the world would see the glory of God.[2] Beginning and ending each day with the Shema, wearing the fringes, celebrating the weekly feast of Shabbat, engaging in the pilgrimage walk to the holy city of Jerusalem, celebrating the prescribed festivals, and celebrating the rhythm of Jewish life were powerful moments that reminded them all of God's gifts and expectations.

Three celebrations each year taught key events in Jewish life: Passover (*Pesach*), Pentecost (*Shavuot*), and Booths (*Sukkoth*) (Exod. 23:14-17). Passover taught the events of the slavery and freeing of the Hebrew people from Egypt. As the evening ritual was spoken, event after event of the struggle for freedom was remembered. The memory of freedom so worried the Romans, for it was the memory that encouraged some to enact it. In turn, Pentecost reminded the people of God's gift of Torah. Fifty days after Passover, the people remembered their obligations to live God's way. Again, see the risk for the Roman oppressors: the people affirmed that God of the covenant was the true object of their worship, not the military gods of Rome. Finally, at harvest, the people celebrated the Festival of Booths, constructing tents, as is done today, to remind the people that they were utterly dependent on God in the desert where they wandered for forty years. God provided food and water; without God's care, they would have perished. Note how these three yearly celebrations teach the full story of a people chosen by God, freed by God, cared for by God, and given a vocation by God. The ways of the community powerfully taught the people that being holy as God is holy was their business—their responsibility (Lev. 19:2).

Community of Faith in Christian Education

Communities profoundly teach as we participate in them. Anyone who has moved from one town to another, or even more, from one country to another, knows that life ways are different. One learns expectations and ways of being by simply living in a community. All of us, as infants, learn to talk as we grow up in our families—a large vocabulary and the syntax of the language are learned by simply communicating.

The power of the community was reemphasized in the history of Christian education in the early 1970s in two works, one by C. Ellis Nelson, *Where Faith Begins,* and the other by John Westerhoff III, *Will Our Children Have Faith?*[3] Both emphasized that congregations teach through their full lives: music, worship, mission, evangelism, social action, education, and fellowship. Children and adults learn the faith as they participate in the practices of the faith. As a congregation faithfully embodies the gospel, people learn the meanings of the gospel. Therefore the power of the community of faith to teach is immense.

The work of John Westerhoff III addressed how worship teaches, how the Christian year teaches, how actions for social justice teach, and how practices of stewardship teach. He argued that churches failed children by relying on inadequate Sunday school instructional strategies where students learned very little, not growing into thoughtful, practicing Christians. In contrast to the "schooling/instructional paradigm," he proposed a "socialization/enculturation paradigm" that recovered a catechetical approach to education. "Christian education focuses on the total life of persons in the faith community and it is the deliberate, systematic and sustained efforts of that faith community which enable persons and groups to evolve Christian life styles."[4]

In particular, Westerhoff argued that Christian education needed to focus on "rituals, experiences, and actions." Rituals were best expressed as the rhythm of the Christian year and the regular Sunday liturgy that rehearsed the basic meanings/stories of the tradition. Rituals both assisted people in moving through the life cycle, for example, baptism, confirmation, commitment, vocation, and so on, or in reinforcing the basic meanings of life, for example, our dependence on God, our call to faithfulness, and our expectations for service and vocation. Experiences were particular moments within the life of the community where the deepest meanings of that community were enacted—when the stranger was welcomed, when the child was accepted as a child of God, and when the community discerned how to use its resources for faithfulness. The actions of the community of faith in its wider world taught much about its commitments.

The work of Nelson and Westerhoff was important for the field of Christian education. They not only recovered past commitments of the field, but they offered a direction for how the community of faith could be intentional about its teaching as it planned its community life.[5]

The Goals of the Faith-Community Approach

Many congregations have taken seriously community-of-faith approaches to Christian education and have sought to enhance their practices of Christian education. Let me begin with examples of two ordinary congregations and then further develop the approach.

St. Paul's Church is located in a large urban center. The church provides many programs and has many ministries. While the congregation has a clear statement of its ministry and mission, the leaders realized that life in the congregation is much like the life many of its members live in the wider world—abundant opportunities with little coordination. Members had to choose among competing alternatives, both within and without the congregation. Children of members tended to attend Sunday school somewhat regularly, when there was not an outside conflict (soccer, dance, or visiting grandparents). Children's classes used a lectionary-based curriculum; therefore, they were connected to the themes reflected in worship, yet children under second grade always left the sanctuary for a care and craft experience after the reading of biblical texts, and a children's sermon. Furthermore, there was little correlation across the themes of adult classes, and thus there was no unified adult curriculum. Only one of the adult classes studied the lectionary.

After consideration at a church board meeting and with the

70

establishment of an action task force, leaders decided to seek coordination across the congregation. They focused on the seasons of Advent and Lent, connecting education, worship, and spiritual formation. The lections for the Sundays of both Advent and Lent were chosen as the texts for all children and adult classes as well as for worship. A worship planning team was organized working with the pastoral staff to connect worship and education. Furthermore, a teacher-training event for all adult's and children's teachers taught the content of the biblical passages. Finally a devotional book was developed for individuals and families on the themes encountered in the texts. The plan has been in place now for three years, and people are beginning to ask how the mission life of the congregation can also be connected. St. Paul is slowly enhancing and coordinating its educational and ministry life using the community-of-faith approach.

Faith Congregation is located in a near suburb of an urban area. As a result of a church-planning process, the congregation determined that "Living the Faith in Church and World" was the theme of the congregation. Members noted that it was hard to make connections between good intentions that arose in congregational study and worship with daily living. Vocation became the focus of the congregation's ministry. Several efforts sought to address this lack of connection. First, each sermon was planned to end with questions of vocation and discipleship. Second, small covenant groups were established, meeting monthly and focusing on how people were living the faith. Third, after the first year of the program, the call to worship each week began with individuals requesting prayer for special projects in which they engaged (their vocations). Finally, the themes that were being raised in worship became a set of concerns for the church's mission committee to consider a coordinated response. Again, Faith Congregation's ministries are being affected by the community-of-faith approach.

While many religious educators have advocated and developed the perspectives of the community-of-faith approach, Maria Harris, in her book *Fashion Me a People*, offered theological language to talk about the challenges of educating in community: "We find the image of God as a potter fashioning a people both from the Hebrew Bible and the New Testament. . . . We are held in the divine hands, and the grace of God, and the Spirit of God abides within us, enabling us to become what we are called to be."[6]

Using classic terms, Harris defined the ministries of the church where education or fashioning occurred: *koinonia* (community), *leiturgia* (liturgy),

71

kerygma (proclamation), *didache* (teaching), and *diaconia* (service). Each of these tasks of the church pointed to unique opportunities to plan and engage education and to influence a person's vocation as well as that of the congregation itself. Education was so much more than schooling, it was a process of attending to the life of the congregation, organizing it, and enabling it to be a faithful communicator of the power of the gospel.

Charles Foster further focused the community-of-faith approach when he described the educational task of a congregation as providing a catechetical culture. "By linking the notion of catechesis to congregational culture I am suggesting it is something more than a mode of instruction and the congregation is something more than a voluntary association of people held together by common values, beliefs, and practices." Catechetical culture connoted an environment "conducive to forming faith in and through the interplay of a congregation's formal educational structures and informal educational patterns."[7] Through repetition, the meanings of living as a Christian are rehearsed in a congregation over and over. In a poetic manner, Foster envisioned the dynamics of congregational learning:

> In their reverberations we encounter the faith of our ancestors "living still" (as the hymn writer put it) and anticipate the faith of still unknown descendents in the rhythms of our heartbeats, the exercise of our imaginations, and the engagement of our commitments in spontaneous and routine expressions of compassion, love, and justice.[8]

Foster focused on three essential practices of the catechetical culture: the practice of hospitality (inviting people into the life and mission of the congregation), the practice of celebration (attending to the grace of God in relation to human living), and the practice of conversation (cultivating learning and reflection throughout the life of the congregation).[9]

Let's step back. That the community of faith teaches is obvious. People learn as they engage its life and ministry. As they are called to reflect on whether and how the church is seeking to be faithful and fulfilling its responsibilities, people are learning to live as Christians in the world. Yet, here is the difficulty. How does one learn the criteria by which one judges the faithfulness of the community of faith? Moreover, if the community of faith is not faithful, if its content does not match its proclamation, then the teaching of the faith is confused.

Examining the correlation of faithfulness and practice is of utmost importance in organizing a program of Christian religious education. Looking outside the Christian tradition, a very similar effort at a community-of-faith approach is being developed within the conservative Jewish tradition.[10] Historian and liturgical scholar Lawrence Hoffman has been the motivating force in a project called Synagogue 2000 (now Synagogue 3000). Hoffman argues that synagogues cannot simply serve people's needs in a program-centered manner; rather, they need to become genuine places of spiritual experience—of vital Jewish life, thought, and practice. Synagogues need to be places to provide "authentic Jewish experiences that appeal to those in search of identity."[11] Going further, he argues that "Synagogues that cannot provide authentic Jewish sustenance are in trouble."[12] In a style like Harris's, Hoffman looks at the Jewish tradition to discover those places and tasks that are most crucial to the development of faithful identity.

To communicate in a creative way, he makes an acronym of the name *Pisgah*, the mountain where God's vision came to Moses. He argues that attention to six elements shapes the instructional program of a congregation:[13]

- P—Prayer (the traditional prayers of the community rituals as well as personal prayers to God)

- I—Institutional change (examination of the life of the congregation and its impact on people's lives)

- S—Study (intentional engagement with the Torah and the writings and the history of the development of the Jewish community and traditions)

- G—Good deeds (service to neighbors and to the wider community)

- A—Ambiance of the sacred (attention to the presence of God in our daily lives)

- H—Healing (caring for the lives of individuals and the wider community's needs)

73

How do the people pray and worship, attending to the liturgies of the tradition? How do people learn to be faithful in daily life? How does a congregation assess what is crucial for its life together as a teaching and faith community? How are decisions made? What is studied and how is it studied? How does the community embody its convictions into deeds in the wider community? How is the power of God encountered and recognized within the community? How are people healed, and how do they participate in actions of healing in the world? These are clear and forceful questions about how a community shapes its identity and teaches.

Look at the parallels to Harris and Foster and think about your own congregation. How are proclamation, study, liturgy, fellowship, and service constructed? How are hospitality, celebration, and conversation connected? Who decides, and how? What difference is made in the participants' lives, as well as the lives of those outside the community? Asking such questions enhances the life and ministry of a community of faith. Such intentionality also better makes the congregation an educating community.

Practices of the Faith-Community Approach

Diana Butler Bass has identified in her study of vital mainline congregations that faithful and vital congregations teach the Christian tradition, live Christian practices, and are concerned to discover and live God's vision for individuals and the world. In particular, she discovered ten "practices" at the heart of these vital communities: (1) hospitality, (2) discernment, (3) healing, (4) contemplation, (5) testimony, (6) diversity, (7) justice, (8) worship, (9) reflection, and (10) beauty.[14] While these activities do not seem strange, Bass concluded that intentionality is what is important. She saw individual congregations planning for Christian education by asking what practices would help them understand and be faithful.

These ten practices were not present in all congregations, but several of them were present in each. For example, discernment was practiced in some congregations as a specific means of planning. Spiritual formation and spiritual reflection were connected as congregations sought to make their decisions based on prayer, theological reflection, and discernment. In fact, some congregations taught members approaches to discernment for use in their daily lives and work.

Another is beauty, where members of congregations intentionally asked how their space for worship, fellowship, and gathering taught the faith. How does the art that is present teach the values of the community? The great cathedrals of the world, with their statuary and stained-glass windows, taught every time people entered them. Bass discovered churches asking how their spaces taught and communicated the faith.

And a third is testimony. A congregation developed a regular practice of testimony—"of having people talk about their experience of God."[15] Scheduled as a part of the regular worship service, individuals were invited to give a testimony of God acting in lives. The testimonies were not judged, nor emulated; rather, they simply became examples of people's understandings of God's presence in their lives. Testimonies provided a rich context for focusing on what matters, on the difference that the life of faith can make.

Bass identified ten practices. An educator might want to ask in the midst of a congregation how any one of them might become a reality. Moreover, the educator would want to develop contexts where the theological integrity of the practice was considered. The focus of the community-of-faith approach to Christian education is intentionally using, constructing, and organizing a set of "faithful practices" as the curriculum for the life of a congregation. Attention makes the difference as leaders openly, purposefully, and comprehensively ask how the life of the congregation can be enriched as a comprehensive plan for community education.

Research on practices has become important for the field of Christian religious education. They are defined in many ways. For example, practices, as defined by Craig Dykstra, educator and retired vice president for religion at the Lilly Endowment, are

> those cooperative human activities through which we, as individuals and as communities, grow and develop in moral character and substance. They have built up over time and, through experience and testing, have developed patterns of reciprocal expectations among participants. They are ways of doing things together in which and through which human life is given direction, meaning, and significance, and through which our very capacities to do good things well are increased. And because they are shaped, patterned, and ongoing, they can be taught. We can teach one another how to participate in them. We can pass them on from one generation to the next.[16]

75

Dykstra lists fourteen Christian practices. With considerable depth and nuance about each, he highlights the following: worship, telling Christian stories, interpreting the Scriptures and tradition, praying, reconciliation, encouraging one another, service and witness, generosity, suffering with others, providing hospitality and care, listening and talking to one another about experiences in life, struggling together, criticizing and resisting powers of evil, and working to create and sustain faithful social structures.[17] Note several parallels between the Dykstra and Bass lists. While few of these practices are novel, Dykstra wonders to what a degree they really are part of the lives of Christians. He worries that the ministries of too many congregations are not robust enough to really challenge the patterns of consumer culture.

Practices are crucial to knowing who we are, our commitments, and our efforts in the world. For example, a couple celebrates holidays and anniversaries as special times to remind them of their story and their loyalties to each other. If these practices wane, the relationship itself may be challenged and the deepest meanings that hold them together may be forgotten. The same is true with faith. Christian faith is a particular kind of faith with particular understandings and commitments. It is a way of life, or to use the words of this book, it is following the way of Jesus. Of course, it has been developed over two thousand years, yet its basic practices focus back on patterns of new life, of redemption, and of community that emerged from that historical matrix in which Jesus lived.

In an effort to further define and illustrate the power of these practices, Dykstra has initiated Practicing Our Faith. This project has produced books, videos, and resources to assist individuals and congregations in reclaiming and enacting the practices of the faith.[18] Practices give focus to the life of the congregation, again becoming their curriculum, drawing on theological reflection on the meaning of Christian life in the midst of the world. As congregations make intentional decisions about their lives, they are creating a rich environment for forming people in the way of faith.

Charles Foster suggests a place for a congregation to begin: "event-centered education."[19] He knows how our goals for Christian education have become therapeutic or marketing (as our wider culture) as the denominational agencies delivering Christian education have shrunk or collapsed. Recognizing how difficult it is for a congregation to go it alone and to develop a comprehensive strategy, he suggests we make key *ordinary events* of the life of the parish rich, multifaceted, and educative. For example, while preparing for the celebration of Christmas, make it an "event" with short-term study sessions, with resources that can be used in families, with service projects, and with liturgical celebrations that all cohere and maintain an educational focus. He describes event-centered education in the following way: "It begins with *preparing* people to participate in [the concrete events of congregational life]. . . . It continues with the act of *participating* in the event itself and concludes with the *recollection and critique* of the experience to discern and respond to claims it may have on our lives."[20]

A congregation I know chooses a book two or three times each year for the whole congregation to read: "One church, One book." The book then becomes the content for several small group discussion groups in many formats and settings. Group leaders are trained to focus the study and to lead dialogue and conversation. The worship life of the congregation attends to the key elements of the book. Finally, action projects are gathered that flow from the emphasis of the chosen book. Thus a congregation is taking concrete steps to coordinating practices so that the life of the community of faith itself teaches.

Intentionality and purposefulness are at the heart of the community-of-faith approach to Christian education as leaders develop the educational potential in specific aspects of the life of the congregation. Which strategies are chosen is not really important as long as the practices are deeply rooted in the Christian tradition, its story and life. What is important is taking a set of elements, assessing their role within the life of the congregation, enriching their impact, and coordinating with parts of the life of the congregation. This whole process, from assessing to enacting to coordinating, becomes a curriculum for the congregation.

We know communities influence the way we see and experience the world. We know that they teach. The community-of-faith approach asks us to use this knowledge to enrich, connect, and enact the practices of Christian faith in the congregation in such a way that those who are influenced by its life grow and mature in the faith.

Community of Faith in the Way of Jesus

Community was at the heart of the message and mission of Jesus. He, like others in his time, sought ways to be faithful in the midst of a world

77

that was unfaithful. Compromises were necessary with the Romans at every moment and time. Using Roman coins meant being captive to the Roman economy. Paying taxes meant sustaining the Roman war machine in its expansionism. Considering how to worship in a way that would not bring the ire of the Romans down on the temple altered worship practices.

All of the groups in Jesus' time were seeking how to be faithful to the community the God of Israel had established. The Qumran community, for example, considered any involvement with the Romans as too much of a compromise, as faithlessness; therefore, they withdrew to the wilderness, where they studied, prayed, and lived outside the ordinary patterns of commerce. Simply the act of withdrawing acknowledged the power of the Roman community to shape the world.

The high priests and leaders in Jerusalem sought to be faithful to the traditions and to extend the expectations and mission of the Jewish people. The Pharisees sought ways to extend the faith of the Torah and the obligations of Shema to all of life. Yet they, too, had to find ways of being faithful and challenging the too-easy compromises of their contemporaries, particularly the Sadducees, without stimulating the force of Roman power.

In fact, one of the biggest complaints about Jesus was the community with whom he associated. Jesus was identified as "a glutton and a drunk, a friend of tax collectors and sinners" (Matt. 11:19). It is also said in this verse that Jesus "came eating and drinking." When "tax collectors and sinners" came to listen to him, the good people of the community objected: "This man welcomes sinners and eats with them" (Luke 15:2). The good people were aghast at his easy acceptance of people who had a history of unfaithfulness or outright complicity with Rome. The Jesus community included those they would never have expected—those who had proved themselves unclean.

Many of the stories about Jesus and food have to do with building community—providing abundance in the midst of scarcity, being hospitable, and uniting a large crowd into a banquet. The feeding of the crowd of five thousand is recorded in all of the Gospels: Matthew 14, Mark 6, Luke 9, and John. Here a child provides five loaves and two fish that are multiplied. Again, Mark 8 and Matthew 15 tell a second story about feeding four thousand, using here seven loaves and some fish, with an abundance of food remaining. Furthermore, many of his teachings about eating and drinking challenge accepted patterns of community building. He subverts the ordinary practices of eating at table—telling those who have honor and are expected to sit at the head of the table to choose a lower place (Luke 14:7-11). He tells people not to invite those who are expected—"friends, your brothers and sisters, your relatives, or rich neighbors"; instead, "when you give a banquet, invite the poor, crippled, lame, and blind" (vv. 12-13). Invitations went to the least expected and not to those for whom the honor system demanded respect or recognition.

Similar advice continues in his parable about a banquet where all the guests refused the invitation and embarrassed their host. Jesus has the host change the guest list: "Go to the highways and back alleys and urge people to come" (Luke 14:23). In fact, when one person heard Jesus teaching about table etiquette, he simply shouted out, "Happy are those who will feast in God's kingdom" (Luke 14:15). In Jesus' stories about eating and associating, the community reaches out to include those who are to be brought in at the end time—at the time of God's kingdom. Community therefore is not so much constituted by historic realities as it is by the vision of God's hope and the experience of God's presence.

Without a doubt the charge of associating with tax collectors, the operatives of Rome, and sinners, must be true, as often as they are repeated in the Gospels. Moreover, being a "glutton and drunkard" must also reflect practices that others could criticize. Jesus pointed his hearers to the presence of God in their living. Such a presence meant that they were to live the realm of God now.

In the Lord's Prayer (Matt. 6:9-14; Luke 11:2-4), Jesus focuses on bringing God's kingdom to earth, on feeding those who are hungry, on forgiving the debts of those who were poor, and of living by God's protection. He further tells his hearers not to be anxious, for God takes care of them . . . God "delights in giving you the kingdom" (Luke 12:32). He adds: "Sell your possessions and give to those in need. Make for yourselves wallets that don't wear out—a treasure in heaven that never runs out" (v. 33).

Community is not based on expectations and realities of the Roman overlords; rather, community flows from the grace of God. Here Jesus' advice is no different from that of many other faithful leaders, priests, Pharisees, and prophets in his day. The prayer of the Shema and its expectations required the people to remember God's creation, God's liberation, and God's presence and care. The people's ultimate vocation was to live faithfully even in these times of oppression—for oppression had been repeated time and again throughout the history of the Jewish people. The Shema and the practices of remembrance pointed people to desire "first and foremost God's kingdom and God's righteousness" (Matt. 6:33).

Being around Jesus must have been in many ways a contradictory experience. He so trusted in the presence of God. He saw God acting in many moments of healing, of release, of forgiveness, and of feeding. He saw God in his own actions of healing and forgiveness. He called people to celebrate. Several scholars have said that Jesus' entry into a village was an invitation for a party. The best wine would have been brought out, as would the best food, for he reminded them of the banquet of the realm of God. Living near him must have meant a community of joy, of celebration, and of grace. Yet it also meant living faithfully. No excuses were allowed. Seeing God at work meant the people were expected to act in new ways, as if they were the faithful and righteous community. Compromises with Roman power simply blocked possibilities of new life. Followers knew that when they called him "savior" and "prince of peace," terms that Augustus Caesar had already bestowed on himself, they were directly challenging the Romans and risking their lives.[21]

Without a doubt, challenging the compromises and living dependent on God's grace is an imperative in the way of Jesus. Therefore, community is defined by grace, by sharing, by love, and by common responsibility. This vision was such a part of the early Christian community that they continued to live it after his death. Luke recorded in Acts: "The community of believers was one in heart and mind. None of them would say, 'This is mine!' about any of their possessions, but held everything in common" (4:32). As the community of believers grew, offerings were taken for the poor, again challenging accepted patterns in Roman culture. Deacons were installed to take the gifts of the table to the widows. Scholarship has shown that in Rome many communities of believers—diverse people, many with simple jobs—lived together in tenements, sharing their resources, and studying and eating together. Even wealthy believers would provide food for community gatherings where people would connect across class. Members transcended accepted definitions of inclusion; for example, communities included Greek and Jew, slave and free, male and female (Gal 3:28). Communities often cared for the sick in their midst, thus vastly improving the health of the community.

The Church didn't clean up the streets. Christians didn't put in sewers. So you still had to live with a trench running down the middle of the road, in which you could find dead bodies decomposing. But what Christians did was take care of each other. Their apartments were as smoky as the pagan apartments, since neither had chimneys, and they were cold and wet and they stank. But Christians loved one another, and when they got sick they took care of each other. Someone brought you soup. You can do an enormous amount to relieve those miseries if you look after each other.[22]

They invited in strangers. Even in the shadow of Rome, they shared resources to pay a friend's bond, to provide freedom from slavery. At least some of these early communities of the way of Jesus were living abundant lives, providing support for the weak, and sharing the food and wine of the table in the world.[23]

We may want to ask whether Jesus' vision was a realistic vision and why the early patterns of the community of the way of Jesus passed away when Christianity was accepted as the religion of Rome, yet that is precisely the question Jesus earlier had for his hometown community. God's grace, healing, feeding, and release called for a new community, one living the vision and hope of the kingdom, one seeking righteousness.

Community of Faith as Approach to Christian Education

We human beings so easily lie to ourselves. We distort the realities of our lives and of the communities in which we find ourselves. Charles Foster is correct as he seeks to understand the plight of Christian education. Foster argues that there has been a "cultural captivity" of church education. It has too often sanctioned "the cultural status quo" rather than embracing "the transformational message of the gospel for the emancipation of people from their spiritual, social, political, or economic bondage."[24] The result is that the teaching of the Bible becomes irrelevant to everyday life, and the goals of the church's education focus on marketing and consumption, rather than the full offer of transformation and new life present in the gospel.

81

In the early 1980s, Charles Foster, Robert O'Gorman, and I completed a historical research project examining the goals and commitments of the church's education, in both Protestant and Roman Catholic contexts. The goal of Christian religious education at the founding of the United States was to offer "reading, writing, arithmetic, and religion" to children of the poor, excluded from schools. While Christian education was to teach the faith, its goals were focused on the renewal of the social order, for example, challenging slavery. We discovered that this focus of seeking justice in the social order has slowly been domesticated throughout the history of Christian education to "church business"—providing sufficient education to the children of the faithful to participate in the life of the church. In denominations, the agenda of addressing the social order has tended to be passed on to other church boards or committees, for example, committees for missions or church and society, rather than remain a task of Christian education.[25]

Without a doubt, the congregation teaches through its life, but what does it teach? Simply, church business is not enough. Unless a congregation is embodying the missional commitments of the gospel for the humanization of people and the renewal of the social order, it is shirking its responsibility. Unless it focuses on teaching the way of Jesus, its agenda can be captured by politeness rather than mission.

To return to Jesus' assessment of the community in his hometown and to the compromises made by the religious leaders in Jerusalem, only part of the good news of God's gracious intervention in the world was being spoken. He felt they were focusing on the past, rather than on the transforming vision of a God who promises healing, banquet, community, and justice. A fundamental question for the community-of-faith approach to Christian education is whether the congregation is carrying and teaching this power of redemption.

We know this is possible, but we also know that too often congregational life is "branded" by the same realities of consumer society, military solutions to problems, and growing divisions and hierarchies.[26] A church will teach in its hidden curriculum the values and perspectives that control its life—whether those are values of the faith or not. A church will teach by what it ignores and about what it refuses to speak. For example, if war and peace are not discussed, then the congregation teaches that these have nothing to do with the faith. Unless there is intentionality about the message being embodied and its faithfulness, the very practices of cultural socialization infect the church itself. Cultural therapeutic solutions or marketing strategies tend then to replace seeking new life following Jesus.

The first task of any educator working from within the community-of-faith approach is to ask how the congregation is a "place of redemption" living the way of Jesus.[27] What is being taught? What are the commitments of the church? How does the congregation conduct regular theological reflection about its life and commitments to know what it teaches? What are its explicit, hidden, and null curricula—its purposes, its teachings, and the questions it refuses to ask? Congregations as places of redemption do exist and do teach with their lives. Theological examination and assessment is a first step in any community approach to Christian education.

We too often fail when we think that the introduction of a practice of Christian living is sufficient. For example, teaching people to testify may mean that they focus on culturally defined blessings, rather than God's transformative calls to new life. How do people learn the theological integrity in their testifying? Introducing a practice is not sufficient by itself. What is necessary is theological teaching about a practice and the testing of the practices. As mentioned earlier, Dykstra has developed in the Practicing Our Faith project a rich and nuanced way of defining Christian practices.[28] Theological conversation about the integrity of practices is crucial for the faithfulness of the community. Assessment or congregational theological analysis is the first step in enacting a community-of-faith approach.

The second is to ask, where do we see God graciously present in our midst? Where is God challenging us to faithfulness? Or as Mary Elizabeth Moore has so well stated, "Where do you see signs of God's blessings or surprises in the community? . . . What destruction, danger, or threats do you see in the present situation, or on the horizon? . . . What wild imagination do you have for your community's future?"[29]

Or, to add the words of another Christian educator, Kenda Creasy Dean, where do we see these "God sightings" in our daily living?[30] Again, theological questions about redemption, forgiveness, hope, abundant life, and faithfulness push the community of faith to define itself. Note how this process of making explicit the commitments and calling of the congregation is itself a theological education project.

Third, the congregation seeks to embody this vision within its life and

83

within the community it affects. Here is where the practices identified by Dykstra, and the ten signs of renewal discovered by Diana Butler Bass, or the categories provided by Westerhoff or Foster, can be very helpful. Not only do we think comprehensively about how a congregation teaches, but we need to ask, where are those moments of power that give life to the congregation and its ministries?

For Foster this is an "event-centered" approach to education. We look at how an ordinary practice is coordinated with a new and renewing practice to communicate the mission of the church. How do worship, study, and mission cohere? What is it that the congregation wants to embody? Again, such decisions are themselves theological education moments when leaders in a congregation with the people of God seek to be faithful, to respond to God's calling, and to shape the concrete dimensions of their lives.

To follow the way of Jesus, these moments will be moments of mission, forgiveness, redemption, healing, or celebrating. Just as the first communities of the way of Jesus needed to learn how to serve each other, congregations today need to fulfill the same tasks.[31] Acts records moments when those early communities of faith were growing as witnesses to the redeeming actions of God in the world. Acts also records moments of faithlessness, when members stole from the community. Paul's Corinthian correspondence records moments of conflict within the community when groups wanted their own way and excluded others.

The community needs to engage in disciplined theological reflection about its life together. Too often I fear denominations, particularly mainline denominations, are caught in the research mode, seeking to find out how to grow the denomination and make it effective again. Study after study is repeated with list after list defined of renewing strategies. We already know what makes a congregation vital—it is changed lives. It is places where new life is present when brokenness seems the reality, where grace offers new chances, where healing occurs, where communities are reborn and reshaped. Church growth is not the issue; rather, growth in faith is. The task is not competition for market share; it is renewal by the spirit. It is transformation. It is birth of communities of redemption.

Extending the Community-of-Faith Approach

In chapter 2, we encountered the "spiritual but not religious" and the "unaffiliated and unconcerned." These are people who rarely attend church, or if they do, they do so for ritual occasions. This group also includes people whose families have been so far away from the church for so long that they really do not know what occurs within a congregation. When they do attend, for a special reason, often they are not able to understand the liturgical practices of the community. While it would seem that a community-of-faith approach does not touch this group directly, I will suggest some ways of ministering to this group—of teaching.

First, some in this group are very willing to attend a congregation to support friends, during a wedding or funeral, or even family members when there are special events such as baptisms, christenings, or confirmations. In addition, some in this group do attend on holy days, such as Christmas or Easter. What might the community-of-faith approach suggest to us?

Let's look at baptisms or christenings. How can the purposes of these events be extended to education? For example, children being confirmed are participants in an extensive educational process helping them know Christian faith, its practices, and expectations. Moreover, parents of children being confirmed or those being baptized are expected to attend educational sessions explaining the meanings of these rituals and how parents can support their children. These very instructional meetings attended by parents offer an opportunity. An additional session can be scheduled where the parents, or even the confirmed, invite participation of their wider family and friends. Such a welcome and hospitable session could speak about the meaning of being baptized or confirmed and of choosing to become a member of the church. What it means for a child to become a member, what expectations are set for the child, and how family and friends can be a support for the child can be discussed. Of course, some—perhaps many—friends and family members will not attend these invitational settings, yet the offer has been made and the seriousness of the transition named. Moreover, parents and participants often like to have "souvenirs" of such services. A bulletin including the ritual and the meaning of the practices can be produced and shared as a gift as well as an educational invitation.

A similar strategy could be used to reach out to those supporting a family through a marriage or a death—group meetings and educational handouts. For example, I attended a wedding in a Jewish synagogue a few years ago where several of the visitors were not Jewish. The couple provided a copy of the service and defined the practices of the day and the meanings of these practices for themselves and the wider Jewish community. Such sheets of information are one introductory way to extend the meanings of being educated in and shaped by a community of faith. They can also be coupled with further information about the life and ministries of the congregation. They can further point to education that is offered online about Christian marriage or the Christian understanding of death and loss.

Moreover, additional opportunities are similarly made available by expanding ritual celebrations. How about celebrations of graduations or of jobs or vocational choices? Such moments of transition provide opportunities for education to friends and family outside the church, who will attend because of their love and support of a person.

Important religious holidays: some people attend only at these liturgical celebrations of Easter or Christmas. Honoring the worship integrity of these times, "event-centered" educational strategies help us think about options. Invitations can be shared throughout the community describing worship services, educational events, and ministries being connected at this time of year. These invitations can include references to further education available on the church website. Educational materials, like the souvenir bulletins mentioned earlier, can be placed in the congregation to share the meanings of these crucial events for those outside the community. Follow-up mailed materials and visits to people who attend can further enhance the welcome. Moreover, such follow-up actions communicate that a community of faith is committed to its values and understandings and openly desires to share them.

Community service events: whenever a congregation extends its ministries to the wider community is again a moment for "event-centered" education. A free farmers' market for people in the community can be coupled with information about the church and its faith commitments. A neighborhood fair is again an opportunity to point people to the ministries and commitments of a congregation. The presence of church leaders at schools in tutoring and service programs is also a time when the values of the faith are embodied. An additional example, many churches have preschools and day care programs that draw people outside the church who are "spiritual but not religious" or "unaffiliated and unconcerned." The preschool itself provides an opportunity to extend the religious education of the children to parents and guardians through support groups and educational events. For example, one church connects the preschool with the outreach mission of the congregation. As families are asked to participate in these ministries, education is conducted demonstrating why these are part of the identity and vocation of the congregation.

Finally, one the best ways a congregation teaches to those outside is the way it lives its life—the ways it is faithful. Does it serve the wider community? Can it be called on when people are in need? Will it support and encourage through actions like tutoring or community? I was amazed a few months ago when speaking to churches in a "district" denominational workshop. Only one of the forty-five churches attending had a tutoring or outreach program for a local school, and only two of those attending had even visited with the school administrators or with their own members who taught in the school. We teach as a community of faith as we live as a community of faith in the wider world.

Evidently this occurred in the early church, who sought to follow the way of Jesus (see James 2). The letter of James tells about a church that paid attention to the rich who visited, but ignored the poor. The author of James says: "You do well when you really fulfill the royal law found in scripture, *Love your neighbor as yourself*" (Jas. 2:8). He continues:

> What good is it if people say they have faith but do nothing to show it? Claiming to have faith can't save anyone, can it? Imagine a brother or sister who is naked and never has enough food to eat. What if one said, "Go in peace! Stay warm! Have a nice meal!"? What good is it if you don't actually give them what their body needs? In the same way, faith is dead when it doesn't result in faithful activity. (Jas. 2:14-17)

The early Christian community taught as it extended the table of fellowship to those outside, as it provided care for the sick and support for those who were lost. The biggest challenge of the community-of-faith approach is the challenge to actually be and live the community of faith in the world.

Conclusion

Jesus embodied the practices of his Jewish faith. His life flowed through the year of remembering God's gift of freedom, of care in times of despair, and of the Torah's plan for organizing life. Daily he prayed the Shema, seeking to put love of God ahead of all else. Daily he felt the cords and knots of his prayer shawl remind him of God's expectations for his people to be "light," to be an embodiment of God's promise for humanity.

Many around him, too, organized their lives and even sought to extend the dimensions of the law to all of life. For Jesus and for the early communities of the way, it was the in-breaking power of the spirit and grace of God that called them to be reborn, to new life in the midst of a world that sought to suck life out of them. The community teaches without a doubt, but community education is stunted without deep knowledge of the tradition, without instruction, without study, and without theological wisdom. To that we now turn.

Chapter Five

Study: Instructional Approach to Christian Education

Throughout his ministry and his travels, Jesus was "tested" on his knowledge of the Jewish tradition and was "graded" on his interpretations of how the tradition offered hope in a troubling time. He was continually asked questions: What is the greatest commandment? How will I find eternal life? Who sinned? Do we pay the temple tax? Will you give us a sign? Are your miracles from God or the demons? What does God require of us? Disciples and Pharisees, ordinary people and advocates for temple authorities, the rich and the poor, and the sick and demon-filled all had to know.

Over and over Jesus showed his respect for the traditions.

> Don't even begin to think that I have come to do away with the Law and the Prophets. I haven't come to do away with them but to fulfill them. I say to you very seriously that as long as heaven and earth exist, neither the smallest letter nor even the smallest stroke of a pen will be erased from the Law until everything there becomes a reality. (Matt. 5:17-18)

Jesus also expected those asking questions to answer them with their living. When asked about the greatest commandment, Jesus answered in the traditional manner. Quoting the Shema, he answered that loving God is first, above all else—"with all your heart, with all your being, and with all your mind" (Matt. 22:37; Deut. 6:5). He then pointed to the full spirit of the Shema, "Love your neighbor as you love yourself" (Matt. 22:39; Lev. 19:18).

Jesus taught through his actions: healings, exorcisms, and feedings. For example, when the disciples of John the Baptist came to speak to him, he answered them by pointing to the results. "Go, report to John what you hear and see. Those who are blind are able to see. Those who were crippled are walking. People with skin diseases are cleansed. Those who were deaf now hear. Those who were dead are raised up. The poor have good news proclaimed to them" (Matt. 11:5; see Isa. 35:5-6; 61:1). Those who saw him forgive and heal a man whose friends lowered him down through a roof were taught that faith, forgiveness, and healing were inseparable (Matt. 9:1-8; Mark 2:1-12; Luke 5:17-26). Those who benefited from his feeding crowds of hungry people learned what abundance in the midst of scarcity meant (Matt. 14:12-21; 15:32-39; Mark 6:31-44; 8:1-9; Luke 9:10-17; John 6:5-15). Moreover, his healing of a man possessed by demons named Legion taught the people that even the power of Rome was limited (Mark 5:1-20; Matt. 8:28-34; Luke 8:26-39).

Jesus also taught through aphorisms and parables. He had an amazing ability to take the ordinary moments of life and draw fresh insights that deepened the ways of Israel, just like many other rabbis. To teach through parables, he had to know the people well and to see the depth and power within the tradition itself. He had to listen to God's grace guiding him. For example, he described a method with which people broadcast seed across a field—some was eaten by birds, some "scorched" by the sun, some choked by thorny plants, and some bore fruit. Taking an ordinary moment of the year that his hearers knew well, he drew them in. He reminded them about which seeds germinate into fruitful plants and which conditions provide the exact amount of light and water. Through these images, he taught about the realm of God. He expected abundance. The crop increased thirty, sixty, and a hundred times (Mark 4:1-20; Matt. 13:1-23; Luke 8:4-15). From the ordinary, hope and possibility are made apparent. Isn't this pattern of teaching followed in many of the parables: reminding people of the realities of their world, gaining their assent and understanding, and offering a problem-posing question or image to invite a fuller understanding of God's presence and grace—almost as if he was educating for transforming moments?[1]

Jesus honored both the traditions and the experiences of the people. From the ordinary, Jesus pointed to the presence of God's grace calling for new life in the midst of a world where the people were daily challenged.

Instruction in Christian Education

Elizabeth Caldwell uses a powerful metaphor as she speaks about instruction in faith—"making a home for faith."[2] Through instruction, children, youth, and adults are invited into the stories, the commitments, the practices, and the expectations of a people. They are empowered to be "at home." We all have experienced entering a stranger's home and not knowing where to sit or how. Can we relax? Do we have to worry about our children touching things? What is off-limits? Sometimes in another person's home, we are so anxious that we are tight and uncomfortable, or we offend. Yet when we are home, we know where everything is. We relax into furniture. We know the rules. We can be ourselves. This is what Elizabeth Caldwell describes—instruction offers us a home for faith.

Her image is on target. I have seen this homemaking in the lives of our grandchildren. Those who have attended a church preschool are learning to become comfortable with many of the stories of the faith, stories of Jesus. They have lived the rhythm of the Christian year in their classrooms, moving from Christmas to Easter and to Pentecost. They have learned songs, shaped crafts, prepared for performances, and gathered mission gifts. Concepts were present, but within narratives. Actions were expected. In fact, my daughter tells about how our grandson comes home and "preaches," teaching the family what he has learned.

Those who have attended a Jewish day school have had an even richer religious environment—of course, it is a full elementary-to–high school curriculum. Making a home for faith: each day begins with reciting the Shema, remembering from whom life flows and to whom loyalty is owed. Through the celebration of the holidays and liturgical life of the Jewish community, children are led through Rosh Hashanah, to Yom Kippur, to Sukkoth, to Hanukkah, to Purim, to Pesach, and to Shavuot, learning the primary stories of the Jewish way of life. Each week the children celebrate Shabbat in the school and study the Torah text for the week. A child is invited to reflect on the passage and interpret it for others, thus practicing beginning theological skills. Through Hebrew language study, they are taught to read the Torah. Through *Tefillah*, they are taught the prayers and the rituals so that when they sit in synagogue, they are at home; they are insiders. The day school makes a home for faith.

Let's look at two other examples of the instructional approach. Second Baptist Church made an interesting decision a few years ago. They decided to make membership in the congregation and baptism easy, but to require a rigorous plan of adult and youth faith education for those who join. By easy membership and baptism, they have highlighted that God's grace is open to all. If people feel God's grace in their lives and want to become members, all they have to do is ask. New members affirm their faith in front of the congregation by answering yes to three simple questions: (1) Is God calling you? (2) Will you seek to be faithful? and (3) Will you continue to grow in your faith? Those who have never been baptized are invited to a believer's baptism. Coupled with this "easy membership," the third question, "Will you continue to grow in your faith?" is taken seriously. The congregation has developed three twenty-week courses that make up "The Church's Teaching Series," which each member is expected to attend. Once the series is completed, each attendee receives a certificate of discipleship. New members are then asked to continue to learn as a part of a small teaching/learning group and to join a mission team that also reflects on its work.

The first course focuses on understanding and reading the Bible. Fifteen biblical stories have been chosen, and through reading and study, members are introduced to Bible study skills. The second focuses on understanding and living the faith. Here again, fifteen faith themes from creation to kingdom to redemption are chosen. People are introduced to how these theological concepts have been used in the history of the church. In addition, the class teaches basic skills of theological reflection. The third course is discipleship, seeking to help people make connections with daily living. Attention is given to stewardship, how we are called to use and nurture the world God has given us. Connecting prayer, study, and service is a theme in the class. It ends with expectations about giving and serving. While not all the new members of Second Church complete all courses, the congregation has discovered that this plan of enhancing the instruction of members also builds congregational leaders. The courses make a home for faith.

St. Michael's is an older parish in a risky neighborhood of an urban center. St. Michael's elementary school has thrived connected to the parish for over a hundred years. While the costs are great, with support from the denomination, from endowment and gifts, and from tuition, they are able to offer a preschool and elementary curriculum. Instruction in faith is the key offering in addition to meeting state education standards in language, mathematics, and science. Church leaders believe that the school is a rich environment to teach children the practices of knowing, doing, and being the way of Jesus. Complementing the activities of the school are monthly workshops to assist parents as faith guides for children. In addition, the children and the work of the school are regularly remembered in weekly worship. Finally, St. Michael's also schedules an after-school day care program for junior-high children. Leaders at St. Michael's have made connections with the local middle school. They send a bus to pick up any children who need day care. This effort not only supports parents, but also reinforces the religious education of youth, many of whom are in the congregation's confirmation program.

Goals of Instruction

Sara Little defined Christian religious instruction as "the process of exploring the church's tradition and self-understanding in such a way that persons can understand, assess, and therefore respond to the truth of the gospel for themselves."[3] Instruction is a complicated process of learning the content of the tradition, making judgments about that content, claiming it as one's own, and living its meanings in the world. It is a depth process of knowing, described best by the Hebrew word for knowing, *yada*. Knowing is an intimate act, much like the love expressed between two people. It is personal, calling people to be deeply connected to each other and each other's ways. In fact, the kind of knowing of which Little speaks requires that we show mercy and live justly because we are deeply connected with God and others (Mic. 6:8).

Elizabeth Caldwell further lists the goals of Christian instruction as the following:

1. "Enabling learners to be grounded in biblical faith"

2. Making the environment for learning a "welcoming space," honoring learning styles of learners and promoting considered reflection and dialogue

3. Attending to methods of teaching that are committed to "conscious listening, responding, critiquing, and questioning"

4. Making connections between faith and life—growing in living the faith[4]

Thus, Christian religious instruction empowers people to know the tradition so well, so intimately, that they orient their lives to it.

How often do we think this intimate knowing takes place in instructional settings in congregations? Do we sufficiently communicate to the people of God that knowledge is crucial for faithfulness? The people at Second Church try to, by requiring it. In chapter 3, we saw people, described by their church colleagues as "faithful," asking questions about faith and living. They drew on the tradition and its meanings, yet even they pleaded for more help from their churches to think theologically. This is the agenda of Christian religious instruction.

What does it take for us to provide the depth knowledge and meanings required for faithful living? I join theologian Edward Farley in expressing fear that much of Christian education practice "occurs in a never-never land between a program of ordered learning (for example, public schools, clergy education) and the general formative influence of everything the church is and does."[5] Farley asks Christian education to "hold before the community the contents of its tradition, bringing discipline to ways of interpreting those contents, and making available tools" of interpretation and criticism.[6]

The people of God are themselves theologians. The responsibility of Christian education is to empower believers to be fully engaged in the nuanced and critical tasks of theological understanding. Such a responsibility is impossible if the people of God are "isolated from the textual riches, methods, and insights of theological education."[7] Theology is not simply an academic field of study; rather, it is a "wisdom" by which a person of faith interprets and engages the world. The word *wisdom* communicates a "habit," a learned pattern of inquiry, critical reflection, and deciding by which a person seeks to be a faithful witness and embodiment of God's redemption. A wisdom, or a habit, to use the title of Little's book, "sets one's heart," focusing the ways people see, engage, and respond.[8]

Just as the "narratives, symbols, and events we call Gospel arose in acts of interpretation" in the ambiguities of history in particular contexts, theology "summons the community to reinterpret."[9] Educator Carol Lakey Hess describes this theological learning process as the encounter of "hard dialogue" with "deep convictions."[10] Theological learning requires sustained effort. Christians are theologians as they are grounded in the traditions of faith, as they are empowered to reflect on the meanings of the faith, as they critique their own present, and as they seek to be faithful in a new time.

Let me use a very mundane example: a technician who is called to a home to repair an appliance must decide what is wrong with the appliance and whether it is worth repairing. There are many brands and styles of appliances. Sometimes presenting symptoms evidence deeper difficulties. Good repair technicians are responsible to those who have called them for restoring the usefulness of an appliance, yet there are limits, financial and otherwise. If a repair costs more than a new appliance, should it be fixed? If a new appliance is needed, will it fit where the old one was? The technician has wisdom, a pattern of previous decisions and the knowledge and experiences to make an informed choice. The technician has a moral obligation to recommend the best decision based on knowledge and critical judgment.

We know this description of "wisdom" is true for many other professions. My brother is a psychiatric social worker. He confronts difficult cases, some involving court-required counseling because of abuse or chronic alcoholism. Over the years, he has gained a wisdom of assessing what is occurring in the counseling situation and of making a decision about how to respond. This wisdom is informed by his training and continuing reading and study, by supervision presenting cases to other social workers, and by reflection on his practice. He makes the best decision possible in the circumstance based on knowledge and critical judgment. Isn't such a process true also for doctors, teachers, and parents?

Something very similar is true for the believer. We are obligated to draw on all the wisdom we have to make a faithful decision. The original expressions of gospel teachings emerged in a particular time and way of thinking. Times change. Original statements may no longer make sense. Throughout the Bible, we see community leaders seeking to understand and be faithful in a new day. Such efforts required study, interpretation, and prayer. For example, the Hebrew people who were captured and sent to Babylon had to consider how they "could possibly sing the Lord's song on foreign soil" (Ps. 137:4). When they returned to Israel, they had to decide how to rebuild the country.

New Testament authors did the best they could to express the transforming power of the way of Jesus in their lives. We are called to do the same today. We are called to use all the tools we have: critical tools of biblical study, approaches to theological reflection, ways of understanding the world in which we live, and our critical, reflective skills to make informed decisions. Christian education has failed if it does not help us in this complex and faithful process of interpretation—of exploring, considering, and deciding.

A friend who teaches in a Jewish seminary described her understanding of the task of a faithful interpreter of the Torah. The person is to study what a text says in its time and context, to explore how it has been interpreted throughout history, to consider the text and its interpretations in light of present understandings, and make a decision on how to live. The person is expected to make the best possible decision about what the text means. Isn't this a powerful way to define the task of interpretation? Christian believers, too, are asked to make the best possible decision using the resources and tools we have to decide what God is calling us to do today.

Processes of Christian Instruction

Christian religious educators have defined processes of teaching and learning that assist the people of God in developing a critical approach to engaging and living the faith. The questions we address are not simple. They require us to use all skills of thinking, deciding, and committing to our best. We will consider the work of three Christian educators: Thomas Groome, Anne Streaty Wimberly, and Dori Ginenko Baker.[11]

Yet, before exploring the processes of Christian religious learning and teaching, let us consider learning itself, using a fun example, an exercise routine. A few years ago, knowing I needed more sustained exercise, I turned to my bicycle. I had earlier (about twenty years before) used a bike for one spring and summer for exercise, and enjoyed it. I thought I had a good bike. Moreover, Chicago has wonderful bike trails, moderate summer and beautiful fall weather, and is flat, thus the ability to improve without an amazing amount of effort.

I began, as many would, pumping up the tires of my old bicycle and riding. After a couple of wonderful days through beautiful forest preserve bike trails, about eight miles from home, I had a blow-out. The blow-out wasn't spectacular; it was more of a whimper, but I certainly did not enjoy walking home, pushing my bike. Thank God for a friend who met me in his car and delivered me to a bike shop.

The clerk was cordial, but barely could contain her derision: "Didn't you know that bikes need to be maintained?" Tires dry out, and furthermore, she noted that my chain was almost rusted thorough. I guess I didn't know the extent of maintenance, nor of safe riding. My dad and Victory Cycle Shop had kept my bike in good shape when I was a child. I asked her to see that the bike was overhauled.

After the "scolding," the flat tire, and the walk, even with a "repaired" bike, I may have simply left it in the garage to get again dry tires, gummy gears, and rusted chains, if it had not been for a friend who invited me to ride. I enjoyed the company and the exercise. The "renewed" bike rode well. Colleagues began to ask me how far I was riding and how fast. I frankly couldn't tell them, so I researched and purchased a bicycle odometer to record my progress. Furthermore, I enrolled in a rudimentary bicycle repair class, learning some basics of bicycle maintenance so I could keep the bike oiled, the gears working smoothly, and the tires well inflated—hoping to avoid future ire from the clerk.

I developed more confidence and more speed. Physical conditioning improved. Also, my conversation (or, more accurately, "showing off") about the sport increased. I learned I did enjoy biking. I enjoyed riding with friends. I enjoyed subscribing to a bicycling magazine and learning even more.

Then, the full conversion: One summer, I watched several of the legs of the Tour de France. The beauty of the country, the speed, the conditioning, and the enthusiasm of the crowd all amazed me. Watching the commercials also introduced me to new bikes and bicycle gear. I began to discuss new bikes with friends and to visit bicycle shops, looking at the options. I grew in my knowledge and facility with biking. Moreover, through riding, I grew in knowledge and facility of the road itself—learning how to take turns, gauge my effort up hills, brake on downhills, avoid cars, and improve my speed. Finally, knowing I had reached the limit of my abilities with the present bicycle, I researched bicycle options and bought a new bike. The process continued.

Note I am describing the development of bicycling wisdom: learning occurred through experience, through trial and error; learning occurred through conversation, consulting friends and experts; and learning occurred through research and study. Furthermore, through practice on the roads, learning continued. I developed some wisdom about biking, enough to make decisions on the road, repair my bike, and even continue to improve my technique. I *explored* my feelings of the enjoyment of riding, I talked with cyclists, and I practiced exercise routines to improve form. I *considered* the knowledge about biking as I read articles and as I reflected on my experiences, often with friends. I learned to better negotiate the realities of the roads around me, the limitations of the bike I purchased, and my own limits. Each day as I rode, I *decided* where to ride, how far to ride, and how to negotiate what I encountered. Learning is a dynamic process, with exploring, considering, and deciding building on one another and deepening one another.[12] Learning results in a wisdom that guides us in making daily decisions.

Don't we do something similar to what I have described whenever we commit ourselves to something new in our lives, our jobs, and our hobbies? My wife, Margaret Ann, is an experienced quilter. She has purchased many resources to assist her work, subscribing to magazines. She watches quilt shows and attends quilt festivals. She has friends who quilt, and they visit quilt stores together. And she is even teaching some of her students to improve their quilting. She has become quite proficient in tackling new patterns and in making new designs come to life. While the content she has *explored* is essential to her work with fabric, she *considers* what she has learned in relationship to her hopes, her time, her resources, and her limitations. She *decides* how to move forward with the quilts she makes. Again, she has developed a wisdom that is continually being refined by the process of quilting itself. She learns from both the mistakes and successes.

Engaging a religious community and learning the meanings and commitments at the heart of the community is very similar. Church historian Catherine Albanese argues that each religion has elements of creed (belief), cult (patterns of prayer and worship), and code (expected ways of living and acting to be faithful).[13] To understand a religion requires us to *explore* these elements in depth so we understand them. Moreover, to live a religious life requires us to *consider* the creed, cult, and codes with the realities of the world in which we find ourselves, our context. We then *decide* how we draw on its creeds, engage in prayer, and live its expectations. Of course, this can be done in a wooden and rigid manner or in a more open and critical manner. Learning is a dynamic process; wisdom develops in the practice. As we learn, we study and *explore*; we then *consider* how what we have learned connects with our lives, and we *decide*.

Christian religious educators have sought to describe teaching/learning processes that empower wisdom. In the processes of teaching and learning in the faith community, people are engaged in theological reflection. Thomas Groome argues that the goal of Christian religious education is to empower people to be faithful in serving the kingdom of God in the world. He speaks about processes of education that move from life to faith and from faith to life. What he proposes is that teaching and learning is a decision-making process informed as we interpret both a person's experiences and the faith story. People approach their lives and the faith with a personal story influenced by their experiences and their training and with a vision of what the world is about and what they are called to do. In turn, the faith has a story, a narrative recorded by witnesses in the past, biblical, theological, and/or ecclesial. The faith also has a vision, a trajectory of what faithfulness means. The process of Christian religious education begins as we consider our experiences, in life and in the church. We probe these experiences. Teaching and learning then call for us to explore the story and vision of the tradition, of the church's narrative. We also probe this for meaning. But learning that affects our living and formation as Christians then occurs as we put faith and life in relationship. Through prayerful discernment alone and in community, we decide the meanings that direct our lives and we live them.

Teaching and learning involve both content and processes. While it is absolutely necessary, simple content learning is not sufficient. In other words, without the content of life and faith, we have nothing on which to draw for reflection and discernment. But content alone cannot define daily meanings; it is simply one element in the midst of a complex, dynamic living process. *We need structured and guided processes in the midst of a community of learners that assist us in discernment.* Not any process will work, but a theological education process empowers us to think and discern the deepest commitments of our lives, commitment to God and to God's creation. Groome's "shared Christian praxis" model is such a structured and guided process.

Anne Wimberly's process of "story-linking" is very similar. She begins with a living experience and/or a story from the biblical witness. The goal is to link Bible and life. She probes the meanings of a biblical story; examines life experiences, both a person's and those in her or his heritage; and links biblical, personal, and corporate (or family heritage) stories into decisions for living. This process was discovered in her historical research on slave narratives and within the life and ministry of the African American church. Her ancestors, she discovered, connected their histories, their communities, their contemporary experiences, and the biblical witness to decide how to respond. For Wimberly, connecting contemporary decisions with the realities of African American history and drawing on the wisdom of the elders are essential. Teaching links the individuals' stories with their people's histories and with the biblical and theological traditions.

Both the work of Groome and Wimberly are structured and guided theological processes to assist Christians in developing abilities of theological wisdom and discernment that will lead them through their daily responsibilities. Content is crucial for both, and so are the processes of discerning.

A third approach is described by Dori Grinenko Baker. This approach is designed for young adults and seeks to empower their vocational choices. It was developed from her own work as a hospital chaplain and in her research with young women. *The Barefoot Way* teaches young people and their mentors strategies that will enable them to build the wisdom to face questions and issues in their daily lives.[14] Her method is called L.I.V.E. It is much like that of Groome and Wimberly, with a clarity and attractiveness for youth:

1. Listen—Listening deeply to stories and questions. Asking oneself to seek to put on "God ears" for the listening.

2. Immerse in the feelings—Immersing oneself in the feelings brought forth by the story or question. Connecting it with stories and moments in one's own living.

3. View it wider—Asking questions such as: Where is God in this story? To what scripture passages or theological resources or ideas am I drawn? Think of Christian practices like hospitality or witnessing. Note how this fits into what one thinks of as God's story.

4. Explore Actions and "Aha" Moments—Asking oneself, so what now? Think about insights and connections that are found. Note how one will respond and engage in living into the story of God in the world.[15]

The power of this approach is that it can become a regular process of Christian wisdom seeking.

The approach can be both a guide for personal reflection and a process of teaching and study. It becomes richer and more effective as the community gathers around youth, listening to them, noting their novel insights and passions, questioning the connections made to the tradition, enlarging options, and supporting them on their journeys of faith.

Paralleling the work of these scholars, in *Educating Christians*, Margaret Ann Crain, Joseph Crockett, and I offered a summary model of theological teaching or wisdom. We described the approach as a fluid spiral with no fixed entry point, moving from considering to exploring to discerning, or from discerning to exploring to considering, or from exploring to considering to discerning. The process is fluid, not static. *Considering* has to do with paying attention to one's own questions, feelings, perspectives, and commitments, of drawing deeply from our experiences. *Exploring* has to do with attending to and remembering the theological and biblical tradition and knowledge from culture and study. *Discerning* is that interpretive move when we make connections and decide how we are planning to respond and live by the light we have gained from both personal and group reflection and guidance.

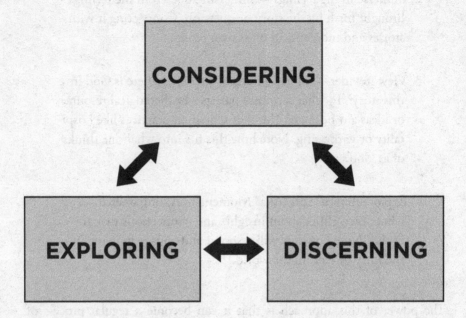

The process is dynamic. It can be used for personal reflection or in a classroom or retreat setting as a model for planning teaching.

For example, beginning with exploring: A teacher chooses a text from the Bible—the parable of the sower. Activities are developed to help learners explore, thinking about the intentions of the Gospel writers in telling the story and how the passage connects to what we know of Jesus' message. Learners are invited into strategies of biblical study. They ask questions of the text. They wonder how it was heard by its original audience as well as how it is heard by a contemporary reader. The text is "explored" as fully as possible.

Yet, as the exploration occurs, we also know that the learners are personally considering the parable. They are thinking about it and are feeling some of its powerful messages. The text points people to its message of grace, of how Jesus believed that God's grace was working through the ordinary moments of living. A teacher develops strategies to assist the learners in considering feelings, previous understandings, and alternate meanings.

Finally, before the end of the teaching session, the teacher offers ways for the learners to decide meanings for their understanding and living. For the process to be complete, learners need to name how they will enact the commitments and ideas they have explored and considered in their daily living.

The process is engaging and dynamic, but all three elements, exploring, considering, and discerning, need to be present. Too often congregational instruction focuses only on content. While using good strategies for exploring, the lack of attention to considering and discerning limits the impact of the teaching/learning experience. Learners are not helped to test insights and connect them to previous understandings. In addition, too many congregational teaching sessions end before any decisions are made. The process of developing theological wisdom is incomplete.

When all three of the elements in the model are engaged, people are practicing theological wisdom. When people first begin the theological reflection process, the references from scripture and theology may be limited, the ability to consider what is occurring in one's feelings may be limited, and the ability to decide and take responsibility might be anxiety producing. Yet, as the approach is practiced and tested, enriched with direct teaching of the faith tradition, and decisions are made, learners enhance their abilities to draw from the faith and engage it in living. We develop a theological wisdom. Learning is more powerful when we consider our feelings, ideas, and commitments; when we explore the theological tradition and our knowledge in depth; *and* when we make decisions about how we will live our faith lives.

Preparing for Teaching

As any good teacher knows, planning for teaching is essential, whether we teach in a classroom, retreat, or youth gathering. We ask: What do I want people to learn, encounter, or do as a result of a teaching/learning session? Learning goals focus our purposes for teaching. Planning builds on both the content we are teaching and the learners we are encountering. On the one hand, all the skills we have developed as theological educators are tested as we explore a text and develop its meanings in its time and in the present. On the other hand, learning fails if we do not know the learners.

Developmental research empowers us to know what is possible in their learning. For example, young children do not engage in complex critical reflection, what Piaget called *formal operational thinking*. Their thinking is more episodic and narrative, more concrete than abstract. In addition, people have differing learning styles. For example, Howard Gardner has conducted extensive research on "multiple intelligences": musical, linguistic, logical-mathematical, visual-spatial, bodily-kinesthetic, naturalistic, interpersonal, and intrapersonal.[16] Thomas Armstrong, for one, builds on Gardner's work by offering strategies to teach using these intelligences.[17] Research shows that if we use more than one learning style in our teaching, we will touch more of the learners in a group. While there are many different approaches to defining learning styles, what they all communicate is that we need to attend to our learners and the ways they learn.

After we have examined the content to be taught and our students, we are ready to make specific decisions about what we will emphasize and teach. Here is where we specifically define what the teaching/learning session is about and how to teach so its goals are achieved. We ask:

- What will we teach?

- How will we use and enrich the environment for learning?

- How will we structure the teaching/learning session?

- How will the session flow?

- On what resources and practices will we draw?

- What do we hope students will learn?

We then teach!

Finally, we evaluate and consider the decisions we made in the teaching session. What did people indeed learn? Did the session achieve our goals? Were there unintended consequences? How will we build on this learning in future sessions? We move from evaluation to think about the learners with whom we work and our practices and planning as a teacher.

A lesson-planning process often looks something like this:

104

1. Context—describing the context and the learners (whether classroom, mission trip, retreat, youth gathering, and so on)

2. Content—exploring and describing the content to be taught

3. Learning goals—focusing on learning, being clear and limited, deciding what we hope will be learned

4. Environment—attending to room arrangement and enrichments of setting for teaching/learning

5. Flow of the teaching– deciding on timing, strategies, and aesthetic shape

   a. Beginning—focusing the learning community
   b. Flow or process—using the "considering, exploring, discerning approach"
   c. Ending—Sending out the learners

6. Evaluation—Noting signs of student learning; considering what one learned about learners, oneself, the teaching and learning plan, and theological education and theological wisdom; and defining options or steps for the future

Instruction in the Way of Jesus

Jesus was an amazing teacher. He connected with people's experiences. He questioned, told stories, used parables, and challenged his hearers. Jesus *lived* the faith and drew people into their own processes of interpretation. He assisted people in developing habits of thinking and seeing, theological wisdom. The parable of the sower again is an example. The ordinary was used to stimulate thinking and critical reflection that called the hearers to more faithful ways of living.

In Jesus' society, as we have seen, there was considerable conflict about how the Jewish faith tradition was to be lived. The leaders in Jerusalem, particularly temple leaders, worked hard to keep the ritual life of the community alive, while they cooperated with Rome—in an effort to protect and preserve what they thought was important. In fact, we know that many groups and individuals were risking much. The feeling of risk and fear makes its way into the New Testament as Luke tells the story of Rabbi Gamaliel's address (Acts 5:33-39). The events about which Gamaliel, an honored rabbi, speaks are real and dangerous. Gamaliel seeks to prevent further conflict that would set off the Romans.

> Fellow Israelites, consider carefully what you intend to do. . . . Some time ago, Theudas appeared, claiming to be somebody and some four hundred men joined him. After he was killed, all of his followers scattered, and nothing came of that. Afterward, at the time of the census, Judas the Galilean appeared and got some people to follow him in revolt. He was killed too, and all his followers scattered far and wide. Here is my recommendation in this case: Distance yourself from these men. (Acts 5:35-38)

Records show that both Judas the Galilean (approximately 6 CE) and Theudas (approximately 40 CE) were messianic prophets who led revolts against the Romans and were put to death and their followers punished.

Jewish leaders had to assess how they could preserve Jewish worship and some elements of self-control. Without a doubt, this same argument was spoken by rabbis and leaders after the fall of the temple.[18] Many stayed as far away from messianic and revolutionary movements as possible, fearing that they would bring further Roman destruction. Clearly this destruction is exactly what occurred in the Second Jewish-Roman War in the early second century. The high priest in Jerusalem became a follower of Simon bar Kokhba and joined the revolt against Rome. Roman Emperor Hadrian reclaimed control. He made circumcision illegal and began building a temple to Jupiter on the holy mount of the Jewish temple.

The Jewish rebellion seemed the right decision for many when victory after victory returned territory to Jewish control and leadership. In fact, coins were even minted that proclaimed, "Freedom." Yet, again, as in earlier Roman justice, the military totally destroyed the territory, led Jewish survivors away as prisoners, and barred Jews from their holy land.

The Pharisees were explicit claiming that reflection about the tradition was essential. The written Torah was holy, but it dealt with a time in Israel's past. To be fully faithful, the Pharisees developed an oral Torah, which sought to extend the expectations of the Torah, articulating how to be faithful and respond to God in each new day and time. In a similar vein, James, Jesus' brother, sought to maintain the faithfulness of the Jesus community in Jerusalem amid multiple competing groups under the watchful eye of Rome. Here he and his friends were killed in 62 CE, over the objection of many faithful Jews.[19] The Romans saw him as a threat, as the leader of a rebellious messianic movement challenging the authority of their rule.

Note that all of these groups have a wisdom, a way of interpreting text and times. Their ways differed, which brought them into conflict. Simply having a theological wisdom is not sufficient. How do we test the insights gained? The great biblical prophets conflicted in their advice from conclusions of temple prophets working for the rulers. Theological wisdom is always risky, yet it is all we have. We are required to seek to understand. Those of us calling ourselves Christian engage theological wisdom asking:

- Does it open us to the grace of God, as Jesus taught?

- Does it call us to live the faith as fully as we can?

- Does it encourage us to look for the realm of God in our lives?

- Does it keep us open to the transforming power of God's new creation?

Jesus embodied a stance, in many ways, not very different from the Pharisees'.[20] In Matthew we are given a glimpse into his religious teaching. He sought to extend the meanings of the tradition for his day. Note both the honoring of tradition and the critical reflection to understand what it meant for a new time. Specifically, Matthew has Jesus saying, "You have heard that it was said to those who lived long ago . . . But I say to you . . . " (Matt. 5:21-22). Throughout this reporting, Jesus notes what was said "long ago" and connects it to the contemporary situation. He speaks about murder and anger, about adultery and dishonoring another, about divorce, about swearing allegiance and retaliation, and about love.

107

In each, he sought to help people live faithfully in the present. He grounds his argument in the expectations of the Jewish community that reconciliation with neighbors was essential before reconciliation with God was possible.[21] He calls people to live faithfully—not showing only outward signs. Through considering, exploring, and discerning (critical theological reflection), Jesus was embodying how a faith lives in a new time, even a conflictual time. He was helping people make a "critical" and "responsible" home for faith. This form of critical reflection on the tradition demonstrates how one achieves a theological wisdom that fosters living the tradition in a new time.

Instructional Approach to Christian Education

Without a doubt, instruction makes a home for faith. People are able to participate as full members of a faith community. But, as in the last chapter, what happens if the community has it wrong? What happens if community practices are exclusive, shutting down the experiences of God's grace? Or, what if the community's creed, code, and cult simply do not adequately address the contemporary context? Here is where critical reflection needs to be added to simple knowing and participating in the faith. As Elizabeth Caldwell says so well, Christian instruction focuses on methods of teaching that are committed to "conscious listening, responding, critiquing, and questioning."[22]

For example, the problem the Pharisees had with the Sadducees' beliefs and actions was that they too easily compromised with the impositions of the alien Roman state. They thought the Sadducees compromised the faith. This compromise was also a problem for Jesus. As he challenged their ways of life, the Sadducees resisted, seeing his actions as dangerous.

Sadducees, mostly wealthy and well-connected people, had a clear set of beliefs and a code of conduct for the community. They denied that circumstances had changed to require an extension of the words of the written Torah; therefore they rejected the oral Torah that was so important to the Pharisees. They managed many of the activities with Rome, collected taxes, participated in temple leadership, and served on the Sanhedrin, and thus were seen by many of the people as complicitous with Rome and as corrupt. Yet, in their minds, compromise was the only option with Rome. Gaining as much advantage for their faith in the midst of the Roman realities of control was a deeply lived conviction. In hindsight, we know their judgments about the risks of challenging the Romans were in many ways accurate.

Even so, their at-homeness with the compromises had a limit. Herod Archelaus, after the death of his father, Herod the Great, sought to install the symbol of Roman control, the eagle, on the temple. That was a sacrilege that had to be challenged. It was outside their religious world. When a group of Pharisees removed it, Archelaus was outraged and massacred over three thousand for this seditious plot. Sadducees could no longer stand aside. Their values and commitments were also brutally trampled upon. Even with their conflicts, Pharisees and Sadducees joined together in the direct protest to Rome about Archelaus's cruelty. Their protests were honored, and he was removed.

We cannot adequately live a faith or engage in theological wisdom unless we are growing in understanding and knowledge of the faith and its practices. Understanding creed, code, and cult is essential. Rigorous, ongoing, systematic, and structured education is necessary. Yet, practicing a faith is not a rigid simple repeating of what one learns. To be faithful requires a critical and nuanced practice of reflection (of considering, exploring, and discerning) in the midst of seeking to live and practice that very tradition.

Philosopher of education Walter Feinberg has completed a comprehensive study of religious schools and their efforts at religious instruction. Feinberg's analysis assists us in understanding the elements of critical and reflective religious instruction. Feinberg has examined Islamic, Jewish, and Christian schools. Identity is a crucial aspect of all. They help children and youth know to whom they belong.

> Once a child is placed in one religious tradition rather than a different one . . . perspectives are set, horizons shaped, understandings circumscribed, boundaries constructed, epistemic foundations established, relational possibilities circumscribed, roles marked off, and a collective identity stamped. . . . He or she will take on many of these practices as second nature and may find those of other groups to be alien or incomprehensible.[23]

Honestly, this is what being at home in a religious tradition can mean.

While the schools have different practices that fit their religious commitments and traditions—for example, Jewish teachers allow for more arguing and disputing among students than do teachers in Lutheran schools—the schools seek to bring order out of the chaos of children's lives. They define truth, help students become familiar with religious practices, and provide ways for students to learn how to live faithfully and make faithful decisions. The schools "are expected to transmit doctrine and shape belief, to craft souls, and to refine consciences"—creed, cult, and code.[24] Yet, many of the schools limited testing the boundaries of the tradition. While critical thinking was often encouraged, more often it was restricted and controlled. Teachers ended conversation when it approached critiquing the tradition itself.

Here is the theological question that those who follow the way of Jesus must answer. Simply knowing and enacting the bounds of a tradition may result in the same criticism Jesus had of the Sadducees. They engaged in theological wisdom, defining boundaries of what was acceptable and what they sought to preserve. Nevertheless, the very preserving missed profound, transformative actions of a living God calling people to new ways, consistent with the past, but more vital and profound. That is what the Pharisees sought to do and what Jesus sought to do. He was furious with his disciples when they put limits on the power of God and when they sought to take advantage of their familiarity with him. Did not, for example, James and John ask Jesus to put them on his right and left hands in the kingdom (Mark 10:35-45; in Matt. 20:20-27, their mother makes a similar request)? Did not Jesus chastise the day laborers who were angry at the landowner for his grace, unable to see that God's grace transcended what anyone expected (Matt. 20:1-15)?

A critical engagement with a tradition leads us beyond simply repeating it, to encountering the dynamic dimensions of redemption and grace that call for new ways of faithfulness. Interestingly, Feinberg found just such a practice in two of the schools. In those schools, religious instruction had all of the dimensions of teaching code, cult, and creed, yet it pressed for an "overcoming of self-centeredness through service to others and spiritual transcendence."[25] For example, critically examining church teachings was an exercise in engaging students in critical reflection about their own personal experiences. . . . Students at [X high] are responsive to these messages, and when it comes to social justice will often go beyond them. . . . They are quick to spot injustice and respond to it, sometimes collectively; and they are willing to organize to address an injustice.[26]

What happened in these schools is that students entered into the dynamics of a tradition, not simply repeating it. They lived its dynamics into their own time and the future. They were not simply learners of a tradition, or recipients of it, but they were creative, participatory agents within a tradition into its power, revelation, and witness for their time and the future. They were fully critical theologians themselves. They lived the dynamism of grace and redemption, seeking to be as faithful to a dynamic and living God as possible.

The church's doctrine can be presented as a "platform" from which to criticize the wider society and as "unchanging and absolute truth"; or it can be experienced as "an evolving institution" whose life is informed, and ability to criticize the wider culture is empowered when students have the "opportunity to reflect on the doctrine itself and the interpretive possibilities it may provide."[27] Helping students become agents of the life and of the future of the faith community, agents of the living way of Jesus, is a profound way to think of task of instruction.

Students need to explore the creed, cult, and code of a tradition and to continue to grow in understanding and living, but they also need to consider alternative points of view within the tradition and the contexts in which they developed. They need to interpret and discern faithfulness in a living way. They need to realize and ask, what does it mean to live faithfully in a genuine pluralistic world, where differing views and perspectives must be negotiated? This latter is critical, for without a living dialogue about the future, the powers of hierarchy and of lethargy simply limit options.[28]

Extending the Instructional Approach

Again, how does Christian religious instruction touch the "spiritual but not religious" or the "unaffiliated and unconcerned"? Too many people in these groups have only experienced religion demanding a rigid, unitary response. Some, in fact, do not consider themselves "religious" because they have been hurt by religious groups. They have never heard that the church might be "an evolving institution" where adherents are encouraged to criticize the wider culture and reflect on the interpretive possibilities in a tradition.

Helping people gain theological wisdom by becoming agents of the future of the faithful community, or agents of the living way of Jesus, is a profound way to think of tasks of instruction. When have these groups experienced that kind of instruction? I turn back to our discussion in chapter 2 of theologian Linda Mercandante's work. Many people in these groups actively carry important theological questions and are open to respectful theological conversations, not even knowing that these are theological or where to have them. They have never had any experience with disciplined, respectful conversation about religion.

Congregations and denominations need to consider ways of making their work more transparent. Work of groups such as Protestants for the Common Good that seek to connect theological reflection with important public issues is crucial.[29] How can local associations of clergy follow this lead and communicate more publicly about the concerns that direct their work? How can excellent theological resources prepared by denominational leaders and seminaries be shared?

Two suggestions: local clergy and seminary leaders can make themselves known to public media. Many issues discussed in the media are at their heart religious and deal with conflicts in values or understandings. Local media, newspaper and television reporters, often need assistance in interpreting the meaning of religious concerns as they communicate particular stories. To know that a religious person with an open and critical perspective was available to assist in understanding an issue would be of interest to these news leaders and would bring a more nuanced perspective into public conversation. Church and seminary websites could then follow up with thoughtful discussions of current issues being discussed.

Second, a church in Chicago advertised on the elevated trains, targeting those who had been hurt by churches, felt excluded by churches, or had their theological questions silenced. On their church website, they prominently place a motto of the congregation: "We love doubters. We love Believers. Come see how we are doing church differently."[30] The invitation is itself a form of religious instruction—inviting people to conversation and connection. They list on their website workshops they have scheduled, for example, "HIV Retreat Workshop." Congregations that communicate that they are willing to talk about profound issues and offer opportunities become settings for Christian religious instruction. The congregation I attend offered for our community a Friday evening lecture and a weekend workshop on the new research on the historical Jesus. It was well advertised, and it was filled by people interested in the topic who turned again to this church for future forums on topics of public concern. Another example, Parker Palmer's new work on democracy, *Healing the Heart of Democracy*, is being communicated by the Center for Courage and Renewal. Public forums are scheduled. This center has invited conversation about the religious dimensions of public service.[31] All are beginning efforts at public religious education.

Conclusion

Jesus, the Pharisees, and the Sadducees knew that rebellion against the power of Rome meant death and crucifixions. They also knew that simply accepting the power defined by the Roman military and political authorities would wipe out hopes of community, justice, and walking humbly (and completely) with God. They had to decide how to navigate this tension.

Elizabeth Caldwell, in a new book, *God's Big Table: Nurturing Children in a Diverse World*, offers an image of what religious instruction in a world of diversity can be—a form of religious instruction that honors the traditions of our faiths, connects us with the dynamics of our faith communities, and assists us in partnering with others who may be very different from ourselves. She suggests that God invites us to come, linger, and learn at a broad and generous table "with friends and strangers," knowing that we will leave with new insights and hopes for the world.[32] Sharing our faith across these boundaries is indeed a way we can learn to live the wisdom of Jesus and listen to the call of a kingdom-bearing and life-giving God.

Chapter Six

Service: Missional Approach to Christian Education

Jesus was formed in a community seeking to live faithfully in the midst of the oppression. He knew firsthand how the Roman overlords affected the people. He knew families who had lost their meager possessions. He had seen the crosses hanging at the sides of the roads, where Romans warned the people not to test their will. He knew families who had reverted to hoarding so that even their neighbors would not ask them for assistance. Even his cousin, John, from whom he had learned so much about repentance and the kingdom, was cruelly imprisoned and beheaded. He confronted death as a social tool for control. In fact, some even wanted to know his opinion of Pilate's murder of Galileans during worship (Luke 13:1-5).

Perhaps his father and he served as laborers in rebuilding Sepphoris (it had been destroyed by the Romans because of the rebellion led by Judah ben Hezekiah at the death of Herod the Great). Just a few miles from Nazareth, Herod Antipas had it rebuilt as the jewel of his kingdom in Galilee. The pain and power of oppression were clearly apparent. He had to know of bandits who attacked Romans to gather spoils, he knew of rebellions and their impact, and he knew the hopes of Zealots to restore Israel as an independent state.

Justice was at the center of many of his parables and teachings. One example is the parable of the woman and the unjust judge. A judge who "neither feared God nor respected people" (Luke 18:2) ignored a woman's plea for justice. He turned his back on her until her persistence became "embarrassing" to him (v. 5). Since he couldn't get rid of her, he granted her the request. Jesus taught of a just God, in stark contrast to the people's daily experiences of Roman injustice.

Note also how Jesus responded to a particularly difficult question about taxes, challenging the powers of injustice. Jesus was asked by a supporter of Herod a politically charged question: "Does the Law allow people to pay taxes to Caesar or not? Should we pay taxes or not?" (Mark 12:14; see also Matt. 22:15-22 and Luke 20:20-25). The question was a provocation because refusal to pay taxes resulted in immediate Roman punishment. For example, in the early first century, a man we know as Judas led a group of people to refuse to pay taxes. He argued that God alone deserved worship. Pointing to the image of Caesar on a coin, he argued that paying taxes substituted worship of Caesar for worship of God. The Romans quickly responded by murdering Judas and scattering his followers.[1]

Answering the question was risking death. Jesus, requesting a coin, asked whose inscription and image were on it. The people responded, "Caesar's." Then Jesus answered, "Give to Caesar what belongs to Caesar and to God what belongs to God" (Mark 12:17). What did he mean? Clearly Jesus was claiming that God was other than Caesar, which was itself a treasonable offense, yet a word that many Jews spoke. But more than that, Jesus indirectly asked, what is from God? Any Jewish hearer would have known: since God created and God gave life, everything belongs to God. In fact, to give Caesar what he deserves is to say, "Give him nothing" because "nothing" belongs to Caesar, since all belongs to God. By whose authority do we live? By God's and God's alone. Caesar may kill, may tax, and may oppress, but nothing can challenge that all belongs to God. Jesus could not avoid engaging the world the Romans constructed.

Mission in Christian Education

From the vantage point of her ministry as Christian educator at East Harlem Protestant Parish in New York City, Letty Russell published in 1967 *Christian Education in Mission*. Living in Harlem in the 1960s, she saw the effects of poverty, class, racism, and sexism. In this book, she focused a conversation occurring widely about the purposes of Christian education. Her ministry occurred "in a Christian community set in the midst of poverty, failure, and despair that has nevertheless learned to give thanks."[2] East Harlem Parish was a network of storefront ministries committed to both service and renewal. Russell argued that the whole parish educated, worship to fellowship to education to service; thus she reflected the community-of-faith approach. Yet, her primary focus was mission. The church was "a witnessing community . . . a matrix for teaching and learning in the context of God's mission of restoring people to their true humanity."[3] While the parish may have been struggling in a wilderness, its leaders and members knew God was with them, calling people to true humanity and new creation.[4]

This missional approach to Christian education has developed and expanded in many contexts. Its goal is empowering all to "true humanity" and calling the wider church to partner with God in restoring "new creation." Therefore, it has variously been referred to as liberation, emancipatory pedagogy, social transformation, and prophetic education, yet the goals are the same—true humanity and new creation.[5]

The approach has been built on the work of Brazilian educator and activist Paulo Freire. He developed a way of education to empower peasants to address oppressive realities that stole from them the ability to participate in creating their own futures. After a military junta in the late 1960s, Freire was jailed, sentenced to death, and ultimately exiled, later joining the office of education of the World Council of Churches.[6]

Freire was clear that education must be grounded in the contextual realities of people's lives. At the heart of his faith was the commitment that human beings were meant to be partners in the creation of their worlds. Freedom to create and responsibility for creating are core beliefs of his vocation of "humanization"—affirming personhood and overcoming alienation from both our work and our worlds. Oppression steals from people the ability to create a world where their personhood is respected.

Freire feared that churches too often either complied with oppressive regimes religiously reinforcing their power or sought some kind of simple reform that did not adequately challenge the powers of money and force that defined realities for others. He called for a prophetic church to challenge oppressive structures and to seek social change.

Freire's pedagogy is problem-posing education, where people are invited to engage the realities of their lives, mutually consider those realities, and cooperatively act for change and humanization.[7] Freire's work has affected Christian religious education, for both those who seek emancipation and those who call the powerful to prophetic, transforming education.

Two ordinary examples of churches that embody missional education: St. Andrew's is located near one of the poorest neighborhoods in a large urban center. School failure is significant. While children succeed in the first few grades of elementary school, failure becomes a pattern after fourth grade. By high school, 60 percent have dropped out. St. Andrew's is a mission-minded, Afrocentric congregation with a creative leadership staff. Denominational sources as well as private and public foundations fund their work. The church sponsors an after-school program in a storefront near the elementary school. But recently, it has expanded its mission by officially partnering with the school, with the support of the principal and the local school council. The church provides school supplies, after-school tutors, and even transportation for parents to attend school functions. In this partnership, members of St. Andrew's respect publicly accepted guidelines and refrain from evangelism.

Yet, in its after-school program, the church takes a different approach. From 3:00 to 7:00 each day, students engage in religious education. With parental agreement, the church picks children up and takes them to the church, where they are fed, taught, and loved. Furthermore, St. Andrew's has hired a social worker, who meets with a parent or grandparent of each child, seeking to find ways of supporting and enriching the lives of these primary adults. Computer education, study skills, identity formation, and religious education help the children know their true humanity—that they are loved children of God.

The school connection has profoundly affected the congregation. Church members seek funds to support the program; its experiences are at the heart of preaching and self-understanding; and parishioners tutor, volunteer with the local school council, supervise interns from a local college, and provide transportation and support for parents and grandparents. The effort to help children know and claim they are "children of God" has become the primary metaphor for redemption and faithfulness in the congregation. Without intending to, the church's ministry of outreach has reshaped its whole ministry. The problem posed of assisting children's education has empowered the members of St. Andrew's to consider the transformative dimensions of the gospel.

A second example: First Church is a more traditional congregation in a near suburb of a large urban area. Once a large and powerful church in its denomination, its building began to deteriorate as its membership dropped. The lively group that remained refocused their efforts as an open, multicultural congregation. Attention to mission has transformed the church. The work of a youth leader to gather youth in mission, returning year after year to serve people in Appalachia, has been the catalyst. As youth have prepared for the trip and returned witnessing to its transforming power, supporting the youth has become central to the life of the church. In response, adults, too, have scheduled a mission trip during the school year, modeling their trip on the work of youth.[8]

While traditional activities of worship, Christian education, fellowship, and pastoral care are accomplished well, mission has become the metaphor of the congregation. Now the church has added a children's mission experience as well as a partnership with a congregation in Africa where they have also worked and served. A mission coordinator has joined the pastoral staff, to enhance the church's service in its local neighborhood.

In a particularly transient area near a university, 60 percent of the congregation are new members in the last five years. Such change has meant that those who join enter thinking the mission program has always been central. From a ministry engaged by youth, the church is redefining itself around the image of mission. Those in mission are the yeast for the whole—addressing the true humanity of those served and of the members.

Goals of the Missional Approach

Empowerment and partnership (solidarity) are the goals of the missional approach to Christian religious education. Both reflect restoring "true humanity" and God's "new creation" for people and congregations. Missional Christian education addresses directly the world in which people find themselves and seeks to enable them to examine and claim what is expected of them as faithful Christians. As Allen Moore has summarized it, Christian education is prophetic, helping people "locate themselves in the injustices of the world with new awareness and form a new Christian consciousness for themselves."[9]

Studying a group of black youth in a large urban center, Evelyn Parker described how faithful Christian education needs to become emancipatory. Because of racism, sexism, and classism, the youth experienced "skepticism, cynicism, and despair." While many of those she interviewed were able to speak theologically about salvation and God's presence, only rarely were they able to connect God's gracious activity with efforts to confront racism. She writes, "Their agency to dismantle racism . . . was absent. . . . None of them talked about racism in light of their deeply held theological beliefs."[10] The content of the faith was separated from action. The youth she studied had lost what Freire would have called the ability to create history—to be agents in history. Typical Christian education seems to miss agency. While the youth had been taught personal spirituality, they had not encountered a direct connection between theological teachings and the ability to address systemically the racist dimensions of everyday living.

To offer an alternative, Parker examined how elders, or faith models, had learned initiative and leadership. She knew it was present in the civil rights movement. Turning to elders like Fanny Lou Hammer, Sojourner Truth, and Daisy Bates, she examined their resilience. What she found was that the church through its education had offered them an "emancipatory pedagogy" rooted in emancipatory hope. An expectation that the "hegemonic structures" that define and control can be transformed empowered them to act as God's agents bringing in "God's vision for humankind."[11]

She identified several key values that Christian education needs to engage: "oppositional imagination, self-worth, loyalty, moral agency, and holy rage." Emancipatory pedagogy weaves together Christian understanding and spiritual practices with practices of social justice. "Emancipatory hope fosters an intrinsically woven life of both pious and political living, where critical consciousness and critical action sit at the core of a way of knowing, a way of meaning-making."[12]

Anne Streaty Wimberly's research with slave narratives further defines Christian education for mission, or what she terms "education for liberation and vocation." She has well documented that a theological reflection process, story-linking, offered people hope and an identity as children of God. Furthermore, she defined an agenda for Christian education to empower and build solidarity:

1. Know one's life as gift—being a valued human being

2. Gain the ability to maintain basic necessities of life

3. Be equal partners and beneficiaries in life-building processes of nation

4. Be treated justly and respectfully

5. Gain the ability to see possibilities and break out of restricted ways of thinking and acting

6. Share stories with self and others

7. Be changed by God in Jesus Christ

8. Be aware of other's needs and willing to respond[13]

Other Christian educators have concurred that missional education means addressing directly the realities of daily living with faith resources. Katherine Turpin, for example, demonstrates how youth are caught in the consumer culture and "branded" by its messages, defining how they understand themselves and others. Their faith cannot be engaged without addressing branding.[14] Christian education combines social and theological analysis.

Finally, Daniel Schipani points to an exemplar church educating with its whole life. Reba Place, a Mennonite community, educates as it confronts the "dominant values" of consumer culture in the United States and dominant patterns of power. By doing so, the church "increases learners' awareness for the need for communal and social transformation and enables them to participate in such change." Reba is an economically diverse community of faith, that includes an intentional living community, where worship, education, small groups, and mission all become united around an alternative way of seeing, being, and living.[15]

Critical consciousness about one's own living situation, theological reflection connecting God's vision with human realities, and the development of social action for restoring "true humanity" and joining God's new creation are goals of missional education. Empowerment and partnership go hand in hand. As Letty Russell has stated, freedom from oppression opens the way for freedom for partnership with God and others.[16]

Processes of Missional Education

Enacting missional education begins with an acknowledgment that faith and life cannot be separated. There is no pure and detached reading of a text. Each interpreter and learner is grounded in a context and culture. Events of the day are always in the background: a medical diagnosis, a child's illness, a new job, a mortgage coming due, or a community crisis. Both teachers and learners need to acknowledge the realities of their lives.

Furthermore, beneath these everyday realities is culture. Our cultures profoundly affect the ways we see, understand, and live. The cultures of Galilee and Judea were very similar but were also different. Such differences caused fundamental misunderstandings. In fact, didn't those in Judea wonder whether anything good could come from Nazareth (in Galilee) (John 1:46)? I am certain that Romans could not understand the Jews' need to worship Yahweh. Why would anyone want to worship only one God when there were so many? Particularly, why worship a God whose people had been defeated? Rather than risking the ire of any God, Romans admitted them all into their pantheon.

The power of culture is illustrated by the Japanese author Shusaku Endo, in his powerful novel *Silence* about the introduction of Christianity into Japan. He reveals all of the misunderstandings people had of this "foreign faith" as well as the birth of deep faith commitments that developed despite loss of family connections and military oppression. For many years, believers suffered at the hands of the powerful. Faith was maintained in silence, passed from one person to another. More and more, as that faith was maintained, it took on a particular character, related to the wider culture. He therefore has argued that most Western portraits of Jesus make little sense to a Japanese cultural perspective. Therefore, his biography *Life of Jesus* offers an alternative, a brotherly Jesus who relates to a mothering God.[17]

Our cultures shape everything about our lives—our language, our customs, and our perspectives. In a multicultural world, we of course learn from others and see differences. We also are forced to recognize that some have sought to triumph and control others. Postcolonial analysis pushes us to name how much of the faith we have been given is the result of cultural power and control, rather than the expectations of God.[18] An example of this reality is a discussion of Asian images of Jesus produced by Australian media.[19] In it, theologian Peter Phan grounds the meaningfulness of Asian images in their ability to connect Jesus with the realities of people's lives (inculturation). Theological understandings are taken into the living realities of people's lives, reexpressing the faith. It is obvious: culture shapes what we see, how we know, and how we interact. If we do not connect understandings to our cultures, they remain alien—too strange to make sense.

Religious education is about living. Creed, code, cult, and community, to use the characteristics of religious communities defined by Catherine Albanese, cannot be separated.[20] To think we can is to deceive ourselves. Studying a creed is a form of prayer. Praying is informed by our beliefs. The community in which we study, pray, or serve shapes our responses. Living faithfully is goal. Remember: love and serve God and your neighbors. Such was Jesus' prayer, learned from his parents and his community, repeated each morning to set an agenda for the day and each evening to reflect on the challenges and gifts of the day.

Grant Shockley, a United Methodist educator, has challenged churches. He argued that too many deceive themselves by making church about church business, rather than connecting with the world. As such, they have missed really being the church—offering grace to life. He called for an intentional-engagement approach to Christian education. Its message was clear. Be intentional about the realities of living. Engage the realities of living with the faith.

His agenda for Christian religious education included the following:

1. Biblical integrity (drawing on the profound understandings of justice, of good news, of God's grace, and of human creation as children of God)

2. Radical contextuality (directly and truthfully engaging the social situation in which a church found itself)

123

3. Systematic engagement (work to identify, analyze, correct, or eliminate "destructive structures and/or systems that support and sustain oppression, racism, and sexism"—critical theological awareness and analysis)

4. Educational change (seeking education for action that transforms thinking, being, and doing)

5. Programmatic integration (integrating education, worship, and mission for participation in a theological vision of what God seeks)

6. Laity empowerment (empowering people to become agents of change, rather than sitting responsively in pews)[21]

Shockley argues that Christian education cannot be whole without knowledge of faith content (particularly the stories of God's grace and justice), without contextuality that takes one into the personal worlds of the learners as well as the wider world they inhabit, and without educational strategies that transform thinking, being, and doing.

Shockley points us to the second process of missional education, teaching methods. Several scholars—Anne Wimberly, Katherine Turpin, Evelyn Parker, and Reginald Blount—offer strategies for teaching. Behind each is Paulo Freire's "problem-posing." For Freire, to be transforming, education had to treat all learners as agents. Simply repeating "banking strategies," where a teacher deposits content in learners' minds, continues the pattern of stealing power and initiative from learners. In turn, problem-posing education offers the learners an opportunity to consider, explore, and discern whether and how to learn. Teachers and learners become partners in addressing the problems living poses.

Problem-posing grew out of Freire's efforts to teach literacy to nonliterate peasants in Brazil. Most often these peasants were employed as workers on large estates or were living in subsistence communities. By the powerful, they were defined as "peasants" to fulfill the will of the landowner or the middleman who purchased their crops. Being nonliterate meant that many did not have "word." They did not have the language skills to define their worlds. They signed contracts with their mark—contracts that kept them and their labor controlled.

The method of problem-posing began with listening to the people (ethnography), where Freire and his fellow students/teachers would talk to and watch the people, seeking to understand the "code" by which they lived—their most significant concepts, rituals, pictures, stories, and so on. For example, many of those with whom they worked were "hunters." Hunters, whether using bows or guns, foraged for game to feed families. To find and kill game on the hacienda was forbidden, for the hacienda was the owner's land. People talked about, understood, and told stories about being hunters.

For the next step, the teacher would find a way to "re-present" the most significant elements of the code. When the people saw these pictures, they could immediately relate, telling further stories about their lives and world. Note the significant respect that goes into the teaching as one listens intently and seeks to understand another's world.

Conflicts emerged from their stories and responses. For example, the land belongs to the master, or at least he says it does. Before lands were fenced, they were open for all. Now they are off-limits. We need to feed families. The only places we can go are the roads between the haciendas. Game does not neatly walk down the road for us to gather. Yet, to be caught hunting on owned land is bad, and those who get caught are bad. See how the worldview of the powerful, the oppressor, is, as Freire says, "introjected," inside the "peasant." In other words, the oppressed take on the characteristics, often the negative characteristics of the powerful— totally without awareness. That the world of fences and landowners is a "constructed world" is not recognized. Rather, people think it has to be this way.

Here is the moment of opportunity, where the problem is posed, the process of education engaged. Again, through a code of some kind (Freire used slides), people may see and engage conflicts in a worldview. They may recognize that the world is created and they, too, have a part to play in its creation. Remember Freire was teaching literacy. As people learned to read, they gained a sense of self-awareness and self-understanding that pushed them to act in different ways. His approach was so successful that when a military junta took control of Brazil in the 1960s, Freire was seen as dangerous.

125

The impact of his posing problems was immense. Freire reports a conversation with a member of one of the literacy circles, a person Freire respectfully calls a "sower of words:"

> We asked one of these "sowers of words" . . . why he hadn't learned to read or write before agrarian reform. "Before agrarian reform, my friend," he said, "I didn't even think. Neither did my friends. Because it wasn't possible. We lived under orders. We only had to carry out orders. We had nothing to say." He replied emphatically.
> "Before we were blind, now the veil has fallen from our eyes. . . . Before letters seemed like little puppets. Today they say something to me. I can make them talk."[22]

Of course, my description is much too fast. And frankly, the bifurcated view of some as powerful and others as not ignores all of the levels of power in between. Yet, when people make a decision and take responsibility for it, they become agents in their worlds. They are world creating. We know how the space for decision making and world creating is reduced in our world. Miss a credit payment and who pays? Lose health insurance and who pays?

It is apparent how this approach has been used with the oppressed, those without voice, to raise awareness. Yet, how negotiations then occur to develop shared participation in building a shared world is very tricky and difficult. It is similar to the reality that all of Jesus' neighbors had to deal with each day. Education opens up the processes of faithfully participating in world creation. Freire names the impact of problem-posing education. "In problem-posing education, humans develop the power to perceive critically the way they exist in the world *with which* and *in which* they find themselves; they come to see the world not as a static reality, but as a reality in process, in transformation."[23]

For Freire, transformation means acting to make the world different. By acting and reflecting and then acting and further reflecting, we engage the world—we show we are most human.

What Freire describes is very similar to Evelyn Parker's emancipatory pedagogy—to empower youth for leadership (agency). She believes, as faithful Christians do, that the world is open to "new life" and "new creation." God is redeeming the world. God calls us to participate in this re-creation. That is what God's agency (God's kingdom) is all about—the power to build and care for a world. This power to build is what the Romans sought to kill with crucifixion. In fact, Freire expressed his own faith when he affirmed: "It is only in the authenticity of historical praxis that Easter becomes the death which makes life possible."[24]

Problem-posing is the pedagogical process of missional education. It is an invitation for teachers and learners to join together. Problem-posing is a way to call all Christians to consider, explore, and discern what God is doing in their worlds. Yet, as Christian educator Mai-Anh Le Tran comments, there are only a "few developed pedagogical practices for sustained engagement in systemic change."[25] Developing such practices is an essential agenda for the field of Christian education.

Frankly, one of the most used, most provocative, and most misused is mission trips. Sometimes these trips become charity without sufficient action-reflection to respect those encountered as well as to learn what God is doing in the interaction. Moreover, when churches schedule trips shifting from one location to another, too often "tourism" results.[26]

Tran suggests a way to make contextual or cross-cultural encounters promising is to make partnership and solidarity possible. For her, participatory action research offers the guide. The taken-for-grantedness of our everyday lives is so extraordinarily powerful (what Freire termed *introjection*) that we need a spiritual practice to assist us in being self-reflexive and truly receiving the gifts of grace and challenge in encounter. She suggests one needs to (1) learn how to see in the new context, (2) make sense of what one sees, (3) see oneself and the wider world as the other sees, (4) risk deep scanning and reflection (thus spiritual), and (5) name what one is learning in context so it can be tested, challenged, and refined.[27]

My description sounds too simple. With God's grace transformation does occur. Margaret Ann Crain tells about the mission experience of First Church, described in the beginning of this chapter. The quality of theological reflection coupled with humble prayer have resulted for some in genuine transforming God moments. Margaret Ann tells the story of Emily, who has since partnered with colleagues in Ghana to listen for God moments together. With mutuality and respect, they engage mission together and seek ways of educating others in the call of vocation.[28] The five practices of transformation include the following:

127

- Building heartfelt community that incorporates similarity *and* difference

- Experiencing and naming God as an ongoing act of shared theological reflection

- Integrating transforming mission experiences

- Using the language of call and vocation at key moments in the community's life

- Reversing hierarchies of age and status as youth lead the congregation in its commitment to mission[29]

With prayer, we Christian educators need to continue to learn, risk, and refine the processes of missional education themselves. Missional education is not an add-on. The whole life of the congregation teaches, all of its ministries. Missional education occurs "through active engagement and critical reflection, dialogue and action focused on important concerns for daily living."[30] In fact, the very process of missional education is a problem posed to educators and pastors who seek to be faithful to the transformative possibilities of empowerment and solidarity. Posing problems in the midst of our worldviews and taken-for-granted assumptions about church is an invitation to new life and new possibilities. Mission education seeks to restore true humanity and new creation.

Mission Education in the Way of Jesus

At the heart of the mission of Jesus was the proclamation of the realm of God—"Now is the time! Here comes God's kingdom! Change your hearts and lives, and trust this good news!" (Mark 1:15). Marks of God's activity were expressed as Jesus answered questions from the disciples of John the Baptist. As we think about the encounter, remember that Jesus was John's cousin. He was baptized by John and learned from him. Therefore, the questions were from within the family. Moreover, John's disciples were familiar with Jesus' work (Mark 1:16).[31]

To answer, Jesus turns to Isaiah and lists the marks of God's realm:

- Blind see

- Crippled walk

- Skin diseases are cleansed

- Deaf hear

- Dead are raised up

- The poor hear good news

An additional mark is spoken of by Jesus in his hometown—prisoners are freed (Luke 4). Each of these marks is described in some detail in the Gospels through Jesus' healings and exorcisms. Most are also included in the instructions Jesus gave to his disciples when he sent them out on their own missions: "Make this announcement: 'The kingdom of heaven has come near.' Heal the sick, raise the dead, cleanse those with skin diseases, and throw out demons" (Matt. 10:7-8).

As we review the stories of healing, exorcism, and new life, Jesus points to God's action. God is making things new. Jesus and the disciples are joining God and invite others to join God. For example, Jesus restores the speech of a man made mute by a demon (Luke 11:14-26). His healing is accomplished by the "finger of God" (NRSV). This image "finger of God" is a traditional term describing how God pushed the Egyptians to free the Jews and how God completed the tablets of commandments that Moses brought to the people. "The finger of God" is God's freeing and God's covenant—times God builds and defines community.[32]

Restoring community or building community is therefore at the heart of God's realm and of the healings of Jesus. Restoring community is also true for those who ask for forgiveness. Relationships are built. Note how the healing of the paralytic connects healing, forgiveness, and community. Note how Jesus gathers "tax collectors and sinners," eating and drinking with them and celebrating their new way of living (Mark 2).

Restoring community is nowhere clearer than in the healing of the man with the skin disease (Matt. 8:4; Luke 5:14). Jesus instructs him, "Go and show yourself to the priest and make an offering for your cleansing, as Moses instructed." Illness severed community. Being received by the priest would allow the man back into community. We don't know what happened with the man, but we know what the intention was—to restore community (Luke 5:14).

Furthermore, "Proclaim release to the prisoners" (Luke 4:18) restores community. Interestingly, in Hebrew poetry the phrase "proclaim release to prisoners," parallels the earlier phrase, "preach good news to the poor." This, too, is a mark of the kingdom. While there is no direct evidence of Jesus freeing prisoners, it is interesting to note that in Jesus' day, people became prisoners because of theft, as today. Furthermore, imprisonment was a result of failure to pay debts. And most of all, it was the result of disorderly conduct and sedition.

Any direct confrontation with Rome is subtle in the Gospels. The writers knew how dangerous that would be. When they wrote, not only had Jesus been put to death, but also James, Paul, and Peter. Furthermore, Rome had destroyed the temple in Jerusalem and left the city shattered. Yet the following events are still listed: Jesus was charged with sedition by the Romans—proclaiming that he, not Rome, was the true "king of the Jews." He challenged Rome in the discussion of Caesar and taxes. He called the demons he cast out of the pigs "Legion," the name of the Roman army. He staged a riot on temple grounds, challenging temple authorities, collectors of Roman taxes. His followers referred to him as prince of peace and savior of the world, terms that Romans used to refer to Caesar.[33]

"Preaching good news to the poor" or "proclaiming release to prisoners" clearly focused on debts and resistance. Jesus knew that in the environment created by Rome, peasants (the poor) were most vulnerable. He knew that many had been turned into day laborers, losing their lands, and others became indentured servants on previously owned lands. The plight of the poor was immense. He prayed with them that God's realm would come, that debts would be forgiven, and that daily bread would be provided. These petitions were central aspects of his proclamation. But how about "seeking release to prisoners," or, in other words, righteous people who were imprisoned for challenging Rome? Did Jesus also pray for this and engage in this activity? Clearly, John the Baptist had. He seemed unafraid of power: "You children of snakes! Who warned you to escape from the angry judgment that is coming soon? Produce fruit that shows you have changed your hearts and lives" (Matt. 3:7-8). We know that Jesus honored John for his integrity and prophecy (Matt. 11:11).

Rome had disrupted the Galilean community. Without a doubt, Jesus preached that righteousness was possible even in the world that was filled with demons (defined for some as Romans).[34] Righteousness was a gracious response to God's in-breaking kingdom. Jesus' actions of "preaching good news to the poor," are efforts to rebuild community—to invite back into community those who had been excluded.

As Jesus pointed to God's actions, the Gospel writers in turn point to Jesus' actions—restoring health, shalom, to both individuals and to the community. Shalom, God's gift of peace and health and hope, is wished on each person at each Shabbat. After the prayers of loyalty to God and prayers of blessing, participants wish each other *"Shabbat shalom,"* or peaceful Sabbath or the peace of Sabbath. The greeting *Shalom*, appropriate at all times, wishes God's peace, righteousness, health, and wholeness on each person. It is the recognition that God is at the heart of community, hope, and life. *Shalom* is also a word for "truce" or "treaty." Shalom evidences the depth of community and responsibility to and with others.

Without a doubt, for Jesus, the marks of God's realm restore, redeem, or build community. God is building community. Yet, note: refusal to accept the gifts of healing and new life blocks community. This was true in Jesus' own life. The Gospel writers did not have to remember the times Jesus failed, but they are very honest. In his hometown, he was unable to do any miracles, only a few healings (Mark 6:5). Their disbelief stood in the way of new life. The rich young ruler went away "saddened" because he would not accept the hope and freedom of the kingdom (Mark 10:22). After Jesus had exorcised the demon, by the finger of God, the bystanders didn't welcome the man to health or listen to him talk; they demanded a "sign from heaven" and claimed that Jesus was cavorting with demons. Furthermore, when Jesus healed a blind man, the crowd again refused to believe (John 9; see also Luke 18). Those around distrusted the healing, even denying the man had even been blind. They called him a sinner. And many disciples, it appears, "turned away and no longer accompanied him," because Jesus expected too much (John 6:66).

The mission Jesus conducted and on which he sent his disciples was the mission of the realm of God—to build and restore community. As a result of healing, feeding, and exorcisms new life was given to many. These were marks of the kingdom of God, marks of God's gracious nearness to everyday life. Yet, in spite of it, some heard, some had lives renewed, and some responded. Others turned away.

Missional Approach to Christian Religious Education

What a challenge to the church today. Mission restores community; resistance to righteousness and to others, blocks community. There are so many parallels between the experience that Jesus had and ministry today. In some places, Jesus was unable to perform miracles of healing and community. Many fought over whether the "markers" of the kingdom were real. Resistance is seen in his own disciples and in his own family.

Mission follows the marks of the kingdom—healing, feeding, and releasing. Mission is following God's lead into the actions of restoring lives and communities. Any discussion of missional education begins with recognition that it will be accepted by some and rejected by others. Some, perhaps many, will wonder if the alternative vision proclaimed, the inviting of those not wanted, or the enacting of hope is really what mission means.

The process of reflecting on mission is itself profoundly educational. We must remember that mission education is simply that—it is a process of education. The very process of considering and deciding about mission is profoundly educational. It is a process of discernment: asking, where is God in our midst? This question is not vague. Clear hints/marks are given to assist us:

- Healing the sick

- Giving sight to the blind

- Offering hearing to those who are deaf

- Forgiving those who have sinned

- Proclaiming release to prisoners

- Preaching the good news to the poor, the least of these

- Restoring community

- Enacting shalom

When congregations are asked to define their missions, some will be clear and expansive, yet others will focus on what makes them happy and secure. That is simply a reality. Defining a congregation's mission is not easy, yet the process is educational. Asking how we discern where God's kingdom is occurring within our communities or where we can join God in ministry pushes a congregation to listen to their community. Remember Freire's process begins with listening. The first step is analysis: What is occurring? What is needed? Where is hope emerging?

A second step is discernment, or theological reflection. Where are the markers to which Jesus pointed? Many congregations have ministries of feeding and clothing people with needs. Honoring that gift, theological reflection further pushes to consider the systemic realities that caused the hunger and poverty. Or, to seek parallels to the time of Jesus, congregations can ask: Where is the presence of Rome limiting the way community can be built and shalom offered? Such analysis is quite difficult. For example, what does it mean that millions of people in the United States do not have access to health care, or if they do, it is only through emergency rooms? If shalom is a marker of God's kingdom activity, how do we work to commit ourselves with others to provide healing ministries? Some communities have been profoundly led to address healing by the hiring of a parish nurse or deacon engaged in health care. Learning the needs in the community have led them to ask, to seek to discern, new ways of living mission. This means educating for systemic action.

A friend, David Merritt, who for many years was an executive in Christian education in the Uniting Church in Australia, has commented that many churches are willing to systemically study issues, like hunger alleviation, yet the way they study gets in their way. What? Too often people get caught in the study, examining and debating, almost to no end. He has suggested that education functions better when understood as a process of *mission strategizing*. Beginning with a concrete decision to follow God's activity, study occurs to fill out the activities of the mission. An example I have used before is the work of my colleague Reginald Blount. He clearly enacts what Merritt describes. Dr. Blount called his congregation to provide school backpacks filled with required school supplies for children who were unable to afford these for themselves. The mission was decided. They knew they would be unable to provide all needed, yet they started. This effort built confidence in the community, claimed their vision, and led them into additional study to address poverty. The gathering where the backpacks are to be given out has turned into a community fair, where resources meet people. Moreover, reflection further called the congregation to offer a weekly, free, summer farmers' market in a food desert. Beginning mission is itself an educational process that asks about the vocation God expects of us. It calls us to further reflection and social analysis.

Mission education is rooted in biblical and theological study. Attending to the dimensions of mission and systemic change in the biblical witness is crucial. Too often, if we are honest, a study of poverty, abuse, peace, or economic justice is resisted in a congregation. Instead of accepting this resistance, mission education calls us to point directly at the biblical witness and experience. In fact, as we have seen, the political situation of the time of Jesus has been kept from many people for a long time. Simply knowing this political situation, how the gospel emerged in relationship to it, its results, and its parallels to today are amazing learnings for many people and can empower ministry. In addition, the practices of the earliest Christian communities and the ways they sought to ameliorate the economic and political system their communities faced is also a powerful moment for education and commitment to mission.

For example, there has been increasing violence in the days in which I am writing this manuscript against faith communities. In Oak Creek, Wisconsin, many were killed as they participated in worship at a Sikh gurdwara. Muslim worship sites have been defaced and attacked in the Chicago area. Regular acts of violence against Jewish synagogues occur. The right to worship, the right to pray, the right to provide social services to a community, and the right and responsibility to partner with others in caring for the earth are all values that we respect and honor. As the Reverend Jacob Dharmaraj, president of the South Asian National Caucus for United Methodists, has said, "Ignorance about people of other faiths and cultures among average Americans is a heavy burden that only education and awareness can alleviate."[35] He adds that depth theological reflection is crucial—an understanding of church that "defines the Body of Christ in relation to the adherents of other faiths rooted in the Kingdom of God." Without such theological reflection about mission, the church will simply remained confused as to how to respond to those different in our midst.

Problem-posing is the key strategy. Missional education focuses on the values that direct our living. Jesus was disappointed with his home community. Their fear profoundly controlled the ways they responded to his reading of the text of Isaiah and his call for them to transcend the limitations of their present—their values blocked their actions.

We should not be surprised. Like others in Galilee, their lives had been profoundly disrupted, as were traditional patterns of interaction and community support. Fear and loss are the results of such despair. Evelyn Parker has shown that such loss of hope privatizes faith and blocks action for change and for others. Remember Parker's work: without emancipatory hope, anger and cynicism result. People look to what they can acquire and protect, rather than how God is calling them to freedom and to responsibility.

Directly addressing emancipatory hope and its vision is crucial. To follow Parker, one of the first things we must do is teach that God is making a difference in the world. Many forget without a reminder. She then advocates that we listen intently to their "oppositional imagination, self-worth, loyalty, moral agency, and holy rage." This task is exactly what she has been doing in recent research studies published in *The Sacred Selves of Adolescent Girls: Hard Stories of Race, Class, and Gender*.[36] This hard listening is essential within our congregations. Only then can we hear people's concerns and the blocks to abundant living. Resistance is in fact a gift in education, because it opens us truthfully to another, instead of hiding differences in withdrawal.

The Uniting Church in Australia has completed a study of values shared by Australians. Similar studies have been conducted elsewhere. The authors, Philip Hughes, Sharon Bond, John Bellamy, and Alan Black, found a shared widespread hope for "depth and authenticity" in relationships and for "a world at peace, honesty, true friendship, and equality." But they also discovered four competing "value orientations":

1. The importance of national security, politeness, and cleanliness

2. The social environment—equality, freedom, social justice, broadmindedness and helpfulness

3. Self-enhancement—excitement, enjoyment, wealth and success

4. Spiritual values and the importance of a spiritual life[37]

That these values conflicted did not surprise them. They cannot be held together. People who held national security and self-enhancement as primary were less likely to engage in work for "a world at peace," even though they hoped for it. The researchers concluded that conflicts in our values need to be made transparent. Problems need to be posed so that we wrestle with our identity as children of God and followers of Jesus' way. Otherwise Christian education will be trapped in "avoidance responses."

Mission education teaches by engaging in concrete acts of charity, justice, healing, and community. At the heart of Jesus' ministry were concrete acts of healing and restoring community. Not only is this our call, but it is also an educational practice. People learn as they are mentored in living the good news. Jesus, as we know, mentored his disciples, because he sent them out to precisely embody these practices in their ministries—to offer God's peace, to provide hospitality, to heal, to free from demons, to raise the dead, and to offer good news (Matt. 10:5-15; Luke 9:1-6; Luke 10:1-12).

In contrast, too often we are either numbed by the enormity of the pain we see in our world, immobilized by the complexity of the problems, or frightened of others who hold very different life experiences and perspectives. Numbness, inadequacy, and fear lead us to lament that the world is broken and no clear solutions offer hope.[38]

While lamenting is very important, our work does not end with lamentations. The Bible is amazingly truthful about the pain of loss, about confusion, and about the fear of facing uncertain futures. Jesus cried over Jerusalem (Luke 19:41-44), he acknowledged that poverty endured (Mark 14:7), and he was, for a time, defeated by the power of Rome. His disciples were killed and scattered. Some followers turned away, and others even turned to the powers and principalities to give them comfort.

Yet, laments are not where the followers of Jesus end their work. They ask: What does the gospel mean? What do the hopes for new life mean? Paul said we see in a "glass darkly" (KJV), or, "Now we see a reflection in a mirror; then we will see face-to-face. Now I know partially, but then I will know completely in the same way I have been completely known. Now faith, hope, and love remain—these three things—and the greatest of these is love" (1 Cor. 13:12-13).

"Seeing a reflection"—we all see glimpses of hope and possibility. Glimpses inspire us to proclaim that God is making things new. Therefore, we follow a conviction of Jesus, recorded by John: "I assure you that whoever believes in me will do the works that I do. They will do even greater works than these" (John 14:12).

Therefore, the call is to "do the works that I do." As we have seen, disciples who follow Jesus seek to follow God's openings of shalom in the midst of the world. We look for where the sick of body, heart, or mind are healed, where those blinded by fear and confusion are given sight, where those who are deaf to others begin to listen, where those who have sinned are forgiven, where those imprisoned by their choices and the powers of the world are being freed, and where "good news" is offered and communities are being restored. We learn by participating in practices of charity and justice. As Charles Foster has clarified in *From Generation to Generation*, practice learning occurs through engagement as people mirror the actions of others. Practice or habit learning, "in contrast to cognitive memories, are social and historical, embodied and contextual."[39] We learn the practices of mission by participating in mission.

The power of practice learning is what John Wesley offered Methodists—a method to grow in grace. He spoke of the "means of grace" that assist us in growing in the faith. Some of the means of grace helped a person grow in relationship to God and God's call—prayer, fasting, Bible study, and celebrating Eucharist. Other methods helped people grow in the Christian life—the practice of covenanting in small groups, finding colleagues and support. Still other methods called people to embody the grace of God—acts of mercy. For Wesley, these included good works, visiting the sick and imprisoned, feeding and clothing those in need, and working for the abolition of slavery. These means of grace are precisely "practice learning." They are methods of education seeking to orient a Christian disciple into "habits" of Christian living.[40] Of course, Wesley is not unique. Such means of grace have filled Christian practice.

In contrast, too often the experience of many people in churches is passive. People listen to sermons and attend study classes to help them live faithful lives. But living is not learned simply by giving attention. Growth in faith requires embodiment and action. We learn as we fully participate in the rituals of the community, as we practice leadership for the community, and as we engage its mission. That is the witness of the members of First Church and St. Andrew's that we met at the beginning of this chapter. People learn mission, learn to engage in acts of transformation by joining in mission and transformation.

Paulo Freire argues in his brief essay "Education, Liberation, and the Church" that we learn the prophetic faith of Jesus by developing relationships with those who are marginalized. He writes: "We cannot discuss churches, education or the role of churches in education other than historically."[41] Missional learning is at its heart embodied and historical learning. Freire called for "a new apprenticeship" where those committed to a prophetic church join hands with those who are broken by historical social structures—apprentice to them, learn the world the way they see it. Missional or prophetic education occurs in mutuality and respect. Through mutuality, those in the prophetic church learn that missional education is political. They also learn a vision to empower their work. They learn that the "family that prays together also needs a house, free employment, bread, clothing, health and education for their children, that they need to express themselves and their world by creating and re-creating it, that their bodies, souls, and dignity must be respected."[42] Or in other words, they see God's vision and action restoring community. The Christian life expects us to live missionally. Missional education occurs as we engage in the practices of faith, hope, and love.[43]

Conclusion

To live missional education will mean reaching out and creating agendas of care and hope. Yet, it will also mean more. It means creating coalitions of people, creating partnerships, where people work with others for hope and community. For followers of Jesus, this will mean seeking to follow God's actions into the world. It will also mean building public coalitions—joining for action with people who may be different and motivated by different meanings—to work together for shelter, food, employment, creativity, and dignity. Doesn't this sound much like the agenda Jesus gave his disciples or the one he reported to John the Baptist's disciples when they asked him about his work? As described, I think four educational tasks are necessary for faithful, missional education:

1. Reflecting on mission

2. Biblical and theological study

3. Problem-posing

4. Engaging in concrete acts/practices of charity, justice, healing, and community

At the heart of missional teaching and learning is spiritual formation—learning to trust that God is working ahead of us. We know that many left Jesus' community. That is what the Gospel writer John recorded in his own day in the late first century. Yet, in contrast, those with hope, emancipatory hope; those who held on to the profound presence of God's grace and forgiveness, were able to face the profound challenges brought by the militarism and hegemonic relations of the Roman Empire. The early Christians developed communities cutting across ethnicity and economics to provide healing, feeding, and community-restoring ministries in their midst.[44]

The very process of engaging mission, of deciding about it, of exploring theologically and biblically, and of addressing perspectives and values may be itself transformative. Too often time is wasted, good intentions shattered, and fear instilled by well-meaning leaders who challenge without listening and plan without engaging.

Paul's vision was that the "powers and principalities" could not resist the grace of God. Honestly we know they have, but we also know the grace of God empowers us to begin, and education assists us in enhancing and developing the processes for learning and the consequences.

Section III
Into the Future: Teaching the Way of Jesus

Jesus asked his disciples, "Who do people say that I am?" Furthermore, he inquired of them, "And what about you? Who do you say that I am?" (Mark 8:27, 29). The question still remains for all of us: "Who do you say that Jesus is?" Being disciples was amazingly difficult for Jesus' companions. Is it any easier for us? The Gospel writers tell us that the disciples argued about who would be first in the kingdom of heaven (Mark 10:35-45). They seemed dense. Jesus had to give them private tutoring sessions to help them understand. We too, through our confusion, ask: "What does it mean to be a follower of Jesus?"

What do we teach, and how do we teach it? The Gospel writers tell us that Jesus sent twelve disciples out to announce "the kingdom of heaven"— to "heal the sick, raise the dead, cleanse those with skin diseases, and throw out demons" (Matt. 10:7-8; see also Luke 9:1-6). Luke adds that Jesus additionally sent out seventy-two other followers: to offer God's peace and blessings, to heal the sick, and to proclaim "God's kingdom has come upon you" (Luke 10:1-9). And when they returned "joyously," Jesus, too, "overflowed with joy" (Luke 10:17, 21). Like the Twelve and the Seventy-Two, we are sent out to teach, to offer peace, to heal, and to point to the realm of God. Moreover, Matthew reminds us that God is pleased with those who serve the hungry, the thirsty, the stranger, and the naked (Matt. 25:31-46). Even more, he calls for us to teach more and more people to be followers (Matt. 28:16-20)—to teach offering God's peace and blessings.

His disciples and his early followers went out into a world of political and military domination; we go out into a different world, yet one still filled with domination, division, and violence. Jesus and his disciples pointed to the work of the realm of God in the world. They saw that this rebuilt relationships and communities, that it healed and cast out evil. With hope and assurance they faced into their worlds. We, too, need to face into ours. How does the "way of Jesus" shape our identities, our communities, and send us out in mission to the world? What does it mean to follow the way of Jesus? How do we accomplish our work as teachers?

These two questions focus the task of this final section of the book. Chapter 7 summarizes the way of Jesus that can be gleaned from witnesses to the transforming grace of God known through Jesus. Chapter 8 provides an agenda for the practice of Christian education. Through historical study, biblical exegesis, theological reflection, and educational scholarship, we have reviewed what we know about the way of Jesus and how it impacts how we teach and live. Let's rehearse some of the learnings.

Jesus entered his home community with a reputation and a vocation (chapter 1). He was invited to teach in the community's time of prayer and Torah study. Drawing on prescribed texts from Isaiah, he pointed the people to what God was doing in their present. Instead of wallowing in the losses and pain inflicted by Rome, he pointed them to God's grace and called the people to live it. He proclaimed this vocation with such assurance and clarity that the people were amazed. Yet, they found his invitation to see and live God's grace very difficult.

Those who did see and hear were transformed. He gathered around him disciples and worked and worked to teach them to know and live in the midst of God's gracious actions of shalom (chapter 2.) He continued to teach this message of grace through his whole life. Many of these followers found the message too difficult and fell away, yet some became witnesses and guides working to express the way of Jesus in new days and new circumstances.

The activity of God's realm was so intense and transforming that even Jesus had to consider again and again the breadth of his vocation (chapter 3). Looking in on the practices of Jesus and his disciples, we learn processes of prayerfully seeking discernment in each new time. We are called again and again to define and refocus our responsibilities in light of God's activities.

We draw on the support and vocation of the community of faith, now called church, as we learn and live the faith. Jesus, and his followers, drew on the learnings provided them in their communities of origin, to build an inclusive, hospitable, and transforming community flowing from the grace of God (chapter 4). While failing many times, the church seeks to live by the vision of a dynamic, living kingdom of God always breaking into life.

Born in a tradition that highlighted love of God and love of neighbor, Jesus drew followers into processes of interpretation building on the texts of the Torah and prophets to see God's in-breaking, transforming grace (chapter 5). Jesus' followers, in a world of oppression and violence, continued to teach people to respond to a living and redeeming God. These followers of the way drew on Jesus' life and the miracles of God's realm to define their own ministries (chapter 6). Just as the prophets had promised and they saw embodied in Jesus' way, they looked for when and where they could join in God's actions of restoring, redeeming, and building community. They acted as guides to God's realm.

We, too, are called to seek God's transforming grace in the midst of our world, to teach others to see it, and to join God in actions of redeeming community. That is how we answer "Who do people say that I am?"—with our lives.

Chapter Seven

Living the Way of Jesus

The disciples asked Jesus to teach them to pray (Matt. 6:9-15; Luke 11:2-4). This prayer embodies how Jesus saw his world and God's presence as well as his hopes and expectations for his followers. The Jesus prayer, which is recited in most congregations each Sunday, points to the essential dynamics of Jesus' way.

> Our Father in heaven, hallowed be your name.
> Your kingdom come.
> Your will be done, on earth as it is in heaven.
> Give us this day our daily bread.
> And forgive us our debts, as we also have forgiven our debtors.
> And do not bring us to the time of trial, but rescue us from the evil one.
> (Matt. 6:9-13 NRSV)

Matthew and Luke locate this prayer in two different contexts. In Matthew the prayer is part of an extended teaching about religious ritual, beginning with Jesus' criticism of showy and shallow people. Jesus tells his followers not to recite a "flood of empty words," for God already knows what they need before they ask (Matt. 6:7-8). In fact, Matthew connects the prayer to what we treasure and what we worry about. He reminds us that God will provide what we need and that God's gifts are our greatest. Prayer, then, is not for God, to get God's attention; rather, it defines the interaction of God and God's followers. In Luke, after a simple request, Jesus teaches them the prayer and then again follows with a proclamation of God's trustworthiness. God cares about them and will answer when they ask. In both Gospels the prayer is an intimate discourse among followers and God about what is at the heart of faith and living.

Many of the petitions of the prayer refer directly to present experiences, at the same time that they also refer to future hopes. This dual reference should not surprise us because Jesus' teaching is always multivoiced, addressing present experience as well as looking to future expectations. Each petition of the prayer points to aspects of the way of Jesus.

"Our Father in heaven, hallowed be your name." The prayer begins like many Jewish prayers, focusing on the greatness of God—sanctifying the name of God. In fact, the Common English Bible translates this phrase as "Our Father who is in heaven, uphold the holiness of your name." Almost word for word is the *Kaddish* prayer, which is prayed in Jewish worship.[1] The *Kaddish* focuses on how God is present, real, and glorified in life—how God is holy. It is also prayed during mourning to remind the bereaved that even with loss and pain God is present. The believer is reminded that God's greatness will be known in many nations (see Ezekiel 38:23: "So I will display my greatness, show my holiness, and make myself known in the sight of many nations. And they will know that I am the LORD"). The vocation of the Jewish people as God's people was to live in such a way that those who saw their actions would know the greatness and glory of the God they worshiped. Clearly this passage is directed at God, but simultaneously it reminded the disciples of the responsibility to act and live so that others see God's holiness. Holiness is clearly what the followers saw in Jesus. They named him God's presence in the world. For example, Matthew uses the word *Emmanuel*, "God with us," from Isaiah's conversation with King Ahaz about the future of God's people (Matt. 1:23). The way of Jesus extends the work of the people to make God's presence clear and ubiquitous.

"Your kingdom come. Your will be done, on earth as it is in heaven." God's name is exalted when God's activities are seen in the world, when God's transforming presence empowers relationships and community. The phrase is translated in the CEB as "Bring in your kingdom so that your will is done on earth as it's done in heaven" (Matt. 6:10) or simply in Luke as "Bring in your kingdom" (Luke 11:2). This theme of the realm of God (God's activity, God's kingdom) was the heart of Jesus' preaching. Here again it is multivoiced: God's realm is coming now in acts of healing, restoring sight and voice, and releasing people from demons. But also

God's realm is a vision drawing people into the future. The prayer focuses us, as Jesus did, on God's graciousness. "Your Father knows what you need before you ask" (Matt. 6:8). Note the proclamation here: even in the midst of oppression, God graciously seeks us.

"Give us this day our daily bread." The people needed "daily" bread, for many were hungry. Oppression stole from their storehouses; tax collectors searched out what the blessings of rain, soil, seed, and God had given them. Jesus connected to their reality parables about harvest and abundance. Yet, the word *bread* is also used in two ways, pointing to the great banquet, the eschatological banquet, that Isaiah promised.[2] In the villages Jesus visited where he found hospitality, he celebrated with bread, a meal. That celebration was a reality and a promise.

"And forgive us our debts, as we also have forgiven our debtors." The word *debts* also points to two realities. The people were in debt. Their little wealth, which for poor peasants was only their land, was at risk. Furthermore, their land was promising to investors. It could be bought cheaply and gathered into vineyards and orchards. The people needed relief, for which they prayed. Yet, moreover, sins were considered debts. Not living up to God's standards; not living faithfully enough that others could see the "glory" of God in their lives. Luke and Matthew, as the church today, also focus on this dimension of having wronged God; they call us again to live up to the expectations of those who know God's grace.

"And do not bring us to the time of trial, but rescue us from the evil one." Again, used for present and future, the people saw every day the time of trial in the actions of the Romans. They were pushed around. But even more so was a belief of those who held an eschatological Jewish perspective that a cosmic conflict was being fought. For example, this belief centered the Qumran community. Furthermore, note how Daniel, to which Jesus refers several times, locates the cosmic battle in the peoples who have oppressed Israel, thus again pointing to Rome.

Jesus' prayer summarizes the way of Jesus.[3] It focuses on God's grace and our responsibility to look for it and to see it in the midst of living. It focuses on God's realm, here and envisioned. It focuses on real experiences of oppression and God's response.

Method

As we turn to the "way of Jesus," on what grounds do we risk describing the "way of Jesus"? What is the method allowing us to draw conclusions? Let me remind you of what we have learned.

First, while the current historical Jesus work does not and cannot offer us a unified historical picture of who Jesus was and what he taught (does any history, really?), that same research has offered us a wealth of information about the Jewish and Roman context in which Jesus taught and lived and from which his followers sought to define and teach the way of Jesus. The gospel was preached in a **time of oppression and rebellion**.

We know that Israel was a colonized state of Rome. The ubiquitous presence of Roman soldiers to maintain order reminded all of this fact. Elites ruled in the Roman Empire, and the great majority of people were subjugated. Galilee, the home of Jesus and his ministry, was systematically being transformed as its patterns of family, kinship, and village were destroyed by Roman taxation, the development of large fishing industries to serve the Romans, and the consolidation of family farms into large estates owned by the elites and producing wine, olive oil, and food for the armies of Rome.

Moreover, we know the high priest in Rome was approved by the Roman governor and his "vestments" kept under Roman control. Even though a compromise had been reached where prayers to the emperor were not required at the temple, twice daily the chief priests had to sacrifice for Rome and for the emperor's well-being. Rome's agents in the guise of tax collectors and spies made sure that the peasants returned significant parts of their crops in both taxes and payment. **We know much about the climate of oppression and rebellion**.

Second, we know that Jesus, as well as his brother James, John the Baptist, and a list of disciples (from Peter to Paul) **were executed as "criminals" and "traitors."** Jesus was executed as one who claimed the authority to be "king" of the Jews—a challenge to the Roman emperor. The first century is filled with stories of "messianic" leaders who were executed as threats to Roman control—Bannus the bather; Judas, son of Ezekias; a Simon, a servant of Herod; and even another Jesus. Jesus' challenge of the temple was powerful. It disrupted the control of the temple elites. His mocking Palm Sunday entry through the same gate as the Roman governor challenged the authority of the empire. No wonder Caiaphas (Pilate's appointee and confidant) feared his authority.

Third, **the gospels, while theological and religious writings themselves, were efforts to "teach" the way of Jesus**. Like works of any author in any time, they tell stories and commitments from their own viewpoints. Moreover, their stories are filled with their own experiences of resurrection and new life. We can learn much from them about how they sought to teach "the way" and how they shaped the message to communicate in their contexts—similar to our educational task today. We can identify repetitive elements. For example, that Jesus was a *teacher*, that he was known as a *healer* and *exorcist*, and that he *taught in parables*. Moreover, the efforts of the Gospel writers to answer charges reflect realities of Jesus—for example, that he was called a *glutton* and *drunkard* or that he associated with people at the margins of religious and social respectability.

Being a teacher, a healer, and an exorcist, in and of itself, defines elements of the "way." Jesus sent disciples out two by two to "proclaim the good news, 'The kingdom of heaven has come near.' Cure the sick, raise the dead, cleanse the lepers, cast out demons" (Matt. 10:7-8 NRSV; Matt. 10:5-15; Mark 6:6b-13; Luke 9:1-6). And that is precisely what his disciples continued to do—proclaim a healing kingdom that renewed hope and community.

Fourth, Jesus was a **faithful Jew focused on the realm of God**. He daily prayed the Shema and honored Jewish traditions. He kept holy days, for example, the Passover celebration. He remembered the freedom from Egypt—embodied in the Festival of Booths (Sukkoth) and the call for forgiveness and righteousness prayed at Yom Kippur. He wore the phylacteries and prayer shawl meant to remind a good Jewish person of the expectations of God and obligations of the covenant. These phylacteries were even grabbed by people desiring healing.[4]

The words of the law and the prophets were on his lips. When he called the temple "a house of prayer" he drew on the images present in Isaiah 56:7, where God gathered all the "outcasts of Israel," even eunuchs, who were cut off by law from the temple, and "others besides" to Godself. In this little phrase "a house of prayer," he focused on the most expansive and inclusive notions of the Hebrew prophets. That same prophetic quote begins, "Maintain justice, and do what is right, for soon my salvation will come and my deliverance be revealed" (Isa 56:1 NRSV).

The same is true with his proclamations about the Holy Banquet table central to Isaiah. In fact, in Luke's version (Luke 14) of the banquet, the people with status beg off and the table is opened to "the poor, the crippled, the blind, and the lame" (v. 21 NRSV). Jewish historical writings following Jesus' day and in our present help us reclaim the voices of the multiple streams within the Judaism of the Second Temple. While some of his words are transformed in the Gospels, we can identify some that are in direct keeping with these streams of Judaism.

Fifth, historical and sociological research has helped us build on the stories from the early church (some in Acts and in the letters) about the ways the emerging "community of the way" taught and developed that way. In fact, that research suggests the early church sought to **embody the practices of the realm of God—the practices of a way to return to the righteousness of God**. The earliest of Jesus' followers already knew and had experienced educational practices embodied within the Jesus community— Shabbat celebrations, holy days (Passover, Yom Kippur, and Sukkoth are clearly present), teaching of Torah and prophets (*haphtarah*) in community gatherings. In fact, liturgical scholars are quite clear that Jewish practices that emerged in the post-Roman war period (after the temple's destruction) and the early Christian practices drew on common traditions.

Moreover, we know much about the early Jesus communities—the networks of homes, work, and worship described in Acts and Romans. The community, quite small at first, grew because of a deep sense of community, support, and health that frankly stood in opposition to Roman powers of civic organization and responsibility.[5]

By looking for **connections at the intersection** of the research on context, the Roman response to Jesus and his followers, the gospel witness, embodied Judaism, and sociological research, we develop a picture of the "way" from Jesus to his followers—this "way" that John calls "the way, the truth, and the life" (John 14:6) because it offers abundance and focuses our work.

The Way of Jesus

I suggest six conclusions about the content and practices of the way of Jesus. These six convictions focus the educational work of the church today:

1. Loving God and neighbor, the Shema Israel

2. Living in God's grace

3. Looking for the realm of God

4. Calling people to the banquet table

5. Resisting the time of trial

6. Proclaiming the Resurrected One[6]

1. Loving God and neighbor. At the center of the way of Jesus is the daily prayer—the Shema Israel. As a practicing Jew, Jesus would have been taught, as is true today, to begin each day as well as end it with the prayer. Just as Christian schools might pray the Lord's Prayer each day, Jewish day schools open with the Shema. The prayer is so close to one's heart that it is the first prayer taught a child; prayed to open and to close each day; and hoped to be on a faithful person's lips at death. The Shema Israel is prayed on Sabbath before the reading of the Torah and closes the Yom Kippur service. It is a proclamation of faith and a call to vocation. The first part of the prayer, holding together its three passages, is Deuteronomy 6:4-9 (also included are Deut. 11:13-21 and Num. 15:37-41). It is the heart, life, and vocation of the Hebrew people:

> Israel, listen! Our God is the Lord! Only the Lord!
> Love the Lord your God with all your heart, all your being, and all your strength. These words that I am commanding you today must always be on your minds. Recite them to your children. Talk about them when you are sitting around your house and when you are out and about, when you are lying down and when you are getting up. Tie them on your hand as a sign. They should be on your forehead as a symbol. Write them on your house's doorframes and on your city gates. (Deut. 6:4-9)

The total prayer consists of three foci:

151

1. On loving God, learning God's ways, and passing of the traditions

2. On remembering one's identity by wearing the prayer shawl and posting the *mezuzah*

3. On acts of *mitzvah*, the wearing of the fringes to remind the faithful of the 613 commandments of the Torah of moral law and expectations (or, of loving neighbor). *Mitzvahs* are daily reminders to care for and love others.

When Jesus taught his disciples and those he met the Shema and when he wore the "fringes," he reminded people to love God and to love neighbor. These were also his words to the rich young man whom he reminded that God was holy and that God calls us to love.

The Israelite people were called to "sanctify the name of God" (see Lev. 22:32). The *Kiddush Hashem* (Lev. 22:32) means that the people were to live so that others would come to worship the God of Israel. The lives of the people pointed others to God. Jesus was focused on whether people were indeed living the Shema and sanctifying the name—thus his criticisms of those he saw as hypocrites. Luke even has Jesus redefining his immediate family—"My mother and brothers are those who listen to God's word and do it" (Luke 8:21). He challenged the easy compromises people made to culture, to daily expectations and embedded cultural practices, and even to oppression.

The Shema Israel is remembered through practices—the wearing of the fringes, the prayer shawl, and the *mezuzah*. These are thus means of grace that teach us and remind us of the tradition—of God's creation, the covenant to make the people children of God, the freedom offered from Egypt (and future freedoms), and the promised banquet to come. Living is an embodiment of these practices of faithfulness. Therefore, the liturgical year, the rituals, and the laws are means of remembering one's identity and vocation. Remember the three prescribed ritual celebrations—Passover, God's freedom; Pentecost, God's gift of the Torah; and Sukkoth, God's gift of life and sustenance throughout the wilderness. Each reminds the people of their identity, God, God's greatness, and responsibilities (vocation) to live and fulfill God's ways, in all times. What a powerful means of education.

2. Living in God's grace. For Jesus, God's grace was ubiquitous. God created, God gives life, and God cares for life. When Jesus prayed, he called God holy, as was expected; he also knew intimately a sustaining God. He pointed people to God's presence and actions in their lives. As other rabbis in his day communicated, God is so close as to be called "father"; this was also Jesus' address.

Furthermore, as was made clear in Jesus' prayer, God already knows what we need and is seeking to provide it for us. "Ask and you will receive. Seek and you will find. Knock and the door will be opened. . . . Everyone who asks, receives. Whoever seeks, finds. To everyone who knocks, the door is opened" (Luke 11:9-10).

God gives good gifts to God's children. All those who follow the way need to do is ask, seek, and knock, and they will be found.

Is not that also a description of the realm of God in Luke? God plants the kingdom in people's very lives. There it can grow and multiply like seeds sown in a field (Luke 8). When recognized, it turns even noxious weeds (mustard was not a spice bush, but a multiplying weed) into shelters, and it transforms the ordinary (yeast and bread) into something amazing that can feed many (Luke 13:18-20). In the midst of the struggles and brokenness they all saw, Jesus pointed his contemporaries to where God was already working to make life new, to secure goodness, and to make virtue possible.

Jesus used amazing images from everyday life to define God's surprising grace—a noxious weed, yeast that can expand or spoil daily bread, a lost sheep, a lost coin, and even a lost child (Luke 15). In each case, there is a surprise. In the midst of an ordinary world where loss is real, grace demonstrates that new life and new possibilities can be constructed. The possibilities are so amazing that even tax collectors can be forgiven and join the people of God's realm (Luke 5:27-31).

Worry and fear do not add a moment to life, Jesus proclaimed. As God cares for birds of the field, gives life to lilies, and beautifies common grasses, God also is graciously present to humans. Therefore the agenda Jesus set for his followers: "Desire first and foremost God's kingdom and God's righteousness" (Matt. 6:33). Seeing God's gracious realm emerging demands a new vocation from the people—a vocation of risk and righteousness.

153

3. Looking for the realm of God. Jesus taught, "Here comes God's kingdom!" (Mark 1:15). Jesus sent disciples out with instructions to preach the "kingdom of God" (Matt. 10 NRSV; Luke 9). As we have seen, Luke even records a controversy that erupted at a time that Jesus healed a person. Some near complained that it was through the ruler of demons that he cast out the demon. Jesus, in turn, responded that if it was by the "*finger of God*" (NRSV), the power of God, that he had cast out the demon, "then God's kingdom has already overtaken you" (Luke 11:20).

Over and over, God's realm was in-breaking. Seeing the kingdom brought moments of rare preciousness equivalent to selling all that one has. When asked by John's disciples if he was the one, Luke tells us that Jesus pointed to his actions. Seeing the kingdom brought an amazing collection of people together. This continued in the early church as it brought the outcast, the sinners, and the marginalized together.

This message of seeing God's activities is nowhere more graphically present than in Jesus' story of children. "I assure you that whoever doesn't welcome God's kingdom like a child will never enter it." A strange saying: "God's kingdom belongs to people like these children" (Mark 10:14-15). Catholic educator and philosopher Marianne Sawicki says "children" sanitizes the real experience to which Jesus referred.[7] An earlier version of that text better describes the intensity of grace: "Jesus saw some babies nursing. He said to his disciples, 'These nursing babies are like those who enter the kingdom of God'" (*Gospel of Thomas* 22:2). Sawicki argues that in his travel in villages, Jesus saw nursing mothers gathered together feeding newborn infants. As a nursing mother eagerly feeds her vulnerable child, the babies are equally as eager to feed. Sitting near a nursing mother, we often hear the raucous smacking of suckling as the baby consumes the food of life. Suckling is the first gift of life and the essential gift of life. These nursing mothers, Jesus saw, were themselves increasingly vulnerable to Roman oppression. Notice the simile—the babies are vulnerable; the babies are given milk freely out of love. What a powerful image for the grace of God—a baby nursing at his or her mother's breast! In the midst of vulnerability, God's grace enters. The kingdom is a gracious gift.

Looking for the realm of God transforms the ways people act. Life is nourished and a vocation is given—righteousness even in times when despair might be the ordinary response. Just as God dwelled with the Hebrew people through wilderness wanderings, living in tents, signs of

God's dwelling are visible. They are signs of the kingdom! As a baby seeks the milk of a mother's breast, the vulnerable seek the milk of the kingdom. And God is faithful—freely giving the milk of grace.

Good news calls for a response. That is the vocation. Mark retells the story of Jesus and the children: as the disciples attempt to block the children from Jesus, Jesus becomes angry. They are not a waste of time; grace is free and plentiful. Woe to those who make others more vulnerable; woe to those who hoard gifts at the expense of others. In fact, as Jesus pointed to God's activities, those who followed Jesus pointed to his life as a way of seeing God's continuing grace. Woe is a description: those who refuse to see God's realm cannot live the grace.

What does it mean for us to so teach people that they look for and see the kingdom in daily living? A friend of mine, a Jesuit priest, tells me that his spiritual director regularly asks him if he is being formed in the kingdom and looks for and lives the kingdom. This is a particular kind of instruction—formation for God's realm.

4. Calling people to the banquet table. The phrase in Jesus' prayer reads: "Give us this day our daily bread and forgive us our debts." Feeding was a central aspect of the way of Jesus; it was the way he was recognized as risen Lord at Emmaus and in John's fish fry on the beach.

As we have learned, daily bread and debts were real for the marginalized in the occupied lands of Galilee. Patterns of taxation broke up the fragile bonds of kinship in Galilee and forced the poor off the land. The needs for bread and the cries for debt forgiveness were real.

When Jesus entered a village and was received, he and his followers remained, "eating and drinking" (Luke 10:7). Jesus and the disciples miraculously brought food for thousands. When wine at a wedding dinner was expended, Jesus miraculously found the best wine, the reserved wine. Jesus called miraculous bounty from stingy and fearful people. How many of Jesus' parables focus on unjust stewards and fearful religious leaders? How often are the marginalized the heroes? His practices of reaching out to and of providing the staples of life left him with the charge of being "a glutton and a drunk" (Luke 7:34).

Jesus' way was one of "abundant life," calling the people to rebuild patterns of kinship and support. This is precisely what occurred in the early church. Acts records people living and sharing together, with deacons bringing the fruit of the tables to the sick and the widows. Historical research has demonstrated that churches in tenements in Rome consisted of dwellings where people returned from work (often in the fabric industries) to common living and common meals. Some of the strengths of early Christian communities were the ways they welcomed unwanted infants into their midst, supported the sick in times of crisis, and even shared their offerings to buy the freedom of slaves among them.[8]

Jesus could see and the followers could experience the birth of a new community embodying Isaiah's vision of the great banquet where diverse peoples gathered around tables of fellowship and new life, partaking of the richest of foods and finding themselves filled with the presence of God.[9] Banquet tables for "gluttons and drunkards [and sinners]" were a direct challenge to the patterns of wealth, fear, and oppression of Roman control and the complicity of religious leaders.

What does this mean for education? As we work in mission and as we learn from those who are strangers to us, we gather at the wide and welcome table of the Lord. Education is mission!

5. Resisting the time of trial. Trial was precisely what the people were living. Roman soldiers were camped within sight of the Temple Mount. Each high holy season, the soldiers would march from Caesarea Maritima through the Jerusalem city gates in a show of force—to stifle riots and challenges to authority. Those who revolted and resisted were left to die and decay on crosses of state-supported terror. Pilate was famous for his brutality and control.

Matthew records that Jesus warned his disciples to be "wise as snakes and innocent as doves," for they were being sent out as "sheep among wolves" (Matt. 10:16). We know that life for those who lived the way was indeed filled with terror. Many were executed and others were expelled from Rome as "demonic challengers" of the state religion. A variety of emperors, who claimed to be sons of God, punished them for their commitment to nonviolence and their lack of loyalty.

State-sanctioned terror caused Jesus' death. Charged as the "king of the Jews," Jesus was a challenge to the power of Rome and to the complicity of Jerusalem's religious leaders. The people's anger over the complicity of their leaders is evidenced in the first acts of the Jewish-Roman War in the 70s, when the rebels murdered the temple priests. We also know that Caiaphas did not endure long as high priest after Pilate.

The way of Jesus was not part of this rebellion even though Jesus had resisted actions that spoiled faithfulness. Jesus challenged all who did not "sanctify the name." The way of Jesus taught people to find refuge and support in new communities of faith—often on the margins of society—that resisted the requirements of social contracts with empire and included the unclean, the sick, and the sinful.

Education is embedded in practices of solidarity and community where churches reach out into their communities, providing nurture, education, new life, and hope. A storefront church on Seventy-Third Street in Chicago is one such place. From 3:00 to 7:30 each day, the pastor, a Pentecostal teacher with a PhD in education, gathers children from a neighborhood school where the dropout rate approaches 60 percent. She provides safe sanctuary and tutoring and teaches the way of Jesus. Indeed, this is education that resists temptation; education that teaches how to resist the time of trial.

6. Proclaiming the Resurrected One. The Gospels call believers to the vocation of discipleship. Biblical scholar Osvaldo Vena has uncovered a profound image for Jesus beneath the Markan text. He argues that Jesus understood himself as a "disciple of the kingdom"—following God faithfully to where the kingdom led, even into challenging repression.[10] All of us Christians, as Luke implies by his story of the sending out of the seventy, are, in turn, disciples of Jesus, proclaiming, offering, and seeking God's realm. Paul is even plainer. We are to live lives worthy of Christ. Christ lives in us, and we are called to embody the power of the resurrected and anointed one.

Proclaiming the "lordship" of the Resurrected One was not a timid or safe activity for early Christians living in a world where the military victories of Caesar Augustus were proclaimed as the "salvation offered by the son of God." Roman emperors were known as gods; and some, in fact, publicly celebrated their divination. Proclaiming Jesus as messiah ("anointed one") was dangerous. An "anointed one" was one raised up by God, just as David had been anointed for kingship, for God's work and for God's people. Resurrection was an affirmation of the way of Jesus in the world and a recognition that it continued to affect and direct the lives of the people. It vindicated Jesus and his way and continued to point to the vision of the realm of God, of redemptive community, even where people would not expect it. In fact, after proclaiming the list of witnesses to the resurrection and his own encounter with Christ, Paul turns to the very experience of the people in the ecclesial community of Corinth. "If Christ hasn't been raised, then our preaching is useless and your faith is useless" (1 Cor. 15:14). Their faith is the evidence: they have been transformed, they are being remade in the image of God, and they are called to new life and the lordship of the true God. Their faith is proof of God's vindication of Jesus!

In the community of the Resurrected One, people found new life and were transformed. This ecclesial community, using the image of a city, made an amazing difference in people's lives. Loyalties were transformed. The Empire knew these new groups—growing groups—were dangerous because they would not swear allegiance and because they upset the reign of terror and the balance of power that keeps people subjugated. That is how the church teaches—by being the community of resurrection, by challenging empire.

Conclusion

Note what is central to educating people in the way of Jesus. People are called back to the vocation of "sanctifying the name" and "loving God and neighbor." Even in the midst of state terrorism, people together are taught to seek the realm of God. They are called to live by an ethic of abundance and the banquet table, even in the midst of scarcity and oppression. They learn to resist the powers and principalities and, as Paul states, they watch for the children of God to be born (Rom. 9). The lordship of life is given to the Resurrected One, rather than to the powers and principalities.

We live in a world when the church seems too often to be a place of timid, respectable citizens who really are not looking for anything new to come forth. What would it mean to be taught the way of Jesus, the transforming way of new life—to love God and neighbor, to live in God's grace, to seek the kingdom, to set bounty in the midst of scarcity, to learn to resist the time of trial and the empire, and to experience the new life of the Resurrected One?

A friend in Mozambique tells the story of two United Methodist deacons working in the riskiest of all health situations. Tainted water fills streams, and land mines left by the Portuguese at the end of the colonial revolution too frequently explode and maim children. Yet, in this place, deacons teach healthful practices of prenatal and child care, giving children a chance at life. Then they offer communities of education that build networks of care and hope in the midst of corruption and abuse. Or another friend in Kenya tells of church leaders engaged in ministries that directly address cattle-raising, cooperatives, corruption, and HIV/AIDS. In both places, the church is an embodiment of the Resurrected One in the midst of a time of trial.

Faithful church education occurs in the midst of people seeking to make a difference, offering real life chances, and challenging the powers of the principalities. The Jesus way partners with faithful religious colleagues of other traditions seeking hope and justice.

On the eve of Yom Kippur, I received an e-mail from a friend in Israel asking for one last mitzvah before Yom Kippur. He asked for support for a petition to international aid agencies and governments to allow the International Red Cross to have access to settlements where refugees are being held almost like hostages. Another Jewish friend rewrote the High Holiday service to call for us all to work together in the process of *teshuva*, the process of prayer, recognition, forgiveness, and atonement that will assist us in *returning to our highest selves*. An interfaith prayer service in Chicago on *Eid*, the feast ending Ramadan, challenged the rhetoric that we cannot afford to care for and support the most vulnerable of our US society. They focused on recovering the web of support needed for the millions (in fact, 52 million without health care) and the safety net for the least of these.

The vitality of all religious education is giving birth to vision and hope. In fact, the proverb "When there's no vision, the people get out of control" (Prov. 29:18) should really be translated "For a lack of prophetic vision, the people perish." Knowing the way of Jesus is a means of resurrecting that prophetic vision.

Chapter Eight

Teaching the Way of Jesus: An Agenda for Christian Education

The sign on the synagogue read, "Join us. Renew your faith through community, prayer, study, and service. Serve God." Serving God and loving neighbor were its priorities, but the leaders of this congregation knew that required community, prayer, study, and service. These metaphors of community and prayer, study, and service define well approaches to *religious education* to form observant and faithful people.

Christian religious education, in particular, uses them to assist people to acquire an identity as disciples of Jesus, a vocation shaped by the way of Jesus, and the resources to live this risky faith. Christian religious education consists of intentional actions taken by representatives of the Christian faith community to teach the content, values, affections, life ways, and practices of the faith—to empower people to follow the realm of God.

This chapter is an invitation for educators and congregations to look at their practices and ministries of Christian education and assess them in light of the way of Jesus. How else can they be fulsome and faithful? There is no one program of Christian education that can be replicated everywhere. In fact, all of the examples of congregations used throughout this book are faithful and appropriate representations of teaching the ways of Jesus. St. Paul's, Faith Congregation, St. Stephen's, Second Baptist Church, St. Michael's, First Church, Trinity, Urban Village, and Reba Place have significant ministries of teaching and learning that call people to faithfulness. This chapter on teaching the ways of Jesus is an invitation—an invitation to create a ministry of Christian education that is faithful to the identity and vocation to which Jesus and his followers called us to live. It is an invitation to explore how our communities of faith teach with vigor and passion, how our instructional classes and teaching sessions provide a critical and nuanced means of theological education, and how the mission of the church faithfully calls believers and communities to teach and live the realm of God. In the next pages, I will review the approaches to Christian religious education and how they cohere. Using the six elements of the way of Jesus, I will then offer invitations and examples for us to seek to embody in our teaching ministries. Finally, I will suggest how this ministry of faithful teaching reaches into our public environment.

I hope Christian religious educators see much confirmation for their work in these pages. There are not a lot of new strategies to be added. Rather, the task is focusing our work and ministry with purpose on the vision of the way of Jesus, to engage in practical theological reflection and action, and to embody the way in our congregations and settings for education. Over and over, I want to proclaim that the way of Jesus is the essential vision of Christian faith and living. Over and over, I want to proclaim that our congregations and settings for education, from classes to schools to service associations, teach faithfully only as we live and embody this way—as we witness, as Jesus did, to the transforming possibilities of the realm of God.

Linking the Approaches to Christian Education

People are shaped in communities of meaning, communities of memory and vision (chapter 4). Communities define the patterns by which people interact with their worlds. Many learnings are informal and shape expectations. For example, that water is clean and does not need to be boiled are assumptions of those living in the United States. Yet after a crisis, like Hurricane Sandy, when potable drinking water on the East Coast was scarce, those living there had to change their expectations.

The same is true with communities of faith. Many religious believers, Jewish, Muslim, Buddhist, or Christian, send their children to religious schools. Not only do these parents want their children educated in the content of their faith communities, but they also know that the children will acquire particular ways of thinking, feeling, deciding, and living by simply being around others who are immersed in their religious traditions. Learning occurs as people experience the creeds, codes, and cultic activities of the faith. For example, children who attend a Jewish day school study a Torah passage, a *parsha*, at the same time the synagogue is scheduled to read it and organizes its prayer and study life around it. In school, the children interpret that passage. School is thus connected with synagogue and reinforces the values and meanings of the community. Another example: the rhythm of the Jewish day school is so different from the rhythm of US schools. The intentional focus on study of Jewish texts, practices, and Hebrew language, as well as times of prayer, teach different meanings from the flow of a public school. The rhythm of the Jewish liturgical year—from Rosh Hashanah, to Yom Kipper, to Sukkoth, Simchat Torah, Hanukkah, Purim, Pesach, and Shavuot—teaches very different meanings from the rhythm of the US calendar—from New Year's Day, to Memorial Day, to the Fourth of July, to Labor Day, to Halloween, and to Thanksgiving. Other practices and rhythms could be defined for other "religious schools," yet the purpose of all of the schools is similar—to teach children to embody the meanings and values of a particular faith community in a rich interpretive and supportive community.

Christian congregations themselves teach as people worship, converse about values and meanings, study, fellowship, engage in mission, and imbibe the aesthetics of the building. People learn by participating in the life of a community. Practices of faith are taught through the interrelationships of worship, study, mission, prayer, learning, and living.

Our theological analysis of the community-of-faith approach suggested that the primary educational question was the faithfulness of the community. The cultural captivity of the church in the United States has tended to make the church an agent of culture. This is not to critique all the commitments or emphases of the culture, for many are praiseworthy, nor is it to challenge the wide diversity of community voices operating in this culture, representing many religious and philosophical traditions. However, knowing the power of community to "shape" people's character, the community-of-faith approach emphasizes that for specific and intentional Christian learning to occur, the voice of the church must be faithful and powerful. In fact, in Jesus' own time, there were also multiple voices affecting the wider culture, from the intrusive voice of the Roman military, which, frankly, provided many technological benefits (roads, canals, and trade routes), to the variety of voices within the Jewish community itself, and those of a wide diversity of other peoples. In fact, research on the city of Antioch suggests that eighteen diverse ethnic communities lived side by side.[1] While each ethnic group shaped its own members, members of each group also had to cross ethnic boundaries in public life—in many ways, as today, learning as we engage each other.

The redemptive community rooted in the surprising graciousness of God was at the heart of the Jesus movement—where people and systems were humanized and where the excluded found a place of welcome and inclusion. Essential for the church's education is asking the very question of what kind of community the church is living and what message it is teaching. Teaching congregations are explicit about how they live their faith. Are there signs of forgiveness, redemption, hope, love, justice, and new life? The church that teaches cannot avoid the cacophony of the public square or the diversity of faith perspectives seeking public attention. It teaches as it participates in the midst of a public search for hope and humanization. The faith is taught as the community acts and engages others. We ask if the church is powerfully witnessing and living the ways of Jesus.

Such awareness points us to the task of religious instruction (chapter 5). How do people critically learn the content of the faith to assess faithfulness? Jesus was taught well. He honored the tradition and lived its practices. The hope promised in the prophets inspired him. As he offered others the hope of God's great banquet, he expected them, whether in his hometown or in Jerusalem, to live righteously by the requirements of a living God.

He and other religious leaders of his day would have disagreed over some particulars as these same leaders would also have disagreed among themselves. Yet, they held in common many of the same convictions of the Jewish way. In fact, Jesus, as others in his day, led one of the revitalization movements in his community. He expected God's grace to guide people to abundant living even in the midst of Roman power and oppression. He knew a tradition, deftly engaged in parabolic teaching and theological reflection about it, and joined in a living faith dialogue. His perspective was part of the important theological conversation occurring in his day.

Instruction is essential for education. Instruction is *intentional and formal* efforts to teach. Schools are organized for instruction. In fact, in the United States, when we see a need that must be ameliorated, we often add more school instruction. Teenage drivers are seen as dangerous; we add driver's training. Young people do not know healthy ways to express their sexuality; we add sex education. In fact, at my seminary, as is true in any school, when we hear of a lack in our graduates, we usually add a new class.

Instruction in the content of the Christian faith, its history, practices of interpretation, and processes of theological reflection is critical. Congregations' efforts at instruction are too often episodic and shallow, assuming that the teaching of short introductory courses over and over and offering Sunday school experiences that jump from one topic to another are sufficient. This pattern simply does not empower people to engage in a rich, nuanced, and creative theological practice, to learn the depth, richness, and development of the faith tradition.

Jesus was an amazing teacher connecting with the experiences of people and illustrating for them the vitality of the faith tradition. For Jesus, instruction involved parables, prayer, and depth theological conversation and reflection. The power of his teaching was continued in those who followed him, as we see evidenced in Paul's rabbinical reflections on living in Christ, and in the rich theological reflection and theological storytelling of the Gospel writers. Most of the theological conflicts of the early church were born in pastoral practice as people and communities sought to live the faith. The theological development of the church arose as teachers sought to communicate the power of the way of Jesus in new times, cultures, and circumstances. Theological reflection was at the heart of the work of teachers of the faith, as it must be today. Of course, some of the early teachers, as today, were misguided, compromising with power and excluding the very people to whom God offered the free gift of redemptive grace. Nevertheless, others showed the power of seeking prayerfully to communicate the way of Jesus in new times and circumstances—in ways that honored God's grace and call for abundant life and justice. We are called to teach in this fulsome manner.

Religious instruction expects that the people of faith will be honestly and fully taught the ability to read and interpret scripture, to know the tradition and how it developed, to encounter historic moments when profound decisions were made that affect the very character of a living community, and to learn to engage in responsible theological interpretation in community. Congregations have to prioritize the teaching of theological interpretation and help people practice it. To fail affects profoundly the very way Christians participate in public dialogues about the world we share with others.

Mission is both the goal of ministry and an essential process of Christian education or faith formation (chapter 6). For Christians, the goal "serve God" is rooted in the very proclamation of Jesus: "Here comes God's kingdom!" (Mark 1:15). Engaging in mission focuses people on the transforming power of God, or as Letty Russell defined it, joining God in efforts of realizing true humanity and new creation. People are invited to participate in God's gracious redemption.

Mission makes a concrete difference in the world in the ways communities thrive and individuals interact. Mission therefore grounds and focuses educational ministries. In fact, missional education gathers up and gives direction to the other approaches to Christian education (community of faith and religious instruction). Living the faith in our communities becomes the goal and direction of Christian education. Instruction assists us in defining mission, and mission shapes the life of the community of faith.

Jesus and his followers led those around them to engage in theological discernment about the marks of the realm of God: seeing, healing, forgiving, feeding, freeing, offering peace, and building community. Exploring how these very marks call a congregation into living is a profound pedagogical activity. Jesus instructed his disciples to go into the world to heal, cast out evil spirits, and offer the peace of the kingdom. As Luke records, when the followers of Jesus returned, they were amazed by what had happened. As they practiced living the marks of the faith, reflection guided them to grow more fully in the ways of Jesus, in the ways of God's gracious realm.

Moreover, we learned that engaging as partners with the people to whom God calls us (missional apprenticeships) poses for us profound "problems" about the systems and practices of the world. We ask why. We are directed into important biblical, theological, and cultural study about the structures of the world. Just as Jesus' followers and those who preached the way of Jesus throughout the first several centuries had to ask what it meant to live in a world dominated by the Roman war machine, Christians today have to ask hard questions about how we carve our ministries amid the profound pain, violence, and opportunities in today's world. For example, as children and adults raise money for "Nothing but Nets," they learn about malaria, but more, they learn to ask why it thrives in parts of the world and not in others, why it is bred by poverty and neglect, and how the structures of the world can be focused to address the childhood diseases that destroy opportunities and futures (problem-posing).[2] In deep connection with others (apprenticeship), study is transformed from acquiring information to a purpose-driven activity. In fact, mission education is much more like a project, directing service and action, than a school room. Living missionally teaches.

The goal of Christian religious education is following the way of Jesus into the public world. Faithful education is essential to believers. Christian learning occurs through direct teaching and instruction, through participating in the faithful ministries of congregations, and through witnessing in the wider public world.

An Invitation to Live and Teach the Way of Jesus

Again the obvious conclusion: there is no one program of Christian religious education that can be replicated for every place and time. Many, many congregations, faith associations, service organizations, schools, and ministries teach the way of Jesus faithfully and effectively. Each of us called to Christian education is obligated to continue to build the faithfulness and effectiveness of the ministries with which we work. This chapter is an invitation to that reflection on faithfulness and effectiveness. Using the dimensions of the way of Jesus (those defined in chapter 7), I will provide questions, invitations, and examples for us to consider. Faithfulness is always contextual responding to the in-breaking of the realm of God calling us to vocation and discipleship—calling us to form disciples of the way of Jesus. The dimensions include the following:

1. Loving God and neighbor

2. Living in God's grace

3. Looking for the realm of God

4. Calling people to the banquet table

5. Resisting the time of trial

6. Proclaiming the Resurrected One

Loving God and neighbor. Loving God and neighbor is at the heart of the Christian community. It is our vocation. The educational tasks here are those of identity and understanding. How do we encourage and teach the Christian way of loving God and neighbor? How to we remind Christian believers what is at the heart of their faith?

Jesus was formed in a faithful Jewish environment that taught him a way to live. Those who followed Jesus' revitalization movement similarly developed and taught ways of reminding followers to serve God and love others. The movement led by Jesus' brother John in Jerusalem continued to pray the Shema daily, as did many other early Christians. It appears centrally in each of the Gospels. To this prayer, early communities added key practices of reciting the Jesus prayer, baptism, and a common meal. The rhythm of each day reminded believers of their identity as followers of Jesus' way.

Our pedagogical question, then, is: What are the daily practices of prayer and community life that teach and remind us of our identity to love God and neighbor? Multiple identities compete within each one of us: citizen, parent, or consumer, to name a few. Yet, our primary identity is child of God. Just like those in the Roman world, we too often give all to Caesar and live as if the world of Caesar is all there is, yet Jesus reminded us, and his followers taught, that our primary loyalty is to God. God has given us life, called us children, and sustains living. We are reminded to "give to God what is God's." Remembering this identity is at the center of all educational decisions.

Rituals of initiation are a place to start. For Christians, baptism is the primary ritual of identity. In fact, a practice of the early church was to give the baptized a new name—to seal one's identity. Baptism occurred after instruction and commitment. How we educate parents of infants and youth and the wider Christian community to the vows taken by us or on our behalf at baptism is central to that identity. This instruction attends to fundamental questions of loyalty. Remember the baptismal questions: they ask how we will confront evil and counter the forces of sin and brokenness in the world, how we love God and neighbors. Every time a child or adult is baptized in a congregation is a time to remember and refocus these loyalties. Regular efforts to renew the commitments of baptism continue believers' identity formation. Liturgical services of baptismal renewal and other programs, such as a "rite of Christian initiation" for adults, are profound means of education.[3]

Coupled with baptism is the most important educational time in congregational life—membership instruction and membership renewal. When people become members of a congregation, instruction focuses on the meanings of Christian life, the dynamics of a particular community of faith, and ways of making theological decisions in the world. In fact, this is an opportune time to assist persons to practice the processes of theological reflection about their own lives and the world that surrounds them. The strategy used by Second Church, recorded in chapter 5, is recommended. The leaders of the congregation created a three-course introduction to Christian living in which they encouraged every new member to participate. This three-course curriculum was a substantial instruction in the meanings of and critical reflection on Christian theology and practices. In addition, when new members are welcomed into the congregation, older members can be reminded of baptism, membership, and faithfulness to the way of Jesus. At Second, this basic foundation in the faith is complemented in the congregation by a full program of Christian instruction and by action-reflection on mission.

Again, a full and rich instructional program is important to assist believers in growing in the faith. I believe we need to consider how to formalize "schooling" for our members and their families, for example, the patterns of after-school classes for children on the meaning of faith, like those practiced in St. Andrew's and St. Stephen's, or even the sponsoring of parish-related schools. These are rich, supportive environments for critical study of Christian faith and living.

Rites of transition are another means of connecting the faith to critical developmental transitions in people's lives. Early Christian communities gathered food from the common Eucharistic meal and shared it with the sick and frail. Note the power of this action: the sharing reminded all that even during life transitions, particularly of illness and loss, the faith of the community surrounded the person. Rituals of transition should additionally be considered focusing on crucial life moments, like parenthood, marriage, a teen's coming of age, vocational changes, or loss and dying.

Again, living the Shema means that one is reminded daily of God's gift of community, of liberation, and of call. That prayer reminds people of their heritage, identity, and vocation to love God and neighbor. Similarly, *reminding* is an essential responsibility of Christian education as we guide people to claim the identity of God's people in the world.

Living in God's grace. An intimacy between Jesus and God is reflected throughout the Scriptures. At moments of great transition, in the wilderness defining his vocation, on the Mount of Transfiguration, and in the Garden of Gethsemane, prayer and discernment were deep, honest, and filled with emotion. Prayer was essential to the first communities following the ways of Jesus. Prayer is the primary means of remembering that our primary loyalty is to the God who cares for all creation, the God who knows each person as a special child.

The pedagogical question: How do we help people connect with God's presence and call? The primary means are the church's historic practices of spiritual formation. Believers are asked: How do we experience God, how are we dependent on God, and how do we seek to live God's grace? Prayer is the daily way to remember on whom we depend for living and hope. Prayers of thanksgiving are ways of recognizing the gifts of life and possibilities that God has given each of us. Prayers of intercession are a means to attend to the brokenness of the world—in the lives of individuals and the wider communities we touch. Prayers of the dark night of the soul are ways of continuing to reach out, even when God's word is not clear. Furthermore, prayers of discernment when making decisions help us draw on the resources of the tradition, to know that we live, decide, and interact with others as children of God. Finally, the regular praying of the Jesus prayer leads us fully to proclaim Jesus' way—particularly the dimensions of seeking the realm of God, being thankful for nourishment and forgiveness, and living in a time of trial. Too often we live and interact out of habit. The above suggestions are ways for us to "pray without ceasing"—of focusing our attention. Our interactions then are deepened as we attend to living as children of God.

Looking for the realm of God. Seeking the realm of God empowered the ministry of Jesus. He taught it and schooled his followers to look for it. Furthermore, the purpose of the Gospels themselves was to assist persons to remember and look for the realm of God in a time of seeming delay.

The pedagogical question: How do we assist people to seek and live the realm of God? We humans yearn for meaning and vocation (chapter 3). Daily we live out of meanings that shape the ways we act, interact, and decide—that shape the ways we simply are and expect the world to be. We are thus living a way of life. Theological reflection is the process for us to consider, explore, and discern the meanings of God's realm.

People of faith need a rich, full, and nuanced theological wisdom empowering living and deciding. While we may not draw on it for every decision, when our worlds are challenged or when we examine our lives and vocations, we need the resources of theological reflection (much as described in chapters 3 and 5). Without living daily the wisdom of the tradition, we are distracted from our fundamental purposes. A lawyer in a men's group I have attended described his daily practice. As he entered his office each morning, before turning on the light and organizing the tasks of the day, he simply asked God to guide him through the day. He asked to be reminded of his identity as a child of God as he interacted with people. He witnessed that that simple action called him to use the resources of theological discernment more often in his work, rather than just reacting, as he also tended to do a lot of the time. In fact, he thanked the men's group because its regular practice of studying and practicing theological reflection gave him a foundation, a wisdom, on which to build.

We need to help the faithful to practice in small groups thinking theologically about the decisions and tasks of his living. Covenant groups, study groups, and mission project teams are ways. Furthermore, this agenda of theological wisdom becomes a guide for preaching as weekly worship demonstrates connecting faith and living in response to God's good news. The emerging practice of lectionary study groups, where people examine Sunday texts before or after weekly preaching, is a rich means of practicing theological wisdom.

Furthermore, the mission of the church is specifically defined as a response to the in-breaking of the realm of God (chapter 6). Seeking the kingdom is the first question of exploring and assessing a congregation's mission or a person's vocation. Church education helps the people of God use the markers of the kingdom to which Jesus pointed: acts of healing, freeing, feeding, addressing evil, and offering the peace. Specific time must be set aside in congregations for seeking spiritual discernment about how God is calling believers and congregations to follow these markers of care, healing, and justice today. The practices of Christian conferencing and theological discernment are such means of looking for and of defining how to live the realm of God. The language of how we are responding to where God leads needs to be central to the vocabulary of a congregation.

Calling people to the banquet table. Table fellowship was important for Jesus and his followers. They rehearse the promise of Isaiah that God will set a table for all, where the finest foods and wines will give sustenance. In fact, some suggest that Jesus' entry into a community would call for a banquet—setting a table in hope of the realm of God. As we know, it was also at table in Emmaus that Cleopas and friend recognized the continuing presence of Jesus and were empowered for ministry.

The pedagogical question: How are we welcoming those seeking forgiveness and new life, those excluded, and those dismissed into our communities of faith? First, the people of faith need to know the meanings of the banquet table; they need to experience regularly its hope. As was taught in the early church, the people Jesus gathered at table were not the typical ones. Jesus had been called a glutton, and questions were asked about with whom he ate—a motley crew who were not expected or who were unclean. The table of Jesus' way reached into the wider community, gathering those seeking forgiveness and new life. Here then is the only requirement for participation—seeking forgiveness and new life. Christian living transforms.

Congregations teach the banquet table when they embody hospitality. As the congregation engages in worship, service, and witness, the table provides their vision—a table of plenty, where even those who are excluded elsewhere are celebrated. Calling people to the table teaches the wideness of God's care and mercy. God has created all as God's children.

Resisting the time of trial. Jesus lived in a time of trial, as did the earliest Christians. We, too, face times of trial in our personal and public lives. *The pedagogical question asked is: How do we help people face into the world, resisting the powers that control and define?*

Recently I began a workshop asking the group to consider the baptismal liturgy:

- "Do you renounce the spiritual forces of wickedness, reject the evil powers of this world, and repent of your sin?"

- "Do you accept the freedom and power God gives you to resist evil, injustice, and oppression in whatever forms they present themselves?"[4]

To my surprise, even though many in the group were educators, pastors, and Sunday school teachers, only about half even knew of the existence of the questions. Evidently and regretfully, they are not used in their congregations.

Participants engaged in serious discussion about the involvement of the United States in military actions, some commenting that not all interventions were warranted. Others responded reminding the group that early Christians were pacifists and would not participate in loyalty oaths or war making. The conversation also considered personal realities of illness and need for healing and peace in individuals. These two baptismal questions engendered important reflection about the mission of the church and about theological reflection.

As I read workshop evaluations, I was amazed by a couple. Most were energized by the theological conversation and noted directly that we were beginning to talk about the petition in the Jesus prayer about "keeping us from the time of trial" or "from temptation." Yet, a couple read: "I appreciated how the workshop ended. I was worried as we began with all the political talk. The workshop was to be about theology." What does "resisting the time of trial" mean if it is not political? Jesus' followers knew the ire of the Roman war machine. They knew about crucifixions, the destruction of whole villages, and torture. They knew that they were seeking a way in the midst of oppression. In fact, early Christian communities took offerings to buy the freedom of slaves and thereby embody God's healing and redeeming presence.

Just as early Christians had to ask how to live in the midst of their world, we do too. Profound questions of health care, imprisonment, war, and economic opportunity are with us daily. Christian education needs to find ways of helping believers engage in serious theological reflection and action about our engagement as Christians. A colleague told me a story of a doctor who works in genetic research and who was called, over and over again, by his pastor to serve on the church's budget committee. The pastor seemed not even to be aware of this man's potential to help the whole church address crucial questions about the meaning of life and health—an opportunity wasted. Some of the churches we have used as illustrations—Second Baptist, First Church, Urban Village, and Reba Place, for example—provide direct attention to living in a time of trial, to living as a faithful presence in their own communities. They do not shirk being willing to face and engage the most troubling questions of how to live in today's world. In fact, one of them has scheduled a forum of lamentation and reflection about the gun violence in its community as well as the tragic national school and cinema shootings. They hope to be a force for change in their neighborhood.

Resisting the time of trial means finding ways of educating congregants in the skills of theological reflection and ethical analysis. Defining the congregation's missional identity, asking what it means to follow Jesus, and creating ministry teams examining essential questions of human living empowers congregational vitality.

Proclaiming the Resurrected One. The transforming presence of Jesus is living. On this, the proclamation of Christian life is founded: the way of Jesus is a living, God-directed pattern of being. We can embody the identity, live in God's grace, seek the realm of God, call people to the banquet table, and resist the time of trial because the God of all life and creation continues to guide the community.

The pedagogical questions are: How do we affirm a living God? and How are we "light to the nations"? The author of the Gospel of John promised Jesus' followers that they would be led in doing the same works Jesus did, and *even greater* works (John 14:12). Even facing a profound loss, the disciples were called to "remain in [him] . . . and produce much fruit" (John 15:7-8). Isn't that what Trinity Church is doing in its health fair and farmer's market? It is witnessing to a living faith that God calls us to produce fruit of hope and redemption. Isn't that what Faith Church, Urban Village, and St. Stephen's sought to live, or what St. Andrew's and Reba Place embody?

Proclaiming the Resurrected One is precisely proclaiming that the way of Jesus brings hope, community, and shalom to the world, for it points to the realm of God's promises and abundance in the world. It transforms everyday living. It calls us to faithfulness serving God and our neighbors. Even the darkest powers of the world, even oppression and crucifixion, cannot triumph over the realm of God.

Frankly, communicating this power of a living God is at the heart of vital educational practices. As the vitality of the faith is experienced, as transformation occurs, and as lives are changed, we say, "Amen," let it be so. We recognize the power of faith to make a difference. As we remember, in Luke's version, the Seventy-Two returned joyously after offering peace, healing, and resistance (Luke 10:17-24). Seeing them, Jesus was also joyous because he knew they were embodying God's grace. God's grace was alive. His response was a prayer of thanksgiving for the sharing of redemption in the world. Christian education helps the congregation live by the titles of "children of God," "new life in Christ," and "community of redemption"; it enlivens the vocabulary the church uses to define its identity, its call, and its mission.

Extending the Teaching of the Way of Jesus

Almost all of the conversation in the last section has been about Christian education in congregations. That is not surprising because congregations are the primary context where issues of Christian faith and hope are taught and learned (chapters 3 and 4). Many of the suggestions that have been offered focus on helping people daily remember their identity and draw on the resources of the faith to live their vocation as children on God in that daily living.

However, how do we extend the teaching of the way of Jesus with those who have been hurt by religious groups, those who are "spiritual and not religious," those who do not know this faith, those who seek transformation, and even to those of other faith traditions, so we can live and work together in the world we share? In the recent Pew Study, one in five adults in the United States has no religious affiliation.[5] Many of these individuals tend to be younger. Some have been hurt by churches. The resistance of churches to address complex social issues excludes still others.[6] Yet a surprising finding was that many of these same people continue to believe in God; most even pray. A lack of church vitality, a lack of a vision of the life-changing character of the way of Jesus, means that many people live with a kind of low-level knowledge of multiple and diverse religious commitments and real lack of awareness of the critical processes of theological reflection. This is a profound issue for all religious education.

While some suggestions about how congregations reach out to this population have been given before, we need to find additional ways of extending education. Let me offer three:

1. By enjoining public conversation about a vision for the future

2. By entering the debate about and practice of public education

3. By being the church

By enjoining public conversation about a vision for the future. Too often media portrayals of religious communities are closed and rigid. Many may be. Yet the alternatives need to be seen. For example, as a result of the discussions in Washington, D.C., in December 2012, about the budget, Bishop Robert Hoshibata, president of the United Methodist Board of Church and Society, and Jim Winkler, general secretary of the board, produced an open letter, "A Faithful Alternative to the Fiscal Cliff," to the president and Congress.[7] It simply and effectively stated some of the key values of this denomination about government care for the poor, about work, and about peace. It was an invitation to theological conversation. Many other religious and interfaith groups and nongovernmental organizations develop similar statements on a variety of issues. However, there is usually little public conversation about them. The news media rarely covers them, not fitting their notion of "newsworthy." The result is that the public rarely is invited into such educational moments of public religious education and does not engage the deep theological wisdom informing the ways churches seek to speak faithfully to the way of Jesus.

Expanding moments of public religious education is important. For example, how do religious statements become a more significant part of public conversation and the education of the public? One response is within religious communities themselves. Some of the "statements" tend to focus only on legislation and offer conclusions rather than the thinking that undergirds them. Providing the fuller, nuanced theological reflection would more effectively define convictions, illustrate approaches to theological reflection, and invite others into a conversation about visions. Such fuller discussion highlights religious groups as dialogue as partners—thoughtful colleagues.

Yet, a second response must be to find ways for these documents to become more—shared through the media, the Internet, and publication.[8] Basic documents exploring understandings of war and peace, economic justice, immigration and care for strangers, and health care would contribute to our common life together, particularly if they are occasions for inviting the public into conversation and reflection.[9] "How we do this, where, and to what extent as denominations, churches, and religious groups?" are important religious education policy questions. Assisting our members who are in public leadership to clarify religious perspectives as they communicate their leadership is one simple means. Yet more than this, we need to think of ways of inviting and contributing to public conversations about the character of our life together. We need to think of this public leadership as engaging in education of the public.[10] At this point interfaith conversation and common work are essential as people of religious commitment and integrity together seek to build on their commitments to justice and hope.

By entering the debate about and practice of public education. Faith communities teach members their traditions and practices. Congregational education affects the ways their members walk into the wider world. A wider concern for congregations and their leaders is assessing how whole communities are being educated—what is the role of schools, voluntary agencies, the media, gangs and community living, and so forth? Congregations often think about being in mission to a community, yet to what degree do congregational leaders explore and seek to understand the dimensions of community education? How many times do pastors and educators meet with school officials or other agencies of public life? Of course, in many places there are robust connections; yet thinking of affecting ways the community is educating is often a new consideration.

A second concern is the quality of public schools. We care about the effectiveness of schools in nurturing young people in vibrant and health-giving ways. When schools are failing young people and when youth drop out with little hope, churches must care. We need to seek to enhance the quality of schools. While respecting the diversity of perspectives that form public education, congregations can easily assist with ministries that support the public schools—through tutoring, financial support for activities, transportation, and so on. While a particular congregation can take the lead, interfaith religious groups supporting these schools evidences our partnerships in seeking to shape the worlds we share.

Third, churches need to ask how people are being adequately educated in schools about the meanings of religious life and faith (again respecting public diversity). While there are ways for individual congregations to support religious education in local neighborhoods, a wider and more public conversation is needed, perhaps sponsored by public religious networks like the Religious Education Association, denominations, and interfaith groups.[11] How are schools teaching the ways religious people think about their faith and public meanings and engage public life?

Some congregations participate in teaching of religion by sponsoring their own schools offering explicit religious instruction—a few in an ecumenical fashion, most in a particularist fashion—Jewish day schools, evangelical schools, private academies, Islamic schools. These "parochial alternatives" need to be respected.[12] Additionally, some congregations are exploring how they can sponsor "charter schools," either as a "religious ministry" of the congregation or, more often, a partnership with a local community. The Seton Education Partners is one example of groups exploring public and church partnerships.[13] All of these efforts are ways of seeking to provide public religious education.

On a broader note, much misunderstanding has fueled the wider public conversation about religion and education. Popularly, people believe that religion has been excised from schools. This is simply not the case. Many public schools are experimenting with how the Bible is taught, and instruction in differing religious traditions is offered. Open, inclusive study of religion and religious traditions is clearly a possibility in public education. For example, the American Academy of Religion has completed a major report entitled *Guidelines about Teaching Religion in the K–12 Public Schools in the US.*[14] Other religious groups, including the American Civil Liberties Union, have developed guidelines to assist school officials in understanding advantages and limitations in the teaching of religion in public schools.[15]

Educational scholars have written about the need for public conversation about the place of religion in public schools. They have discovered that many of the mainline religious communities who have open and critical perspectives on religious texts, life, and practice have relinquished the conversation about the content of religion in public schools to more fundamentalist religious groups or to the will of politicians. Educators Susan Rosenblith and Beatrice Bailey have called for

required religious studies courses in America's public schools as well as certified religious studies teachers. In a cantankerous and highly diverse religious country, citizens need basic content and critical skills to better appreciate and respect the religious other.[16]

A goal they call for is offering "students a place to build budding understandings of how various religious traditions deal with existential concerns that are of interest and concern within the public square."[17] Denominational boards of education and their curriculum offices should join this conversation. Moreover, they can encourage the development of curriculum resources that can be used to provide open, accurate, and critical discussion of religious issues in the public schools.[18]

Fourth, developing media resources about religion extends public religious education. Denominations usually prepare resources only for their own members. This means that other publishers or secular educators who really do not know the ways of open and critical religious scholarship develop public resources. For example, each Christmas, Hanukkah, and Easter season in the United States, television shows on channels such as the History Channel or National Geographic offer programs on biblical themes. While many of these are excellent and summarize the findings of scholarship, rarely do they invite the public into conversation about approaches to scholarship in religion, theological reflection, and historical study. For example, in late 2012, *U.S. News and World Report* published a newsmagazine in its Mysteries of Faith series, *Secrets of the Bible*. Interesting articles were published on insights about Jesus' life, whether the flood really happened, the life of Joseph Smith, and the Virgin Mary. The articles focused only on conclusions, rather than on how historical and theological scholarship about religions is accomplished. Another example, in December 17, 2012, *Newsweek* magazine published an article entitled "Who was Jesus?" It is a fine essay by religion scholar Bart Ehrman, yet it simply concluded that such things as the manger scene and the wise men were not historically accurate. It tried in limited space to name the differences between historical and theological scholarship, yet one article in one newsmagazine does not have adequate space to engage this issue. There is a hunger in the public for nuanced religious reflection—for asking why. Denominations and interfaith groups could provide these resources. A popular publication prepared for public media and sold in newsstands, like *Time* or *U.S. News and World Report* on Jesus, on Hanukkah, or on mysteries of religion, by a Christian education or interfaith group, could teach in a more depth fashion about the meanings of religious scholarship. It would embody for the public how religious decisions are made and how they affect the decision making of believers.

By being the church. What? Of course, churches seek to be the church. Yet, why is it that the Pew study discovered that people are leaving affiliation with religious groups at the same time they are very interested in spiritual and religious issues? For many, it was because of the rigidity of religious organizations, their lack of rigor, and their seeming captivity in traditional patterns of behavior and historic religious fights. Frankly, many people are bored by churches—too many churches simply lack vitality.

The church best educates the public about the way of Jesus when it embodies the passion and commitments of the way of Jesus. When it is seen wrestling with the meanings of the faith that make a profound difference in the world in which we live. Early churches in the Jesus movement made a difference in the environment of the Roman world by the ways they stood up for their values, welcomed the hurt and outcast into their congregations, faced the anger of Roman power (crucifixion and martyrdom), and sought to enhance the lives of children and communities. In other words, the passion of their caring and the passion of the ways they embodied the ways of Jesus best taught who they were. We are many years from the vitality of this renewing, revitalization movement. Things fall into a more ordinary pattern and are captured in "the ways we have always done it." Such patterns are often without vitality.

Churches who are asking fundamental questions about how they are following the marks of God's realm, living the good news, and embodying the transforming ways of Jesus in the world are teaching the passion and depth of Christian living. Those outside the faith see clearly the meanings of faith and the ways it transforms lives and communities in the actions of these faith groups.

Indeed the best public education for the church is a faithful church living its identity and vocation publicly and sharing the resources by which it makes decisions about faithfulness. Churches that embody the transforming ways of Jesus profoundly teach! They embody the depth of seeking the realm of God, of listening to the voice of God, of challenging the time of trial, and of proclaiming the new life offered in the Resurrected One.

Faithful churches clear about their convictions are the ones who are free to engage in interfaith partnerships seeking together to ameliorate pain and seeking justice. An example of an outstanding interfaith partnership for community justice is the work of Interfaith Youth Core.[19] Groups with deep, but differing religious commitments come together to build communities.

Hope for the Future

I began this study with three affirmations:

1. I believe in the transformative power of "following Jesus." Following Jesus does make a difference in lives and communities. People are changed and communities are renewed.

2. I believe that our understanding of what "following Jesus" means is enhanced with historical study and theological reflection. Christian education grounded in nuanced, depth, and critical perspectives gives content and life to following Jesus.

3. I believe Christianity can partner with people of goodwill in other faith communities to make a difference in our world—to together work for transformation.

I hope these affirmations have been clear and embodied throughout this study.

We Christians are called to follow the way of Jesus. How else can we call ourselves Christian? We have seen in our work and in our personal lives the transforming power of the ways of Jesus. Communities and people are renewed. Yet, we cannot faithfully live this way unless we continue to study, to grow, and to engage in theological reflection about its responsibilities. We are more than two thousand years from the birth of the Jesus movement. As theologians and church leaders throughout the centuries, we are called to make sense of the way of Jesus and to follow it in very different circumstances and contexts. Such a motive inspired many of the church councils and inspired public practical theological reflection. In a robust fashion, historical and theological research today has reminded us of the power and dimensions of this way. It has called us to seek an identity faithful to the way of Jesus and a vocation that follows Jesus into seeking the realm of God. Renewal and empowerment result from taking the path that Jesus offered and his disciples taught, the path of loving God and neighbor, of living in the presence of God, of looking for the realm of God, of calling people to the banquet table, of resisting the time of trial, and of proclaiming the Resurrected One. These dimensions give focus to our work. We need an effective and faithful education that continues to call us to live the ways of Jesus.

Such faithfulness will push us to reach out to other religious communities, to seek to understand their messages and convictions, and to build coalitions of care and justice in the worlds we share. Our Christian way calls us to face into the world, to follow the realm of God, and to work with all our energy for a world where God's hopes and God's renewals are possible. As we care enough to educate our members in the ways of Jesus, we care enough to share our convictions with others. As we care enough to teach the public the importance of partnership among religious groups, we build communities and live our deepest convictions.

In the early church, the church at Colossae struggled to find ways of living the vitality of the faith in a world of many religions and much diversity. One of their teachers, an apostle of Paul, used Paul's authority to point them to what was important as they faced a challenge. The leader thanked them for their faithful struggling, calling them "to live lives that are worthy," to grow in faith, and to give joy to God (Col. 1:10-12). Furthermore, he pointed to the way of Jesus: "Be rooted and built up in him, be established in faith, and overflow with thanksgiving" (Col. 2:7). He defined the way of Jesus as putting on "compassion, kindness, humility, gentleness, and patience . . . the peace of Christ" (Col. 3:12, 15). He encouraged them by describing how this could be accomplished through teaching, through community worship, through study, and through mission and ministry:

> The word of Christ must live in you richly. Teach and warn each other with all wisdom by singing psalms, hymns, and spiritual songs. Sing to God with gratitude in your hearts. Whatever you do, whether in speech or action, do it all in the name of the Lord Jesus and give thanks to God the Father through him. (Col. 3:16-17)

Isn't that the same as today, in a world of much pain and oppression and in a world where we struggle for hope and justice? Let the way of Jesus live in you richly. Teach one another with all wisdom in the many ways you can. Sing to God with gratitude. Whatever you do, be guided by the way of Jesus. Work with others, live the faith, teach others, and seek to follow the realm of God that guides our living and our being. "Join us. Through prayer and community, through study, through service, learn. Learn how to serve God and neighbor."

Notes

Introduction

1. For a full description of the titles attributed to Jesus in the Gospels, see the excellent account of Edward Adams, *Parallel Lives of Jesus: A Guide to the Four Gospels* (Louisville: Westminster John Knox, 2011). In his analysis of each gospel, he highlights the titles for Jesus—prophet, Messiah, Son of God, Son of Man, Lord, and so on. Teacher is a frequently offered title for Jesus (for example, twelve times *teacher* is used for Jesus in Mark, p. 54; in John, there are eight occasions where he is called rabbi, p. 113; and in Luke, Jesus even calls himself "the Teacher," p. 94).

2. *Realm of God* is a synonym for *kingdom of God*, the phrase used in Jesus' day and the one most often quoted in scripture. In the New Testament, "kingdom of God" is not a place; instead it denotes the times when God's acts were present and transforming living. For example, Jesus pointed the disciples of John the Baptist to moments of kingdom of God occurring in his ministry—moments of profound new life, healing, and hope (see Matt. 11:4-6). The good news is God's actions of new life—everywhere God offers grace and life. *Realm* also expands our understandings of royalty and the relationship between kings and subjects. In Jesus' day, the royalty of Rome sought to extend its hegemony across peoples of their world. This was certainly the case for Judea and Galilee. To focus on God's royalty was a profound challenge to the dominant hierarchies. Throughout this book, I will alternate between using *realm of God, kingdom of God*, and *God's acts* to denote this transforming good news to which Jesus pointed.

3. See for example, Acts 2:42, describing practices of the early community of believers: "The believers devoted themselves to the apostles' teaching, to the community, to their shared meals, and to their prayers." As with Jesus' teaching, they relied on the Law and the Prophets (Acts 13:15) as well as interpreting their own experiences with the way of Jesus.

4. The word *rabbi* is anachronistically read back into the dialogue of the disciples. While the word often meant "master" in the first century, it was only after the fall of Jerusalem and the establishment of the great center of Jewish learning at Yavneh that the word

designated a particular class of individuals who officially teach the law. That John, written after this time, would use *rabbi* for Jesus means that he was clearly designating Jesus as a rabbi and master teacher. See Adams, *Parallel Lives of Jesus*, 113.

5. From *The Book of Discipline of The United Methodist Church, 2012*. Copyright © 2012 by The United Methodist Publishing House; ¶130, page 96. Used by permission.

6. Too often those of us in the church, like Jesus' disciples, want to be in control. We are led into triumphalism. But we need to remember that Jesus chastised James and John when they begged to sit on his right hand and left hand in the kingdom. Jesus rebuked Peter for thinking he had a claim on Jesus' power. Without nuanced Christian education, we forget Jesus' challenge to his disciples.

7. Martin E. Marty, "Jews in the *Economist*," *Sightings*, July 30, 2012.

8. Susan Brooks Thistlethwaite, "The Icemen Cometh: Romney-Ryan and the future of compassion in America," August 12, 2012, http://www.washingtonpost.com/blogs/guest-voices/post/the-icemen-cometh-romney-ryan-and-the-future-of-compassion-in-america/2012/08/12/bedd9f48-e4a9-11e1-8f62-58260e3940a0_blog.html.

9. Letty M. Russell, *The Future of Partnership* (Philadelphia: Westminster, 1979), 106.

10. This book also acknowledges and seeks to partner with brothers and sisters in other faith communities working to communicate the depth and power of their religious communities for our world. Working to understand and live a way of life is at the heart of the definition of religions. Parallels are obvious in the other great Abrahamic faiths. For Jews, the way of the Torah and its history of interpretation is the guide to faithfulness. Rabbis are "teachers" who interpret the meaning of the Torah for believing and living. In fact, at Bar or Bat Mizpah services, the interpreter is the child "come of age" who interprets the text for the congregation. The child becomes a full member of the community by demonstrating the ability to interpret living in light of the Torah. The child calls the community to its identity and vocation as people of the covenant, God's people to whom God gave the Torah. A similar pattern is true in Islam. The word *Islam* means "submission to God." Teachers are spiritual leaders who seek to understand and "teach" God's ways as communicated in the Qur'an. See for example the important interfaith text edited by Hanan A. Alexander and Ayman K. Agbaria, *Commitment, Character, and Citizenship: Religious Education in Liberal Democracy* (New York: Routledge, 2012).

11. Johannes Baptist Metz, *Theology of the World* (n.p.: Herder and Herder, 1969). See also his collaboration with Jürgen Moltmann to discuss ministry, the church, and political theology in *Faith and the Future: Essays on Theology, Solidarity, and Modernity* (Maryknoll, NY: Orbis Books, 1995).

12. For a beginning see Amy-Jill Levine, *The Misunderstood Jew: The Church and the Scandal of The Jewish Jesus* (New York: HarperOne, 2007); Richard A. Horsley, *Bandits, Prophets, and Messiahs: Popular Movements at The Time of Jesus* (Harrisburg, PA: Trinity Press International, 1999); Warren Carter, *The Roman Empire and The New Testament: An Essential Guide* (Nashville: Abingdon, 2006); Craig A. Evans, *Jesus and His World: The Archaeological Evidence* (Louisville: Westminster John Knox, 2012); and Seth Schwartz, *Imperialism and Jewish Society: 200 B.C.E. to 640 C.E.* (Princeton, NJ: Princeton University Press, 2004).

13. In fact, scholarship is part of that partnership. This book will use resources drawn from Jewish and Christian contexts to assist in understanding the Second Temple period and the time of Jesus. See for example, Alan F. Segal, *Rebecca's Children: Judaism and Christianity in the Roman World* (Cambridge, MA: Harvard University Press, 1986).

14. Marty, "Jews in the *Economist*."

15. Jack L. Seymour and Donald E. Miller, eds., *Contemporary Approaches to Christian Education* (Nashville: Abingdon, 1982).

16. Jack L. Seymour, ed., *Mapping Christian Education: Approaches to Congregational Learning* (Nashville: Abingdon, 1997).

1. Following Jesus

1. At this time, synagogues were not yet properly places or buildings. Sabbath gatherings most probably occurred in houses and sometimes in public places, a hall, or even the marketplace. The earliest formal synagogue buildings found date from the third or fourth century. See William R. Herzog, *Prophet and Teacher: An Introduction to the Historical Jesus* (Louisville: Westminster John Knox, 2005), 72–74. This gathering was either in the home of a community leader or the village marketplace.

2. Dwayne Huebner, *The Lure of the Transcendent: Collected Essays by Dwayne E. Huebner*, ed. Vikki Hillis (New York: Routledge, 1999), 39, 360–61.

3. See Warren Carter, *The Roman Empire and The New Testament: An Essential Guide* (Nashville: Abingdon, 2006), 66, 72.

4. Seth Schwartz, *Imperialism and Jewish Society: 200 B.C.E. to 640 C.E.* (Princeton, NJ: Princeton University Press, 2004).

5. See John Dominic Crossan, *God and Empire: Jesus against Rome, Then and Now* (New York: HarperOne, 2007).

6. See *Josephus: The Complete Works* (Nashville: Thomas Nelson, 2003).

7. During the Seleucid control of Judea, practicing and worshiping on Shabbat was outlawed, as was the reading of the Torah. To address this ban, the people read secretly at home. In addition, they developed a set of readings from the prophetic books. These became the *haphtarah*—or more directly translated, "after the Torah," to be read in synagogue after the Torah was read. This is a practice today. Jewish scholarship indicates that the practice of reading the *haphtarah* was widespread from its beginning in the Seleucid period. Many of the synagogues in Jesus' day read the *haphtarah* and the Torah. "The custom was instituted during the persecutions by Antiochus Epiphanes which preceded the Hasmonean revolt. . . . When the reading of the Torah was proscribed, a substitute was found by reading a corresponding portion from the Prophets; and the custom was retained after the decree was repealed." (Louis Isaac Rabinowitz, "Haphtarah," in *Encyclopedia Judaica*, ed. Michael Berenbaum and Fred Skolnik, 2nd ed., vol. 8. [Macmillan Reference USA, Keter, 2007], 199). In fact, a reference to the reading of the *haphtarah* appears in Acts 13:15 (also written by the author of the Gospel of Luke), recording an event where Paul preached in Antioch: "After the reading of the Law and Prophets, the synagogue leaders invited them, 'Brothers if one of you has a sermon for the people, please

speak.'" The Law, the Torah, was read, and it was followed by the reading of the Prophets, the *haphtarah*. While today specific *haphtarah* texts are assigned for each Shabbat, that was not yet the case in the first century CE. The earliest Jewish reference to specific texts dates from the second and third centuries (*Megilla*, 4.3; see again the Rabinowitz essay on "Haphtarah," p. 199.) Therefore, synagogues that used *haphtarah* would have their own patterns. The author of Luke clearly knew that both Torah and *haphtarah* were read in synagogues along with sermons and appointed prayers. The Talmud mentions that the *haphtarah* was read when Rabbi Eliezer, who was a contemporary of Luke, was alive ("Haphtarah," p. 199). See also "Haphtarah," *Jewish Encyclopedia*, http://www.jewish encyclopedia.com. The synagogue in Jesus' hometown could easily have had a practice of reading a *haphtarah* passage, and that was Isaiah 61. In fact, that is precisely what Rabinowitz sees in the Luke 4 passage. See also Amy-Jill Levine, "The Gospel According to Luke," in *The Jewish Annotated New Testament*, ed. Amy-Jill Levine and Marc Zvi Brettler (New York: Oxford University Press, 2011), 106.

8. Remember both the Torah and the *haphtarah* were written on scrolls. To read, one had to unroll a scroll. It is very difficult to move around in a scroll. Large scrolls had to be unrolled and rerolled to move forward or backward—not the easy process of turning a page. In Jewish synagogues the Torah scroll is unrolled a bit each week to read the appointed lesson; the next immediately follows—a much easier process. In this passage in Luke, no mention is made of the Torah reading that must have been prior. When Jesus was given the scroll, the text reads, "The synagogue assistant gave him the scroll of the prophet Isaiah. He unrolled the scroll and *found* the place where it was written" (Luke 4:17). The translation of the Greek word for "found" is somewhat ambiguous, yet it appears that it meant that he moved to the marked place for the reading of the text—a very typical practice. The Greek word used is ευρισκω, "to find"; it usually means an accidental finding, or finding something placed by someone else. Jesus is not said to "seek and find" the place where it was written, which normally would have been said if he had chosen the text. Rather, he only "finds" it, perhaps implying that it was marked for the service. While the exact translation is definitely ambiguous, it is probable that Jesus simply read the appointed text for the day.

9. We know that the Gospels interpreted remembered events, parables, and stories of Jesus' life through the eyes of believers a few generations later—believers who had experienced the transforming power of the Resurrected One. What if Luke added his interpretation to an earlier memory—of Jesus' first sermon at home? We know Luke did this often. He was writing years later at a time when the delay of both the expected return of Jesus and of the kingdom of God were being discussed. These events, as well as his deeply held beliefs, affected his writing. He began his writing with the acknowledgment that there were other stories of Jesus' life that he wanted to set straight—telling Theophilus the truth.

10. In fact, this historical memory is also clearly present to Mark. See Mark 6:2-6.

11. Whether this first section of Isaiah was ever included in versions of the *haphtarah*, we do not know. It is not included today. Yet, as the emerging Christian movement would use this text to refer to Jesus and as Christian oppression of Jews intensified,

certain passages were excluded from weekly Jewish readings. It is clearly possible that a text once read in a synagogue gathering in Jesus' time was later dropped from the final determination of *haphtarah* readings. See Hananel Mack, "What happened to Jesus' haftarah?" *Haaretz Daily Newspaper*, August 12, 2005, http://www.haaretz.com/news/what-happened-to-jesus-haftarah-1.166699, where Mack reports an extensive discussion at the 14th Congress of Jewish Studies held in Jerusalem. The conclusion of the scholars was that typically, "the rabbis who instituted weekly readings from the Prophets as part of the Sabbath liturgy excluded all the biblical verses on which Christians based their principles of faith," particularly those used as christological passages. Therefore, "the heads of Jewish communities, who had some familiarity with Christian faith and literature, preferred to refrain from reading the same chapter Jesus read in the synagogue in Nazareth," because it was used by Christians to define his mission. "This point is especially noteworthy given the fact that the chapters preceding and following that problematic passage chapter 60, and the end of chapter 61 and chapters 62 and 63, respectively are read each year in public as haftarot."

12. An online version of the Tanakh is available at http://www.jewishvirtuallibrary.org/jsource/Bible/Deuter30.html

13. Martin E. Marty, "Jews in the *Economist*," *Sightings*, July 30, 2012.

14. I appreciate the argument about redemption and redemptive community found in Marianne Sawicki's two books on the educational development of the Jesus movement. Sawicki seeks to describe how the new life experienced in Jesus was communicated in the proclamation of the resurrection. Those after Jesus could continue to see the miracles of healing, sight, feeding, and release, of intimacy with God, and of new community occurring. *The Gospel in History: Portrait of a Teaching Church* (Mahwah, NJ: Paulist, 1988); and *Seeing the Lord: Resurrection and Early Christian Practices* (n.p.: Augsburg Fortress, 1994). Sawicki asks: "How did the telling transform the quality of human living for ordinary people?" (*Gospel in History*, 7). Also, for a theological description of "redemptive existence," see Edward Farley, *Ecclesial Man: A Social Phenomenology of Faith and Reality* (Philadelphia: Fortress, 1975); and Mary McClintock Fulkerson, *Places of Redemption: Theology for a Worldly Church* (Oxford, UK: Oxford University Press, 2007).

15. I particularly want to thank my colleagues Dr. Osvaldo Vena, professor of New Testament interpretation; Dr. Brooke Lester, director of emerging technologies and assistant professor of Hebrew Bible, and Dr. Dwight Vogel, professor emeritus of theology, for their questions, comments, and assistance with this chapter. They raised important questions about the interpretation of Luke 4, about its relationship to the theology of the author of Luke, and about the translation of the Greek word translated "found," as it is ambiguous.

2. The Imperative for Christian Education

1. *The Jewish Annotated New Testament*, ed. Amy-Jill Levine and Marc Zvi Brettler (New York: Oxford University Press, 2011), 216.

2. For a discussion of the early interpretations of the death and resurrection of Jesus, see Daniel Boyarin, *The Jewish Gospels: The Story of the Jewish Christ* (New York: New Press, 2012).

3. Edward Farley, *The Fragility of Knowledge: Theological Education in the Church and University* (Philadelphia: Fortress Press, 1988), 92.

4. See Margaret Ann Crain and Jack Seymour, *Yearning for God: Reflections of Faithful Lives* (Nashville: Upper Room Books, 2003).

5. Diana Butler Bass, *Christianity for the Rest of Us: How the Neighborhood Church Is Transforming the Faith* (New York: HarperOne, 2006).

6. Diana Butler Bass, "A Resurrected Christianity?" Religion, *Huffington Post*, April 7, 2012. http://www.huffingtonpost.com/diana-butler-bass/a-resurrected-christianit_b_1410143 .html. See a fuller development of Bass's ideas in *Christianity after Religion: The End of Church and the Birth of a New Spiritual Awakening* (New York: HarperOne, 2012).

7. See the outstanding book by Fred Edie that examines baptism and Eucharist as educational practices. Fred P. Edie, *Book, Bath, Table, and Time: Christian Worship as Source and Resource for Youth Ministry* (Cleveland: Pilgrim Press, 2007).

8. *The United Methodist Hymnal: Book of United Methodist Worship* (Nashville: United Methodist Publishing House, 1989), 34.

9. An example is the "Nothing but Nets" project seeking to end malaria in Africa. See www.nothingbutnets.net. This is a project of the National Basketball Association and several religious groups to provide mosquito netting throughout Africa. The result has been a significant drop in cases of malaria. One partner, The United Methodist Church, has committed to seek to eliminate diseases of poverty (see http://www.umc.org/site/c .lwL4KnN1LtH/b.2558027/k.9640/Nothing_But_Nets_Resources.htm).

10. Martin Luther King Jr., *Letter from Birmingham Jail* (Stamford: Overbrook Press, 1963).

11. Joseph E. Stiglitz, *The Price of Inequality: How Today's Divided Society Endangers Our Future* (New York: W. W. Norton, 2012).

12. Peter Singer, *Practical Ethics*, 3rd ed. (New York: Cambridge University Press, 2011).

13. Diana Butler Bass, "The End of Church," Religion, *Huffington Post*, February 18, 2012. http://www.huffingtonpost.com/diana-butler-bass/the-end-of -church_b_1284954.html.

14. Lee Cowan, "Coming Home," *CBS Sunday Morning News*, June 17, 2012.

15. Protestants for the Common Good, "Programs," accessed July 18, 2013, http:// www.thecommongood.org/programs/.

16. See, for example, the United Methodist Board of Church and Society, which authors the *Faith in Action* newsletter; the Just and Witness Ministries of the United Church of Christ (http://www.ucc.org/jwm/); or the comparable Compassion, Peace and Justice Division of the Presbyterian Mission Agency (http://www.presbyterianmission .org/ministries/compassion-peace-justice/).

17. Bass, "The End of Church."

18. Linda Mercandante, "The Seeker Next Door: What Drives the Spiritual but

Not Religious," *Christian Century*, May 18, 2012, http://www.christiancentury.org
/article/2012-05/seeker-next-door?

19. Ibid.

20. John Roberto, *Faith Formation 2020: Designing the Future of Faith Formation*
(Naugatuck, CT: Lifelong Faith Associates, 2010).

21. For Brooke Lester, see http://anumma.com or www.brookelester.com, and for
Jim Papandrea, see http://www.jimpapandrea.com/Jim_Papandrea/Jim_L._Papandrea
_Ph.D..html and www.Romesick.net.

22. Some of the ideas developed before in this chapter as well as the central convictions of this section of the chapter were previously expressed in my article "Religious Education among Friends and Strangers: Contributions of Revisionist Educational History to
Public Living," in *Autobiography and Pedagogical Theories in Religious Education*, ed. Ina
ter Avest and Gerdien Bertram-Troost (Amsterdam: Sense, 2012).

23. Lawrence A. Cremin, *American Education: The Colonial Experience 1607–1783*
(New York: Harper and Row, 1970): xiii. See also his *American Education: The National
Experience 1783–1876* (New York: Harper and Row, 1982); and *American Education: The
Metropolitan Experience* (New York: Harper and Row, 1990).

24. Dan McAdams, *The Stories We Live By: Personal Myths and the Making of Self*
(New York: Guilford, 1997).

25. Dan P. McAdams, *The Redemptive Self: Stories Americans Live By* (New York:
Oxford University Press, 2005).

26. Amy Frykholm, "Culture Changers: David Hollinger on What the Mainline
Achieved," *Christian Century* 129 (July 11, 2012): 26, http://www.christiancentury.org
/article/2012-06/culture-changers.

27. Ibid.

28. James Carroll, *Jerusalem, Jerusalem: How the Ancient City Ignited Our Modern
World* (New York: Houghton Mifflin, 2011), 189–90.

29. Frykholm, "Culture Changers," 28.

30. Lawrence A. Cremin, *Public Education* (New York: Basic Books, 1976), 96.

3. The People of God as Theologians

1. In Mark, she is called a Syro-Phoenician woman after the Roman province for
which Tyre was capital.

2. *Chicago Tribune*, September 23, 2010, sec. 1, p. 16.

3. Evelyn L. Parker, *Trouble Don't Last Always: Emancipatory Hope among African
American Adolescents* (Cleveland: Pilgrim Press, 2003), 125.

4. Ibid., 29.

5. Margaret Ann Crain and Jack Seymour, *Yearning for God: Reflections of Faithful
Lives* (Nashville: Upper Room, 2003), 139.

6. Ibid.

7. In the following pages, the stories of "Julia," "Frederick," and "Delia" are used to
explore the yearnings of the people of God that lead to theological reflection. Parts of

these stories were shared in *Yearning for God*. Where quotations are used from that book, they are noted. Other quotations are from personal interviews. The names are pseudonyms, and the stories are used with the permission of those interviewed.

8. Reginald Blount, in a similar study with youth, has identified the yearnings of identity, intimacy with God, purpose, healing, being mentored, nurture, and courage. Reginald Blount, "In Search of Living Waters: The Seven Spiritual Yearnings of Youth," Princeton Theological Seminary, Institute for Youth Ministry, 2005, http://www.ptsem .edu/uploadedFiles/School_of_Christian_Vocation_and_Mission/Institute_for_Youth _Ministry/Princeton_Lectures/Blount-Search.pdf.

9. Crain and Seymour, *Yearning for God*, 16.

10. Ibid. See a fuller description of Frederick's story on pp. 13–25, 143–44.

11. Ibid., 17.

12. For a fuller description of Delia's story, see *Yearning for God*, 132–35.

13. Ibid., 16.

14. Ibid., 55.

15. Ibid., 56. For a fuller description of Julia's story, see pp. 51–56, 139–40.

16. James E. Loder, *The Transforming Moment*, 2nd ed. (Colorado Springs: Helmers & Howard, 1989).

17. Later in this manuscript, in chapter 5, I summarize this process of theological meaning making, highlighting the terms *considering*, *exploring*, and *discerning*.

18. David Heller, *The Children's God* (Chicago: University of Chicago Press, 1986).

19. Dr. Blount draws on the work of educator and philosopher bell hooks, *Teaching to Transgress: Education as the Practice of Freedom* (New York: Routledge, 1994).

20. See Isa Aron et al., *Sacred Strategies: Transforming Synagogues from Functional to Visionary* (Herndon, VA: Alban Institute, 2010). This book is part of a project to enhance the lives of synagogues with strategies of education and leadership. See also www .synagogue3000.org.

4. Community and Prayer

1. Daniel Boyarin, *The Jewish Gospels: The Story of the Jewish Christ* (New York: New Press, 2012), 102–28. See Boyarin's interpretation of Mark's presentation of Jesus' understanding of kosher.

2. An excellent discussion of "fencing the Torah," taken from the *Mishnah Aboth* 1:1 is provided by Bernard Brandon Scott in his *Hear Then the Parable: Commentary on the Parables of Jesus* (n.p.: Augsburg Fortress, 1989), 230–31: "The Torah is Israel's joy, that which sets it apart from the nations. As the first saying in *Aboth* proposes, 'Be deliberate in judgment, raise up many disciples, and make a fence around the law.' One of Israel's important responses to the law is its preservation, its protection. . . . The Torah is something to be protected, a trust, but it is also a burden." It is to be lived to demonstrate the greatness and graciousness of Israel's God.

3. C. Ellis Nelson, *Where Faith Begins* (Louisville: John Knox, 1971) and John Westerhoff III, *Will Our Children Have Faith?* (New York: Seabury, 1976). The work of both has continued to influence Christian education. Before his recent death, Nelson published in 2008 *Growing Up Christian? A Congregational Strategy for Nurturing Disciples* (Macon, GA: Smyth and Helwys, 2008). In addition to completing a revised version of *Will Our Children Have Faith?*, 3rd rev. ed. (Harrisburg, PA: Morehouse, 2012), Westerhoff has continued to write about liturgy, spirituality, and Episcopal identity. One example is his *A Pilgrim People: Learning through the Church Year* (New York: Seabury, 2004). For a fuller description of the work of Westerhoff, Nelson, and many of the others mentioned in this chapter, see Kevin E. Lawson, "Christian Leaders of the 20th Century," Talbot School of Theology web page, accessed July 18, 2013, http://www2.talbot.edu/ce20/.

4. Westerhoff, *Will Our Children Have Faith?*, 70.

5. See for example the work of George Albert Coe, *A Social Theory of Religious Education* (n.p.: Scribners, 1917).

6. Maria Harris, *Fashion Me a People: Curriculum in the Church* (Louisville: Westminster John Knox, 1989), 15.

7. Charles R. Foster, *From Generation to Generation: The Adaptive Challenge of Mainline Protestant Education in Forming Faith* (Eugene, OR: Cascade Books, 2012), 97.

8. Ibid., 98.

9. Ibid., 98–99.

10. The project Synagogue 2000 has been enlarged to Synagogue 3000. See www.synagogue3000.org. See also Lawrence Hoffman, *Rethinking Synagogues: A New Vocabulary for Congregational Life* (Woodstock, VT: Jewish Lights, 2006); and Isa Aron et al., *Sacred Strategies: Transforming Synagogues from Functional to Visionary* (Herndon, VA: Alban Institute, 2010).

11. Hoffman, *Rethinking Synagogues*, 181.

12. Ibid. 192.

13. See ibid., 91.

14. Diana Butler Bass, *Christianity for the Rest of Us: How the Neighborhood Church Is Transforming the Faith* (New York: HarperOne, 2007).

15. Ibid., 130.

16. Craig Dykstra, *Growing in the Life of Faith: Education and Christian Practices* (Louisville: Geneva Press, 1999), 69–70. Also look at how Charles Foster describes three kinds of teaching/learning processes: *developmental learning* (completing developmental tasks), *practice learning* (preparation for participation in a community), and *discovery learning* (seeking to extend a community's meaning into the future). Foster believes that mainline churches have failed to attend to practice learning. See his *From Generation to Generation*, 29–37, 74–95.

17. Dykstra, *Growing in the Life of Faith*, 42–43.

18. For example, see Dorothy C. Bass, ed., *Practicing Our Faith: A Way of Life for a Searching People*, 2nd ed. (San Francisco: Jossey-Bass, 2010). Or look at www.practicingourfaith.org to see the list of specialty studies on individual practices and those across the life cycle.

19. Charles R. Foster, *Educating Congregations: The Future of Christian Education* (Nashville: Abingdon, 1994). Also see Foster's description of the loss of a compelling narrative in *From Generation to Generation*, 62–66.

20. Foster, *From Generation to Generation*, 104–5. See his fuller description on pages 138–42.

21. See John Dominic Crossan and Jonathan L. Reed, *Excavating Jesus: Beneath the Stones, Behind the Texts* (New York: HarperSanFrancisco, 2001), 49–50, 137, 231–34.

22. "A Double Take on Early Christianity: An Interview with Rodney Stark," July 22, 2004, http://www.jknirp.com/stark.htm.

23. See the description of these early communities and their development in Rodney Stark, *Cities of God: The Real Story of How Christianity Became an Urban Movement and Conquered Rome* (New York: HarperOne, 2007).

24. Foster, *Educating Congregations*, 31.

25. See Jack L. Seymour, Charles R. Foster, and Robert O'Gorman, *The Church in the Education of the Public: Refocusing the Task of Religious Education* (Nashville: Abingdon, 1984).

26. Katherine Turpin, *Branded: Adolescents Converting from Consumer Culture* (Cleveland: Pilgrim Press, 2006).

27. See Mary McClintock Fulkerson's amazing study of the Good Samaritan United Methodist Church that intentionally sought to embody commitments to justice, diversity, and inclusion. *Places of Redemption: Theology for a Worldly Church* (New York: Oxford University Press, 2007).

28. Craig Dykstra and Dorothy Bass, *For Life Abundant: Practical Theology, Theological Education, and Christian Ministry* (Grand Rapids: Eerdmans, 2008).

29. Mary Elizabeth Mullino Moore, *Teaching as a Sacramental Act* (Cleveland: Pilgrim Press, 2004), 223–24.

30. Kenda Creasy Dean, *Almost Christian: What the Faith of Our Teenagers Is Telling the American Church* (New York: Oxford University Press, 2010).

31. For these planning tasks, I would recommend Moore, *Teaching as a Sacramental Act*, 221–28, "Planning for the Future"; or Foster, *Educating Congregations*, 136–55, "A Guide to Revisioning Local Church Education." There are many others, and leaders can create their own. Nevertheless, the task is theological analysis, to look for God's presence and calling and plan and enact ministries.

5. Study

1. See the reference in chapter 3 to James Loder's work on transforming moments in learning.

2. Elizabeth Caldwell, *Making a Home for Faith: Nurturing the Spiritual Life of Your Children* (Cleveland: Pilgrim Press, 2000). See also her "Religious Instruction: Homemaking," in *Mapping Christian Education: Approaches to Congregational Learning*, ed. Jack L. Seymour (Nashville: Abingdon, 1997), 74–79.

3. Sara P. Little, "Religious Instruction," 35–52, in *Contemporary Approaches to Chris-*

tian Education, ed. Jack L. Seymour and Donald E. Miller (Nashville: Abingdon, 1982), 41. Also see her outstanding book on approaches to teaching Christian faith, *To Set One's Heart: Belief and Teaching in the Church* (Louisville: Westminster John Knox, 1983).

4. Caldwell, "Religious Instruction: Homemaking," 79–80.

5. Edward Farley, *Practicing Gospel: Unconventional Thoughts on the Church's Ministry* (Louisville: Westminster John Knox, 2003), 119.

6. Ibid., 129.

7. Ibid., xiv.

8. Little, *To Set One's Heart*.

9. Farley, *Practicing Gospel*, 7.

10. Carol Lakey Hess, *Caretakers of Our Common House: Women's Development in Communities of Faith* (Nashville: Abingdon, 1997).

11. Thomas H. Groome, *Will There Be Faith? A New Vision for Educating and Growing Disciples* (New York: HarperOne, 2011); Anne Streaty Wimberly, *Soul Stories: African American Christian Education*, rev. ed. (Nashville: Abingdon, 2005); and Dori Ginenko Baker, *Doing Girlfriend Theology: God-Talk with Young Women* (Cleveland: Pilgrim, 2005).

12. See the teaching as discernment model of Christian religious instruction presented in Jack Seymour, Margaret Ann Crain, and Joseph Crockett, *Educating Christians* (Nashville: Abingdon, 1993), 151.

13. Catherine Albanese, *America: Religions and Religion*, 5th ed. (Belmont, CA: Wadsworth, 2012).

14. See Dori Grinenko Baker, *The Barefoot Way: A Faith Guide for Youth, Young Adults, and the People Who Walk with Them* (Louisville: Westminster John Knox, 2012). For her book on which the research for this method is based, see *Doing Girlfriend Theology: God-Talk with Young Women*.

15. Baker, *The Barefoot Way*, 112, paraphrased.

16. See Howard Gardner, *Multiple Intelligences: New Horizons in Theory and Practice* (New York: Basic Books, 2006).

17. Thomas Armstrong, *Multiple Intelligences in the Classroom*, 3rd ed. (Alexandria, VA: Association of Supervision and Curriculum Development, 2009).

18. See David Levenson, "Messianic Movements," in *The Jewish Annotated New Testament*, ed. Amy-Jill Levine and Marc Zvi Brettler (New York: Oxford University Press, 2011), 530–35.

19. See Josephus, *Antiquities of the Jews*, bk. 20, chap 9.

20. See, for example, the discussion of Geza Vermes, *The Authentic Gospel of Jesus* (London: Penguin Books, 2004) or his *Jesus the Jew* (Minneapolis: Fortress, 1981).

21. See the commentary in *Jewish Annotated New Testament*, 11–12.

22. Caldwell, "Religious Instruction: Homemaking," 79–80.

23. Walter Feinberg, *For Goodness Sake: Religious Schools and Education for Democratic Citizenry* (New York: Routledge, 2006), 18.

24. Ibid., 46.

25. Ibid., 69

26. Ibid., 72–75.

27. Ibid., 82–83.

28. See Feinberg, *For Goodness Sake*, 212; and also Jack Seymour, "Religious Education among Friends and Strangers: Contributions of Revisionist Educational History to Public Living," in *On the Edge: (Auto)biography and Pedagogical Theories on Religious Education*, ed. Ina ter Avest (Amsterdam: Sense Publishers, 2012), 175–85.

29. Look at the website for the Protestants for the Common Good. They combine theological reflection with analysis of significant social justice issues. See www.thecommongood.org.

30. The website for Urban Village church details the church's mission and its activities, including educational sessions on important public topics. See www.urbanvillagechurch.org.

31. See www.couragerenewal.org. Parker Palmer, *Healing the Heart of Democracy: The Courage to Create a Politics Worthy of the Human Spirit* (New York: Jossey-Bass, 2011).

32. Elizabeth Caldwell, *God's Big Table: Nurturing Children in a Diverse World* (Cleveland: Pilgrim Press, 2011), 6.

6. Service

1. See Josephus, *Jewish Wars*, bk 2. There is an allusion to Judas's actions in Acts: "At the time of the census, Judas the Galilean appeared and got some people to follow him in revolt. He was killed too, and all his followers scattered far and wide" (5:37).

2. Letty M. Russell, *Christian Education in Mission* (Philadelphia: Westminster Press, 1967), 9. For a fuller description of Letty Russell's work, see Barbara Anne Keely's essay "Letty Russell" in the Christian Educators of the Twentieth Century project on Talbot School of Theology's website, http://www2.talbot.edu/ce20/educators/view.cfm?n=letty_russell.

3. Letty M. Russell, *Growth in Partnership* (Philadelphia: Westminster Press, 1982), 12.

4. Ibid., 147.

5. See Allen Moore's distinction in "Liberation and the Future of Christian Education," in *Contemporary Approaches to Christian Education*, ed. Jack L. Seymour and Donald E. Miller (Nashville: Abingdon, 1982), 103–22.

6. See Ana Maria Araújo Freire and Donald Macedo, eds., *The Paulo Freire Reader* (New York: Continuum, 1998).

7. For a fuller description of Freire's work, see Roberta Clare's essay "Paulo Freire" in the Christian Educators of the Twentieth Century project on Talbot School of Theology's website, http://www2.talbot.edu/ce20/educators/view.cfm?n=paulo_freire. For an essay on Freire's understanding of church, see Paulo Freire, "Education, Liberation and the Church," *Religious Education* 79 (1984): 524–45. For an essay on his understanding of Jesus as teacher, see "Know, Practice and Teach the Gospels," *Religious Education* 79 (1984): 547–48.

8. The story of this transformation is found in Margaret Ann Crain, "Staying Awake: When God Moments Echo in Community," 33-56, in *Greenhouses of Hope: Congregations Growing Young Leaders Who Will Change the World*, ed. Dori Grinenko Baker (Herndon, VA: Alban Institute, 2010).

9. Moore, "Liberation and the Future of Christian Education," 110.

10. Evelyn L. Parker, *Trouble Don't Last Always: Emancipatory Hope among African American Adolescents* (Cleveland: Pilgrim Press, 2003), 29, 11.

11. Ibid., 146.

12. Daniel Schipani, "Educating for Social Transformation," in *Mapping Christian Education*, ed. Jack L. Seymour (Nashville: Abingdon, 1997), 26.

13. Anne Streaty Wimberly, *Soul Stories: African American Christian Education* (Nashville: Abingdon, 1994), 24–26.

14. Katherine Turpin, *Branded: Adolescents Converting from Consumer Faith* (Cleveland: Pilgrim Press, 2006).

15. Schipani, "Educating for Social Transformation," 40.

16. Russell, *Growth in Partnership*, 151–61.

17. See Shusaku Endo, *Silence* (Marlboro, NJ: Taplinger, 1969); and *A Life of Jesus* (Mahwah, NJ: Paulist Press, 1973).

18. See Mai-Anh Le Tran, "*HIC SUNT DRACONES* ("Here be dragons"): Global Cartography, Transnational Pedagogy, Religious Formation, and Learning," *Religious Education* 106 (July–September 2011): 425–35.

19. See "Asian Jesus," Radio National (Australia), September 15, 2012, http://www.abc.net.au/radionational/programs/encounter/asian-jesus/4255030.

20. Catherine L. Albanese, *America: Religion and Religions*, 5th ed. (Belmont, CA: Wadsworth, 2012).

21. Fred Smith and Charles R. Foster, *Black Religious Experience: Conversations on Double Consciousness and the Work of Grant Shockley* (Nashville, Abingdon, 2004).

22. Paulo Freire, *Cultural Action for Freedom* (n.p.: Harvard Educational Review, 2000).

23. Paulo Freire, *Pedagogy of the Oppressed*, 30th anniversary ed. (New York: Continuum, 2000).

24. Freire, "Education, Liberation and the Church," 526. See also Paulo Freire in Rex Harris, *Risk: Pilgrims of the Obvious* (n.p., 1975), 11.

25. Tran, "*HIC SUNT DRACONES*," 433.

26. Don C. Richter, *Mission Trips That Matter: Embodied Faith for the Sake of the World* (Nashville: Upper Room Press, 2008).

27. Tran, "*HIC SUNT DRACONES*," 428–35.

28. Crain, "Staying Awake," 33–34, 50–51.

29. Ibid., 36.

30. Schipani, "Educating for Social Transformation," 29.

31. Note also that Jesus was the first to be told of John's death (Matt. 14:12).

32. See also Exodus 8:19 and Deuteronomy 9:10.

33. John Dominic Crossan and Jonathan Reed, *Excavating Jesus: Beneath the Stones, Behind the Texts* (New York: HarperSanFrancisco, 2001), 49–50, 231–34.

34. See how the name of the "demons" in Mk 5:9-13 and Lk 8: 30-33 is "legion," the name of the Roman troops.

35. Jacob Dharmaraj, "The Oak Creek tragedy: A reflection from a 'voice from below,'" General Board of Church and Society of The United Methodist Church, August 27, 2012, http://umc-gbcs.org/faith-in-action/the-oak-creek-tragedy.

36. Evelyn L. Parker, *The Sacred Selves of Adolescent Girls: Hard Stories of Race, Class, and Gender* (Eugene, OR: Wipf and Stock, 2010).

37. Philip J. Hughes et al., *Exploring What Australians Value* (n.p.: Openbooks, 2003).

38. See Douglas John Hall, *Waiting for Gospel: An Appeal to the Dispirited Remnants of Protestant Establishment* (Eugene, OR: Cascade, 2012).

39. See Charles R. Foster, *From Generation to Generation* (Eugene, OR: Cascade, 2012), 79.

40. See Sondra Matthaei, *Making Disciples: Faith Formation in the Wesleyan Tradition* (Nashville: Abingdon, 2000).

41. Freire, "Education, Liberation and the Church," 524.

42. Ibid., 529.

43. The 2012 meeting of the Religious Education Association focused on the theme "Let Freedom Ring"—attending to the role of religious groups in promoting peace, justice, community, and freedom. Several of the essays prepared for the conference explore approaches to religious education approximating and developing this "new apprenticeship." See the proceedings of the conference at www.religiouseducation.net. For example, examine Jennifer Ayres, "Lives Worth Living: Religious Education and Social Movements"; Susanne Johnson, "Class Matters in an Age of Empire: 'Fugitive Democracy' and 'Fugitive Christianity' in the Quest for Justice"; Ryan Nilsen, "The National Farm Worker Ministry as Freirian Apprenticeship"; Meredith Hoxie Schol, "A Habitus of Resistance."

44. Rodney Stark, *The Rise of Christianity: How the Obscure, Marginal Jesus Movement Became the Dominant Religious Force in the Western World in a Few Centuries* (New York: HarperSanFrancisco, 1997).

7. Living the Way of Jesus

1. See the commentary on this prayer in *The Jewish Annotated New Testament*, ed. Amy-Jill Levine and Marc Zvi Brettler (New York: Oxford, 2011), 13, 125.

2. See how Levine and Brettler explain the very ambiguity of the term in their discussions of Matt. 6 and Luke 11.

3. In fact, as theologian Michael L. Cook states, the Lord's Prayer is a very Jewish prayer, reflecting deep commitments to Jewish understandings of God's actions and of God's grace. It is a prayer, Cook says, that could be shared in interfaith setting, except for the fact that Christian abuse of Jews and the use of it by Christians to spread hatred

tarnishes it. Michael L. Cook, *Justice, Jesus and the Jews: A Proposal for Jewish Christian Relations* (Collegeville, MN: Liturgical Press, 2003), 6–7.

4. See Amy-Jill Levine, *The Misunderstood Jew* (New York: HarperSanFrancisco, 2006), 22–25.

5. Rodney Stark, *The Rise of Christianity* (New York: HarperSanFrancisco, 1997).

6. The very decision about how to list these six factors is itself an exercise in pedagogy. I have basically used the order in Jesus' prayer. Many in today's church might begin with proclaiming the resurrected one, thus highlighting the difference that Jesus has made in people's lives and the centrality of Jesus in Christian witness. They would then move to living in God's grace and loving God and neighbor to focus on the nature of Christian life. This version, however, would not have the edge and the transformative character that I believe was true of Jesus' own day and following. In Jesus' day, the attention would have been on resisting the time of trial—oppression was a ubiquitous reality into which Jesus was born. Loving God and neighbor was taught daily through the practices of Jewish life in Galilee. The attention Jesus gave to looking for the realm of God and living in God's grace were the powerful transforming elements that focused the life of the early Jesus community on calling people to the banquet table and proclaiming the Resurrected One, thus focusing the early community on the new life and transformation that came through following the way of Jesus.

7. Marianne Sawicki, *Seeing the Lord: Resurrection and Early Christian Practices* (Minneapolis: Fortress, 1994), 39–50.

8. Rodney Stark, *Cities of God* (New York: HarperSanFrancisco, 2006).

9. Parenthetically, this is why the offense of the Corinthians is so important. They were redeveloping hierarchies and denying the experiences of salvation, renewal, and community that had been true in their experience.

10. Osvaldo Vena, "The Markan Construction of Jesus as Disciple of the Kingdom," in *Mark: Texts @ Contexts*, ed. Nicole Wilkinson Duran, Teresa Okure, and Daniel M. Patte (Minneapolis: Fortress, 2010), 71–100.

8. Teaching the Way of Jesus

1. Rodney Stark, *The Rise of Christianity* (New York: HarperCollins, 1997), 158.

2. NothingButNets is an international coalition of many groups partnering to seek the alleviation of malaria in Africa. Several US churches have participated in the coalition. For more information on the project and its outcomes see: http://www.nothingbutnets .net/.

3. An example of baptismal education is provided in Paul E. Hoffman, *Faith Forming Faith: Bringing New Christians to Baptism and Beyond* (Eugene, OR: Cascade Books, 2012).

4. *The United Methodist Hymnal: Book of United Methodist Worship* (Nashville: The UMC Publishing House, 1989), 34.

5. Pew Forum on Religion and Public Life, *"Nones" on the Rise: One-in-Five Adults Have No Religious Affiliation* (Pew Research Center, October 9, 2012).

6. An interesting discussion of this study by Lee Cowan appeared on *CBS Sunday Morning*, "Losing Our Religion," http://www.cbsnews.com/8301-3445_162-57559432 /losing-our-religion/.

7. Robert Hoshibata and Jim Winkler, "A Faithful Alternative to the Fiscal Cliff," umc-gbcs.org/press-releases/a-faithful-alternative-to-the-fiscal-cliff.

8. While many examples could be given, the open letter sent through e-mail on January 21, 2013, by Kathryn Lohre, president of the National Council of Churches, titled a "Pastoral Letter on the Joint Occasion of Martin Luther King Jr. Day and the Inauguration of President Barack Obama," is a fine representative of public education and communication as she focused on racism and pointed people to the NCC policy statement on racial justice.

9. Let me point to some resources I think begin to fulfill this call. The 1986 US Roman Catholic Bishop's statement, *Economic Justice for All*, is an example. It was a full statement demonstrating rich theological reflection. See http://www.usccb.org/upload/economic _justice_for_all.pdf. The same is true of many other groups, for example, the United Methodist Bishops statement on "God's Renewed Creation," offering partnership and reflection in addressing fundamental issues of living. See http://www.umc.org/site/c.lwL4KnN1LtH /b.5613639/k.47A9/Gods_Renewed_Creation_Call_to_Hope_and_Action.htm. The same is true of some magazines, like *Tikkun*, from an interfaith coalition of "spiritual progressives." See www.tikkun.org. Several religious websites also fulfill this task: Krista Tippet's www .onbeing.org, Interfaith Youth Core's www.ifyc.org, belief.net, the online encyclopedia *Judaism 101* at www.jewfaq.org, educational strategy centers such as Faith in the Public Life at www.faithinpubliclife.org, or scholarly groups, like the Pew Forum on Religion and Public Life at www.pewforum.org and the Hartford Institute for Religious Research at www.hirr .hartsem.edu. Christian education policy needs to attend to how the information from websites like these, as well as deep reflective pieces by denominational staff and NGOs, are made public. As faithful groups engage public conversation with subtlety and depth, the wider public is taught the resources of religion and how religions play a crucial role in public life.

10. Of course, many of the activities of the religious media address this task. Examples also include Internet publications on public religion, like *Sightings* of the Martin Marty Center for the Advanced Study of Religion at the University of Chicago Divinity School, which has an e-mail and Facebook option as well as web presence at http:// divinity.uchicago.edu/rss/sightings.xml; and the Facebook and Internet presence of Public Religious Research Institute, http://publicreligion.org.

11. One group addressing issues of the relationship of religion formation and the education of the public is the Religious Education Association. For their website where they describe their mission, projects, and conferences, see www.religiouseducation.net.

12. For an examination of quality private religious education, see Walter Feinberg, *For Goodness Sake: Religious Schools and the Education of Democratic Citizenry* (New York: Routledge, 2006). See also my "Constructive, Critical, and Mutual Interfaith Religious Education for Public Living: A Christian View," in Hanan Alexander and Ayman Agbaria, eds., *Commitment, Character, and Citizenship: Religious Education in Liberal Democracy* (New York: Routledge, 2012), 226–44.

13. Seton Education Partners work to see how Catholic churches in particular can enhance the education of children in neighborhoods where schools are failing. They advocate for establishing Catholic charter schools that commit to improving educational effectiveness for neighborhood children. For their mission statement and advocacy work, see www.setonpartners.org.

14. *Guidelines for Teaching about Religion in K-12 Public Schools in the United States* (American Academy of Religion, 2010), http://www.aarweb.org/sites/default/files/pdfs /Publications/epublications/AARK-12CurriculumGuidelines.pdf. See also "Spotlight on Teaching about Religion in the Schools" in *Spotlight on Teaching* 17 (March 2002); and the resource center at Chico State University, http://www.csuchico.edu/rperc/index .shtml.

15. See the ACLU's guide *Protecting Religious Liberty in Public School: A School Official's Guide*, www.aclu.org. See also the Bible Literacy Project of the Society of Biblical Literature (SBL) which since 2009 has published an e-journal, *Teaching the Bible: An E-Pub for High School Teachers*, http://www.sbl-site.org/educational/TBnewsletter.aspx; and the First Amendment Center's *The Bible and Public Schools: A First Amendment Guide* (First Amendment Center, 1999).

16. Susan Rosenblith and Beatrice Bailey, "Grappling with Diversity: Finding a Place for Religious Studies in Public Education," *Teachers College Record* (April 5, 2006).

17. Susan Rosenblith and Beatrice Bailey, "Cultivating a Religiously Literate Society: Challenges and Possibilities for America's Public Schools," *Religious Education* 103 (March–April 2008): 156. See also S. Rosenblith and S. Priestman, "Problematizing Religious Truth: Implications for Public Education," *Educational Theory* 54, no. 4 (2004): 365–80.

18. An example such a religious resource for public education is Melissa Lynch, *Parables of the Kingdom: A Curricular Unit for Language Arts on the New Testament Parables* (Bloomington, IN: AuthorHouse, 2012). This excellent resource uses New Testament parables as a way of teaching language arts for seventh graders and up. It teaches this biblical literature as *literature* illustrating excellent skills for literary and biblical analysis and scholarship.

19. Interfaith Youth Core is an advocacy and service organization that works for interfaith education and interfaith public service. For more information on their mission and activities, see www.ifyc.org. See also Eboo Patel, *Sacred Ground: Pluralism, Prejudice, and the Promise of America* (Boston: Beacon, 2012).